ENGAGING STUDENTS WITH MUSIC EDUCATION

'I recommend this refreshing approach to engaging students in the music classroom. The work is based on the personal experiences of the author, and written very much from the heart. Peter Dale has used DJ decks and urban music many times in various classrooms, but had not been involved in this kind of music as either a fan or a musician before. Therefore the book is an open invitation – not a closed shop for the already initiated – to any music teachers who wish to enliven their classrooms and engage even more of their learners.'

– Professor Lucy Green, UCL Institute of Education, UK

Engaging Students with Music Education is a groundbreaking book about using DJ decks and urban music in mainstream schools to re-engage disaffected learners and develop a curriculum which better reflects overall contemporary tastes. Many young learners are 'at risk' of exclusion; this book argues that for such individuals, the implications of such a shift in the music curriculum could be especially positive.

Drawing extensively on the author's own wealth of teaching experience, and bridging the gap between practice and theory, this book demonstrates through case studies that DJ decks can prove extremely valuable in mainstream classroom situations across the secondary school age ranges. Addressing challenging and crucial topics, combining rigorous theoretical analysis with practical suggestions, the book addresses questions such as:

- Are DJ decks actually a musical instrument, and are they suitable for classroom teaching?
- Will Ofsted's school inspectors approve of music teaching involving DJ decks and urban music?
- If we bring urban music into the classroom, will this further marginalise classical music?
- Are DJing and MCing skills recognised within examination specifications, at least in the UK?

Current teachers will find the practical advice on how to incorporate DJ decks and urban music into their classroom especially helpful, whilst educational researchers will be captivated by the critical discussion of the child-centred tradition and a theoretical approach which stretches from 'continental' philosophy to practice-based reflection.

With an insistence that the starting point for music education should always be the interests and experiences of the learners, this book is essential reading for those music teachers and researchers interested in the benefits of non-standard music-making in the classroom.

Pete Dale is an internationally renowned musician. He has taught music at numerous schools, Newcastle University and Oxford Brookes University, and is currently Senior Lecturer in Popular Music at Manchester Metropolitan University, UK.

ENGAGING STUDENTS WITH MUSIC EDUCATION

DJ Decks, Urban Music and Child-Centred Learning

Pete Dale

LONDON AND NEW YORK

First published 2017
by Routledge
2 Park Square, Milton Park, Abingdon, Oxon OX14 4RN

and by Routledge
711 Third Avenue, New York, NY 10017

Routledge is an imprint of the Taylor & Francis Group, an informa business

© 2017 Pete Dale

The right of Pete Dale to be identified as author of this work has been asserted by him in accordance with sections 77 and 78 of the Copyright, Designs and Patents Act 1988.

All rights reserved. No part of this book may be reprinted or reproduced or utilised in any form or by any electronic, mechanical, or other means, now known or hereafter invented, including photocopying and recording, or in any information storage or retrieval system, without permission in writing from the publishers.

Trademark notice: Product or corporate names may be trademarks or registered trademarks, and are used only for identification and explanation without intent to infringe.

British Library Cataloguing in Publication Data
A catalogue record for this book is available from the British Library

Library of Congress Cataloging in Publication Data
A catalog record for this book has been requested

ISBN: 978-1-138-85834-3 (hbk)
ISBN: 978-1-138-85838-1 (pbk)
ISBN: 978-1-315-71805-7 (ebk)

Typeset in Bembo
by diacriTech, Chennai

Printed and bound in Great Britain by
TJ International Ltd, Padstow, Cornwall

TABLE OF CONTENTS

Acknowledgements   *vii*

    Introduction   1

PART I
Engaging disaffected students   **17**

1   Curriculum tensions   19

2   Child-centred learning   34

3   Understanding students   52

4   Inclusion   66

PART II
Working with students and whole classes   **81**

5   Classroom management   83

6   Remixing the KS3 curriculum   97

7	Remixing the KS4 curriculum	112
8	Advanced DJing skills	127
9	Using new technologies	142

Conclusion *157*
Index *161*

ACKNOWLEDGEMENTS

Above all, I want to thank the young people with whom I worked in the North East of England as their music teacher between 2003 and 2012: it is because of them that I wrote this book. I would also like to thank colleagues in that school, even though I cannot name the institution for obvious reasons.

I want to thank the music team at Oxford Brookes University for appointing me as 'Early Career Fellow' in Popular Music 2012-13: without this fellowship, I doubt I could have managed to complete the manuscript of this book, and the additional research I undertook in Oxford and London has benefitted the project immeasurably.

I am also indebted to music colleagues within my present institution Manchester Metropolitan University who have supported me in various ways whilst the book was in preparation: Jason Woolley, Martin Blain, Adam Fairhall, Ben Challis, Angela Kang and Carola Boehm.

I should thank the following individuals for aiding me in my research: Garth Stahl, Jaz Wharmby, Tom Robinson, Spencer Hickson, Brett Gordon, Rory 'Rawz' Campbell and DJ Gary Smith.

I am grateful to my Mother, Mary Rose Bilson, for reading the finished manuscript and correcting some typographic errors. I am also very grateful to my Dad, Jack Dale, whose book collection proved invaluable at numerous points. Both of them have influenced my ideas about education immensely: teaching and, moreover, the love of learning is at the core of their beings, and I must celebrate that fact here.

I also want to acknowledge my brothers Martin, Ira and Joseph, who I always learn from, my children Willow, Walden and Martha, who I also always learn from, and my wife Jo, who is also always a guiding light for me in all things.

The book is dedicated to teachers who work in state education around the world and especially here in the UK: it is not an easy job at all, but you are doing great work and it is appreciated more than you probably realise. I hope that any music teachers who read the work will at least find some of it helpful.

INTRODUCTION

This book is effectively a plea for engagement in music education to be boosted through the utilisation of 'DJ decks' and other methods and modes of music-making which are associated with contemporary urban music. The argument is that, if this equipment were more widely available in school music classrooms and if the music culture(s) which typically utilise that equipment were granted a higher status by teachers and educational leaders, the transformative effects on disaffected learners could be immense. I will not only be discussing DJing equipment; also of great (largely unlocked) potential for the engagement of disaffected learners are not only MCing (rapping, essentially) but also other forms of music-making equipment which are commonly used to create electronic dance music of differing kinds.

What are the music cultures in which the DJ and MC combination are most popular? In this book I will, on occasion, make reference to 'urban' music – actually a hopelessly wide and therefore too vague category, but one which has utility if a broad reference is intended. Slightly more specifically one can alternatively speak of 'EDM' (Electronic Dance Music). However, much EDM has no MC and, indeed, no vocalist of any kind. The EDM bracket, furthermore, is so broad that it has also become problematic. In June 2014 *Rolling Stone* suggested, with good reason, that 'At the moment, electronic dance production is dominating [the charts] and driving chart success'.[1] That given, music teachers should of course engage with the most populist forms of electronically-produced dance-based music. However, mainstream electronically-produced 'chart pop' is not the music which the present book is primarily directed towards: if such music is dominant then certainly some attention needs to be paid to it, but my purpose here is, rather, to explore the educational benefits which arise from introducing more 'traditional' and more marginal/underground forms of EDM into the classroom.

The word 'traditional' is well deserved here. The DJ as creator of something new (as opposed to passive spinner of uncompromised records, one after the other without creative interference by the DJ him- or herself) is a conception which has now been in circulation for enough decades to earn such an adjective. It is common to suggest that 'the DJ-as-artist paradigm' has its roots in the 'sound system' culture of Jamaica (Emsley 2011: 9). According to Borthwick and Moy, sounds systems were first developed in Jamaica in the 1950s (2004: 98). An important contributor to the sound system would commonly be a 'toaster': a Master of Ceremonies (hence 'MC', sometimes spelt 'emcee') who would encourage both audience and DJ to raise their excitement levels. Confusingly enough for a contemporary Westerner, this MC would be known in Jamaica as a 'deejay' whilst the DJ (as s/he would latterly be named elsewhere in the world) would be labelled as a 'selector' (108). In any case, the combination of DJ and MC would become more widely popularised by the 'hip hop' music which emerged from the New York Bronx towards the end of the 1970s. It is here that core DJ skills involving scratching, cutting and mixing were first advanced. These skills have been further developed, honed and/or adapted within a range of forms of electronic dance musics: house, rave, techno, dubstep and so forth.

Whilst the overall dominance of EDM, in North America at least, is a relatively new development, the aforementioned forms of EDM and the combination of the MC with the DJ have not only a relatively long history but also a more marginal one. Take the rave and house musics which came to prominence in the UK during the 'acid house' boom of the late 1980s. The term 'boom' is well justified here – indeed, something of a 'moral panic' (Cohen 1972) effectively assisted the promotion as well as the demonization of acid house in the late 1980s and early 1990s. However, the music did not become widely accepted and institutionalised in the manner in which 'rock'n'roll' and other mainstream areas of post-War popular music arguably have. On the contrary, acid house to a significant extent but also other forms of 'hardcore' dance music have remained peripheral to the pop mainstream within the UK and elsewhere: they have, in other words, remained as 'underground' subcultures. Indeed, the 'happy hardcore' which became central to the music teaching in North East of England schools which this author undertook between 2003 and 2012 (a teaching experience which forms the central basis of the present book) is a music which many find extremely grating on the ear and deeply unpleasant to hear. It is not, in other words, the sort of stuff which one is ever likely to find in the mainstream pop charts.

The music is not only marginal in that (musical) sense, however. The young people with whom I worked in the North East were also living on the margins of society: disaffected, poor, often barely literate, prone to disruption and even violence in school, frequently in serious trouble with the police outside of school; these were the children of the 'underclass', as some will label them. Despite their socio-economic and cultural deprivation, however, a remarkably large number of these young people turned out to have a major creative passion in their lives: DJing with vinyl and MCing along to the 'tunes'.

This, then, is the music culture in which I am most interested within the present book: the happy hardcore or 'bouncy house' music which a fairly large (though admittedly marginal) subsection of contemporary young people in the UK are passionate about. This does not mean, however, that the book is only designed for teaching practitioners in and educational researchers of inner city schools, let alone only those who happen to have a large minority of MCs and DJs who enjoy this minority strand of EDM. Rather, the book is aimed at teachers and researchers of music education at large and is intended to have practical and theoretical value to any reader who is interested in the possibility for school music classes to open themselves up to EDM in general and the use of DJ decks in particular.

How do you *teach* DJ skills? How can *I* teach DJing and MCing when I don't know anything about them? How does this music fit into the curriculum requirements? How do you assess a DJ or an MC? What about members of the class (or other staff, or the music teacher him- or herself, come to that) who can't abide hardcore EDM? What pedagogical principles (music-specific or otherwise) can underpin the introduction of something as foreign as DJ decks into a mainstream school music classroom? Can't they just make this music at the youth clubs or in their bedrooms or at the 'Pupil Referral Units' (PRUs, as they are known in the UK)? What will Ofsted say? What *should* Ofsted say?

These are some of the questions which I attempt to answer herein. The book is divided into two main parts. Part One explores arguments for bringing this music into the mainstream classroom. Rock and pop are now more accepted as being worthy of an educational focus but hardcore EDM, I argue, remains peripheral and little understood by many teachers. Having discussed such curriculum tensions in Chapter One, and having argued that the popularity of this music amongst marginal/disaffected youth is such that music teachers simply can't afford to ignore it, I turn to questions around child-centred learning in Chapter Two of Part One. Is the idea that the curriculum should respond to (and even be structured around) the interests of learners simply 'old hat' in our new century? Are such pedagogical principles just harking back to the 'bad old days' of head-in-the-clouds idealism as propounded by 1960s/70s 'de-schoolers'? Alternatively, could a learner-centred principle have utility for the twenty-first century music classroom – and, if so, how far should one go down the path of (as a teacher colleague of mine used to put it) 'the lunatics running the asylum'? By necessity this includes some historical consideration of the changes in education since around the middle of the twentieth century, and how these relate to music education specifically.

In Chapter Three of Part One, I ask: what are the effects on student engagement when DJing and MCing are offered in mainstream music classrooms with the use of DJ decks? Here I draw fairly extensively on my own teaching practice but some data is offered relating to broader contexts. In Chapter Four, I explore the delivery of DJ-based and MC-related activities in PRUs, youth projects and other settings beyond mainstream education. For the latter purpose, I bring in data from researches carried out in Oxfordshire and the North West of England as well as some case study information about the High School for Recording Arts in Minnesota, USA.

In Part Two, I turn more strongly towards practical teaching questions. In Chapter Five (the first chapter within Part Two) this entails a focus above all on the 'whole class' question: given the ever-increasing pressure on all teachers to evidence maximal engagement and rapid learner progress, how does one 'keep them going' with only two turntables and a microphone as practical resources? At a theoretical level, what pedagogical justifications might there be for, say, basing a lesson around talk and discussion of the DJing equipment and/or the cultures around EDM whilst only a small number of a class are actively practising music-making with the DJ decks?

Chapters Six and Seven within Part Two are focused upon the UK's 'Key Stage 3' (11–14 years of age, wherein every mainstream learner has an entitlement to one hour's music teaching per week) and 'Key Stage 4' (14–16 years of age, wherein music becomes optional as a GCSE or BTEC subject and thus class sizes tend to become smaller, invariably with a larger number of contact hours with each student). The UK's 'National Curriculum' for music education at Key Stage 3 is explored in some depth in Chapter Six, demonstrating that a good level of overall fit can be shown between DJing and MCing skills and the letter of the National Curriculum. Although the overall focus is upon the teaching regulations within the UK, here, much of the negotiation between government policy and actual teaching practicalities can be cross-referenced profitably against the situation elsewhere in the world. (If EDM is music – and it would surely be hard to deny this status to it – there is good reason to suppose that it can be rationalised as a valuable component within any mainstream classroom, I would suggest.) In Chapter Seven, I show that there is some provision at Key Stage 4 for DJing, MCing, 'beatboxing' and suchlike within GCSE and BTEC curricula. However, elements of the content are shown to be of questionable validity. Within this section I also discuss elements of 'Key Stage 5' (16–18 years of age) and university-level provision for music in relation to non-standard music-making skills such as DJing and MCing.

In Chapter Eight within Part Two, I turn to the question of advanced DJ skills: what are they and how does one acquire/refine them? Here, I discuss some of the advanced techniques of 'turntablism', with my own (somewhat faltering) efforts at developing skills such as 'beatmatching' occasionally informing my discussions. (I should remark, at this point, that I am not and have never been an enthusiast of DJing – I learnt the basic skills on the decks so that I could increase engagement in my music lessons, nothing more or less than this).

Chapter Nine within Part Two looks at new technologies such as GarageBand and eJay as well as the relationship between DJ decks and the more traditional instruments one is expected to encourage learners to take up when teaching music at school level. How does one balance the user-friendly activities which can easily be accomplished with new technologies, such as pasting together pre-programmed loops within the GarageBand software, against the somewhat rarefied skills which have been more traditional to music education? As is the case throughout the book, an effort is made to balance practical suggestions with theoretical/pedagogical principles: *what* should we do and *why* should we do it, in short.

Given that a substantial part of the book is predicated on my own experiences as a teacher, I will use the remainder of this introduction to explore, firstly, methodological questions and the rationale for the book and, secondly, my own background not only as a teacher but also as a musician and scholar.

Research methodologies and rationale

Research which relies upon the fallible and inevitably selective recollections of practitioners is always of questionable reliability. As Ivor Goodson puts it with specific reference to educational research, 'personal data can be irrelevant, eccentric and essentially redundant' (Goodson 2008: 10). However, as a long-term advocate of the value of studying teachers' lives and work (Goodson 1992, 2003, 2008, Goodson et al 2010), he adds that 'these features are not the inevitable corollary of that which is personal'. After all, he goes on, 'the elucidation of more collective and generalizable profferings and processes' can often be developed from that which initially is 'only' personal: indeed 'the data the teacher provides' should 'only [be] dispensed with after painstaking proof of irrelevance and redundancy' (Goodson 2008: 10).

Does this mean that research need no longer be distinguished from practice? Not at all; indeed Goodson has cautioned against the 'grasp' of 'practical fundamentalists' who unwittingly 'make the focus of research a victim of historical circumstances' and 'political forces' with 'the teacher's practice [turned] into that of a technician, a routinized and trivialized deliverer of a pre-designed package' (2008: 3). Rather, 'What is urgently required are [researches] which stay close to the teacher's lifeworld and which [also] systematically build the links to history, politics and theory' (2008: vii). The differently specialised work of the practising teacher and the theoretically-orientated researcher are not necessarily to be conflated in a facile manner, then, but in Goodson's view we should nevertheless seek to 'link the personal, the practical and the theoretical in new ways' (2008: viii). In any case, the researcher should not regard teachers as 'villains', 'victims' and 'in some cases "dupes" of the system' (2008: 2).

In line with the suggestions of Goodson, I have attempted to combine theoretical awareness with practical examples in the present book. That said, I have also paid close attention to his warnings that 'The teacher-as-researcher approach suggests a number of problems'. If, for example, 'the teacher becomes researcher of his or her own practice', then this 'appears to free the researcher in the academy from clear responsibility in this process'. In Goodson's view, however, the latter has 'a primary but somewhat neglected responsibility for sponsoring and sustaining the teacher-as-researcher' (Goodson 2003: 51). The academy-based researcher and the school-based teacher, then, should be in a symbiotic and mutually supportive relationship, not an antagonistic one. In fact, though, those who emphasise practice at the expense of theory 'have thrown the theoretical baby out with the bathwater' (2003: 9). In Britain, he asserts, there has been a particularly 'hysterical tone' in response to what is 'normally referred to as "trendy educational theorists" or "theorists from the sixties"' (15).

In summary, I would suggest that Goodson encourages a strong *rapprochement* between educational theory and practice but that he is not necessarily (or not entirely) in favour of the teacher-as-researcher paradigm. Why the need for this *rapprochement*? According to David Scott, the combined effect of the UK's introduction of a National Curriculum, testing at the end of each Key Stage and the increasing levels of prescription by central government has meant that teachers have 'lost some of their capacity to control events in their classrooms, with a concomitant loss of professional status'. Consequently, teachers have 'begun to lose the ability to think critically about the processes which they initiate, and to experiment *in situ*'. Furthermore, 'teachers are now losing their capacity to think in ways which are not prescribed by policy makers. In short, they are becoming educationally illiterate' (Scott 2000: 1).

Scott's analysis tallies to some extent with my own experience of working in schools, and of undertaking a PGCE in the early 2000s. Few if any amongst my PGCE cohort, besides myself, were reading pedagogical/theoretical texts and writing essays with much enthusiasm whilst most teachers, in my years of school teaching, seemed fairly uncritical in their acceptance of the educational policies which regularly appeared during the 'noughties' and the present decade. Actually, the last statement is not quite true; often the teachers were *privately* critical of the seemingly constant flow of (often contradictory) policy initiatives, and they typically offered highly astute rationales for their critique. However, the idea of experimenting in a (professionally) critical manner during, for example, an Ofsted inspection would be anathema because most teachers would be too fearful of the risk of being labelled 'unsatisfactory', I would strongly assert.

Is such an assertion based on mere 'anecdote'? I won't pretend to have assembled a body of objective evidence to support my claim. Methodologically, however, I am inclined to agree with Scott and Usher that 'the scientific paradigm of a singular, convergent and fragmentable reality which can be known by researchers who act independently from the subjects of their research and who produce generalizations and nomothetic statements is not sustainable' (1999: 2). This does not mean that all knowledge is entirely relative, and thus that I am entitled to make any claim whatsoever regarding things I observed in my many years of teaching without the need for any evidence base. Rather, I hope that other researchers who read this book will look hungrily for claims I have made which they can disprove. That said, I think much of what I propose is markedly modest. It would not be hard, for example, to do some quantitative research to show that teachers will very often be privately critical of policy initiatives. One can note, indeed, Brown and McIntyre's observation that teachers' 'responses were hostile' to some specific curricular innovations which they had been obliged to deliver (1978: 19). In any case, I am confident that most practising educators will have no difficulty in accepting the idea that being labelled as unsatisfactory by Ofsted is greatly feared by teachers. (Ironic, really, given that a pedagogy which insisted that errors must never be made on any occasion would be laughed out of any serious educational discussion – being occasionally unsuccessful, after all, is a necessary component of all learning, and great teaching requires a measure of risk-taking.)

To give a singular example, teacher-researcher with a music specialism Di Brady has described the unpleasantness of being told by an Ofsted inspector that 'Your lesson was inadequate as the students did not demonstrate sufficient progress', with the school more broadly being given 'notice to improve'. Brady 'feared that [she] was a failure' as a teacher. However, this sense of defeat was turned around through experimentation with teaching and assessment. The experimentation in question allowed Brady to 'bridge the gap between rich, meaningful assessment and school-imposed procedures based on Attainment Target Level Descriptors' (Finney and Laurence: xxi–xxx). I recognise this experience as being similar to my own in several ways, and contend that other practitioners also will. *If* I am right in thinking that teachers often feel too nervous, given the risk of having their lesson 'failed' by Ofsted, to demonstrate critical experimentations in response to policy initiatives during school inspections (not such a big 'if', I would suggest), such a fear may not necessarily be well-founded. As I will show, my teaching experiments with DJ decks (which are hardly the most obvious vehicles for delivering the National Curriculum requirements for Key Stage 3 music) did not prevent me from gaining 'Good' and 'Outstanding' assessments from inspectors.

Methodologically, this claim could be problematic: inspection-success for an individual teacher, who may have been merely a 'charismatic' anomaly (Moore 2012: 113–5), does not in itself prove that the HMI and Ofsted (and equivalent bodies elsewhere in the world) are more open to critical/experimental responses to national educational directives than some teachers might assume. A larger set of case examples is required, perhaps. If, however, one case suggesting such success can be identified (and the positive impression my classroom made upon Ofsted inspectors and other observers was unmistakeable, I might add), is it not notable? Perhaps autobiography does not make for good research. If, however, Goodson and others are correct that life-history is 'a potent and useful method for exploring educational issues' (Scott and Usher 1999: 122), perhaps autobiographical recollections of individual teaching success *do* have potential utility not only for researchers but also for the consideration of other teaching practitioners. It is the gamble of the present book that such is the case.

Interestingly, Scott and Usher (based on work by Erben) have queried the possibility of a hard distinction between autobiographical and biographical educational research because, in any case, the researcher is always already 'complicit in the account' (1999: 119). 'The researcher or biographer has their own biography, which comprises a set of presuppositions and is presently constituted', Scott and Usher argue, and 'the interpreted account is therefore only one of many interpretations which could be made'. The resulting evidence base consequently 'conforms, to a greater or lesser extent, to particular agendas, and those agendas always make reference to the past of the biographer and to that of the participant' (1999: 119). Such an argument risks accusations of post-structuralist relativism, of course; but it should nevertheless give researchers pause for thought (at the least) before dismissing the admittedly autobiographical content which constitutes significant segments of the present text. If Scott and Usher (and Erben, it seems) are correct, the differing interpretations which readers might make when reading, say, Abrahams and Head's *Case Studies in Music Education* (2005) will tell us at least as much about the agenda(s) of the reader as they do about the concrete cases. (The 'reflective practitioner' is always already something of an autobiographer, we might even dare to say; and this is the case when s/he simply thinks about a teaching experience without even writing it down, arguably.)

In any case, not all the research which I undertook in the preparation of this book was done in a single school and, furthermore, not all was undertaken on my own. Some interviews with young MCs and DJs in the North East region were undertaken jointly by myself and Garth Stahl (then a PhD student at Cambridge University, now a faculty member within the Division of Education at the University of South Australia), for example. I was also accompanied by an undergraduate music student at Oxford Brookes, Jaz Wharmby, when I delivered a DJ decks workshop at a school in East Oxford in 2013. Jaz went on to teach music at Ambitious About Autism, based in the Tree House school in North London, and is near completion of a PGCE at Cambridge University at the time of writing. I found the input of Stahl and Wharmby most helpful and was naturally pleased to see that their experiences of the DJ-orientated teaching and learning, and their observations of the learners themselves, tallied closely with my own interpretations.

In addition to my own teaching experiences, I have attempted to develop a wider picture of the commonality (or lack thereof) of DJ decks being used in mainstream classrooms elsewhere. My first efforts in this regard were highly informal: I simply asked a range of other music teachers on inter-school training days whether or not they had ever introduced DJ decks into their classrooms. I was able to find no examples of other local schools and/or teachers doing this. However, I did discover a DJ specialist at the Sage Gateshead's CoMusica project. Within this project, the CoMusica Arches (at the rear of the Sage Gateshead's main building) turned out to be a hub for local and youthful MCs and DJs. These music-makers were primarily either 'NEET' young adults (Not in Education, Employment or Training) or were 'at risk' under-16s who were being encouraged to put their energies in a more positive and creative direction than they might otherwise be doing. I made recorded and formal interviews with two members of staff within the CoMusica Arches and attended an award-giving event there which was sponsored by the local constabulary.

During my Fellowship at Oxford Brookes I was able to further my investigation by emailing a wide range of Oxfordshire schools and enquiring, firstly, as to whether they were currently employing DJ decks within their music departments and, secondly, whether they would be interested in a visit from me with DJ decks in order to provide a workshop with learners. No schools indicated that they were currently using DJ decks and only one took me up on the offer of a free workshop, delivered in Spring 2013. A separate workshop at Oxford Brookes' Headington Campus with a group of around thirty Key Stage 3 learners from a range of Oxfordshire state schools was held in Summer 2013. At the outset of the session, I asked if any of the various schools the learners had come from had ever featured DJ decks within a music lesson: the indication was to the contrary. Around the same time, I spent an afternoon delivering a workshop for teachers designed to encourage the use of DJ decks in classrooms. In attendance were over a dozen 'Teach First' trainee music teachers all of whom were currently working in schools in inner-city contexts and/or socio-economically challenging circumstances. None of the trainee teachers had ever encountered this equipment in use within the schools where they were practising, nor had they encountered decks during their own (relatively recent) years of schooling. One trainee teacher mentioned that the school where he was currently on placement did own a set of decks. Regrettably, however, these had always remained in a cupboard, because 'nobody knows what to do with them'.

Accompanying me on this teacher training workshop was Bicester-based DJ Gary Smith ('DJ G') who I had liaised with after discovering that he was actually doing some teaching on the DJ decks in a local primary school as an after-school club. I am aware of other schools offering after-school clubs for DJs around the country (see Chapter Four) but have unsuccessfully struggled to find concrete examples where DJ decks have been used for mainstream music teaching. Although my methods are admittedly somewhat *ad hoc*, then, I have attempted to look as broadly as possible (given the constraints of time I had available for this research project) at the provision of DJ decks in music education around specific regions of the UK. Recent research in the North West of England has supported my broad finding: very few (if any) schools in the UK would seem to be using DJ decks for mainstream music teaching. In Oxford, I found a youth music project operating within the Ark T Centre (based within the grounds of and affiliated to the John Bunyan Baptist Church in Cowley). Here, young people who were at risk of exclusion from school could be encouraged to MC, 'make beats' in the EDM mould and, potentially at least, to practice DJ skills. I made recorded and formal interviews with two members of staff (see Chapter Four), both of whom expressed a love of DJing and a willingness to encourage DJs although, at that time, DJing formed a limited element within their work at Ark T. I also attended a performance of young musicians involved in the project in central Oxford, early 2013, noting that the 'grime'-style rapping here was markedly different from the happy hardcore MCing I had experienced in the North East.

Ark T's Youth Music Project, consequent to the way it was working with a range of local schools, was operating along the lines of an informal PRU. One of the two workers in the project revealed that he had also been delivering similar provision in an actual PRU in the Bicester region. Adding to this my investigations and enquiries in the North East and North West of England, and a picture emerges of DJ-orientated and hardcore EDM-orientated opportunities being more commonly provided in PRUs and other non-mainstream education contexts. A respondent within a study of DJ learning practices carried out by Paul Thompson sums up the mainstream situation fairly succinctly: 'There was nothing at all at school in the way of Deejaying equipment and none of the teachers knew anything about dance music. My old music teacher used to call it noise' (Thompson 2012: 48).

This problem needs to be redressed. We don't know exactly what the outcome was for this particular respondent but we can note with interest that, amongst fifty-four participants in Thompson's research project, not one had 'experienced popular electronic music within formal education' (48) – a telling figure for present purposes. What we can confidently say is that one of the largest areas of contemporary popular music – EDM – has received limited coverage within our music classrooms. Indeed, one of the most important and consistently popular tools for this area of popular music, namely the DJ decks, is struggling to get out of the cupboard.

A core rationale for this book, therefore, is to encourage music teachers, now and in the future, to consider employing DJ decks as an element of their teaching, and to encourage MCing in their classrooms. Why, then, hark back to the trendy theorists of the sixties (see comments from Goodson quoted above) and 'all that jazz' when (arguably) all that is really needed is a practical guide? My answer to this would be that the book is not only about this practical example (the use of the DJ decks and so forth): I am also keen to ask what is music education *for*? What *could* it be doing for our young people and our society? *Who* should be deciding which music is most worthy of study? And so forth. I am in full agreement with Alex Moore's assertion that 'The real trick is for theory, practice and experience to operate dialogically *together*' (Moore 2012: xiv, emphasis retained). I hope, therefore, that the 'theoretical' ruminations herein will be of value to practitioners rather than being a distraction: 'food for thought' with relevance to actual teaching situations, that is.

I also hope that the text could be of interest to researchers and policy makers. As regards the latter constituency, such an aspiration may be excessively optimistic: according to Moore, there are 'official official' logics behind much of state education policy but also, 'in the shadows of these official rationales, a set of "unofficial official" reasons that cannot, for political reasons, ever be made explicit' (2012: 37). His hint is that the politicians' talk of empowering young learners masks a key intention of policy makers: 'To what extent can education really empower children, if the social system *within which is takes place* is fundamentally *dis*empowering?' (38, emphasis retained). It's a great question, but it could of course lead teachers towards despair. Fortunately, Moore turns out to retain some optimism: 'although policy implementation may appear to be "top-down", teachers (and indeed students), as active agents in the field, can and do influence policy through choices, actions and dialogues that may not always present themselves very visibly but are nevertheless influential beyond our own individual practice' (140).

We will return to the ideas of Moore in Chapter Two herein, for I find his prioritisation of an 'emphasis on what *learners* do' most inspiring and important (2004: 171, emphasis retained). For now, though, before moving on, I want to note that his is a cautious way of thinking: he is conscious, for example, that 'to oppose some policy … might smack of unprofessionalism' precisely because 'it might hamper rather than help our students – including those who may cause us the greatest concern' (2012: 138). The challenge for teachers, therefore, is to navigate a path between critical thinking and professional pragmatism. My aspiration with this book is also to navigate that path: to propose approaches to teaching music in the twenty-first century in a mainstream school context which neither bow to the not-always-helpful dicta of policy makers nor lose sight of the practicalities which are necessary for classroom survival. ('Survival' as in, for example, avoiding getting the sack, which was always my bottom line: 'will this get me the sack?' Ten times out of ten, I found that my experimentation in the classroom matched up positively to this *sine qua non*; indeed, the teaching experimentations often won me plaudits which may or may not have been deserved.)

The encouragement of an optimistic (or non-defeatist, we might say) pragmatism in educational research is not unheard of. For example, Daniel Cavicchi declares, at the close of a fascinating chapter within Regelski and Gates's *Music Education for Changing Times* (2009: 97–105), that 'Every semester someone asks me, "We can really do this? This counts?"'. He reveals that his response is to 'just say "It ought to" and hope they spread the message' (105). In keeping with Cavicchi's endeavour, I hope that reading the present book might make teachers feel emboldened to take a chance with DJ decks, MCing and the not-always-easy-listening character of even the most marginal forms of EDM and contemporary urban music. Do 'the powers that be' actively encourage us to give prominence to such stuff in our music classrooms? Not explicitly, but perhaps if we read between the lines we can find a fit between the 'official official' (as Moore puts it) rationale for music education and the things we (and, moreover, our learners) actually want to do and hear and create in our music classrooms.

As to the educational research community more broadly, I hope that the somewhat autobiographical data which I offer up herein will not lead them to conclude that the study is flawed beyond redemption. Certainly there is a great deal more research to do in this area – and a great deal more teaching and learning that needs to be done, with the flow of learning quite often being from 'student' to 'teacher' if my experience is anything to judge by. Doubtless, there are areas of my methodology which could be improved, since my scholarly background is more in musicology, critical thinking and philosophy than in educational research. I will have failed utterly if no elements within this book are found to be provocative by the reader, for I always aim to write polemically – not simply for the sake of provocation but, rather, in order to move critical thinking forwards. All that said, I have made some efforts to create a piece of research into popular music in education which, I hope, has at least some legitimacy in the eyes of the specialist theorists of the field. In any case, given my pleas above for the acceptance of a methodological reliance on somewhat autobiographical data, it makes sense at this point, I feel, to offer a picture of my own background not only as an educator but also as a musician: I was not, after all, born to DJ.

About the author

The single most important thing the reader needs to know about me in order to really grasp the significance of the teaching work I have done with DJ decks is that, prior to introducing this equipment into my classroom, I had barely touched those 'wheels of steel' in my entire life. Naturally for someone born in the seventies, I knew how to put the needle in the groove. (Many younger people today do not in fact know how to do this – more on this later in the book.) As a fresher at Sunderland Polytechnic in 1989, furthermore, I had segued from one vinyl record to another as a DJ in the internal radio system (broadcasting, excitingly enough, to a handful of distracted diners in the student union canteen, if memory serves correctly). I once (but only once) took the role of DJ at a commercial club night in Newcastle Upon Tyne, circa 1993. However, the diet of discs in that instance was indie and punk and my role was to play one song followed by another – not to creatively tamper with the musical sound locked into the grooves in any way.

The restricted extent of my experience of DJing is significant because I have reason to believe that many teachers, both young and old, take an attitude that their lack of knowledge of DJ skills and dance culture prevents and/or excuses them from gaining (or needing to develop) any pedagogical capabilities with the decks. On this point we can note that Professor Lucy Green states in *Music, Informal Education and the School* (2008) that 'twin decks for scratching' were not being used in any of the classrooms in which she undertook this immensely influential research. Green adds that this is 'probably because scratching is that much further removed from the popular music into which the teachers were themselves encultured' (48). However, music teachers routinely lead school bands and orchestras which feature musical instruments with which they themselves do not have any expertise. We teach about, say, raga and tala despite most teachers having a very sketchy knowledge of the musical specificities of classical Indian music. We provide lessons on serialism even though we may not have properly studied Schoenberg's methods. Music teachers, at school level, are not likely to be expert in every area of music about which they teach. Furthermore, I have encountered many a young teacher who decides to learn a bit of guitar so that they can accompany singing in class. A comparable basic familiarity can be sufficient to get a lesson started with DJing equipment, I would assert. Wilful ignorance is hardly a good excuse for limiting the musical diet of learners.

I am also not someone who is enculturated into EDM. On the contrary, I grew up with rock and pop: the Wombles, the Beatles, the Smiths, and so forth. I enjoyed playing 'side drum' in the junior school orchestra and then, later, playing bits of electric guitar in the school's jazz big band and senior orchestra, but I was always a rocker, really. When acid house came to prominence, during my late teens in the late 1980s, I took no interest in it. When electronic dance music was at its height of popularity in the UK, in the 1990s, I carried on listening to indie, punk, jazz, soul and folk music; hip hop and techno formed a tiny section within my growing collection of vinyl. Throughout my twenties, I played in rock-orientated bands and dabbled my feet in the industry with a 'DiY' record label I set up in 1992, which mostly issued punk and indie bands.

I began my PGCE in Primary Education in 2001 at the University of Northumbria at Newcastle, at the age of thirty. I had wanted to train for secondary school music teaching, but I didn't have any qualifications except a Grade C 'O' Level: despite the encouragement of my piano and guitars teachers to take grade exams, I had taken none (for reasons of obstinacy and idealism, in brief). When the time had come to fill out UCAS and PCAS forms, around 1988, I gathered that the kind of ('popular', roughly speaking) music I loved was not on offer at any universities or polytechnics (with the possible exception of Salford – but I failed the audition there, I am willing to admit). I opted for Communication Studies at Sunderland Poly as an alternative, and enjoyed my degree studies there, graduating with upper second-class honours in 1992.

During the 2001–2 PGCE year, I discovered that I had changed a lot: reading academic texts and writing essays seriously turned me on, as they say, in a way that it hadn't when I was twenty years old. I began raiding my Dad's large archive of books and government publications. Jack Dale had been an HMI of schools from 1970 until '84, meaning that he lacked the 1967 *Plowden Report* but did have a copy of *Special Educational Needs* (the 1978 *Warnock Report*, that is). The first thing I borrowed was John Holt's *How Children Fail* (1965) which, in my view, remains the book which every trainee teacher should read. The importance of *Plowden* was briefly mentioned in class but it was my Dad who brought it to life, emphasising to me the importance of the report's guiding principle: 'At the heart of the educational process lies the child'. I enjoyed marks in the 80 per cent plus range, although an ICT specialist gave me a mark in the low 40s. (The title he gave us was 'Describe the impact of ICT in your classroom'; I answered honestly by saying that I felt the impact, at that time (2001), was limited and that the most important thing would always be the interaction between learner and teacher.) A maths specialist who was teaching on the PGCE pulled me aside in the corridor one day and asked me what I was going to do with my 'gift for writing'; his colleague told me that he had phoned him at home to read him sections of what I had written.

My broad success in the academic dimensions of the PGCE would eventually lead me to take up an MA in Music in 2003 at Newcastle University. This was partly because I just wanted to read more and write more essays. I was also driven to gain a qualification in music because, after two terms teaching in a Catholic primary school, I had managed to persuade a secondary school to take me on as a music teacher – that given, I thought I ought to try for a music qualification above 'O' Level. Initially I thought landing a music teaching job with such limited (relevant) qualifications on paper was quite a feat, but I realised at interview that it was a one-horse race. The school was on the 97th percentile, nationally, for official measures of socio-economic deprivation: very near the bottom of the heap, in other words. That said, I was extremely impressed with both the Head Teacher and the Head of Music. Over the coming years I would learn an enormous amount from them both until, in 2007, the Head of Music retired. Due to falling numbers in the school in-take, the Head Teacher decided that only one music teacher was now required and I became 'acting' Head – Head, that is, of a department of one.

Not having stepped foot in a secondary school since I left school in the 1980s, I was a bit trepidatious on my first day of teaching in 2003. The morning passed easily enough, because I had not been assigned a tutor group and thus was simply supporting the Head of Music with his pastoral responsibilities for the bulk of the time. I did note, of course, that these children were quite a bit taller and, in some cases, somewhat menacing relative to the primary-age children I had actually been trained to teach. The last lesson of the day was my first real test: one hour with the second from bottom set in Year 8 (12–13 years of age). I got the class to line up outside the block, as the Head of Music had advised me to do. I could tell that we had a few 'characters' here. One boy asked me 'Do you like monkey, sir?' The others began sniggering, and I recall that someone muttered that this wouldn't be the kind of music I would be teaching. I confessed that I had no idea what 'monkey' was and, after some monkey impersonations had been provided by my interlocutor, somebody in the class took pity and explained that it is a type of dance music. I later found out that what is (or was, at that time, at least) known locally as monkey derives its name from a local club, The New Monkey. The questioning went on: 'are we going to use decks, sir?' I was just about 'hip' enough to know that he was referring to DJing equipment. 'Not today', I replied, 'but if that's what you're into then, yes, we can have DJ decks in the classroom'. Uproar ensued: 'really?!'

My first day and we hadn't even made it into the classroom before I had hastily made a promise I wasn't sure whether I could keep. It took more than a year, in fact, but eventually an RE teacher donated vinyl decks, which his daughter was no longer using, and we were up and running: my classroom was transformed, as were my relationships with some of the most disaffected learners in this most challenging of socio-economically and culturally deprived areas.

This book primarily grows out of what I learnt from the young people I worked with in the music department of that school. I took *Plowden* and John Holt seriously: I refused to fear failure, including my own, and as far as I could without risking losing my job, I placed the children at the heart of what happened in my classroom. Ofsted told me a lesson was 'Unsatisfactory', another (four years later) was labelled 'Outstanding' in every category on the inspector's piece of paper and another again (around three years after that) was 'Good'. I tried not to care too much about what they said, because it seemed to me that my teaching was much the same in all three lessons – at least, it was always me at the front of the class, which has always made me wonder how it could be that the inspectors' judgements differed so widely.[2]

In any case, it is certainly true that my teaching involved some success and some failure. My part-time MA in Music, by contrast, went well in all of its elements, resulting in a Distinction grade. I decided to proceed with a PhD, focussing on popular music (punk, to be more precise) rather than music education. I gained a whole set of analytical and philosophical tools, thoroughly enjoying the supervision of Richard Middleton at Newcastle University. Completing the PhD whilst teaching full-time and bringing up three children was a challenge but I just about managed it, even continuing to play gigs and occasionally issue records with my band. By 2012, I was ready to move on from school teaching and took up the aforementioned Fellowship at Oxford Brookes and then, in 2013, a Senior Lectureship in Popular Music at Manchester Metropolitan University. My research profile has been primarily in 'Popular Music Studies', but I have occasionally published journal articles relating to music education. This book may be my last word on school-level music education because, although I enjoyed it and learned a great deal, I think it is the most exhausting work I have ever done. (I must add that successive UK

Governments during my years of teaching have made the job increasingly difficult; and I, like many other ex-teachers, am little inclined to endure more wrong-headed policy making from Secretaries of State who have never taught in their lives.)

If this book inspires one teacher to experiment with DJ decks or, indeed, to listen to their learners and use that as the starting point for their teaching, the book will have served some purpose. I hope it might also contribute to pedagogical debates about what music education is currently like, could be like and should be like. Some of our most disaffected learners are passionate about DJing, MCing and hardcore EDM. We need to learn from them what is important in this music, what the skills involved in making this music are and how we can share the skills and share the music so that our classrooms celebrate the marginal as well as the traditional and the popular.

Notes

1 www.rollingstone.com/music/news/in-the-club-countrys-fascination-with-edm-20140610
2 The 'unsatisfactory' lesson was with the bottom set, the 'good' was with the middle ability and the 'outstanding' was with the top set, we can note – which may tell us something about Ofsted's covert criteria for judgment, perhaps. It seemed to me that the children in the bottom sets were nearly always from the most socio-economically deprived families whilst the top set was, more often than not, made up of children from more stable families. Apparently, however, we are to expect the deprived children to attain as highly as, if not higher than, those whose background is more comfortable. If the more deprived children's attainment is lower, there should be no doubt that it is the teachers and the school who are to blame, or so the Government, the media and Ofsted seem to believe.

References

Abrahams, Frank, Head, Paul D., *Case Studies in Music Education* (Chicago: GIA, 2005)
Borthwick, Stuart, Moy, Ron, *Popular Music Genres* (Edinburgh: Edinburgh University Press, 2004)
Brown, Sally, McIntyre, Donald, 'Factors Influencing Teachers' Responses to Curricular Innovations', *British Educational Research*, 4/1 (1978), 19–23
Cohen, Stanley, *Folk Devils and Moral Panics* (Abingdon: Routledge, 2011, first published 1972)
Emsley, Jason, *The Laptop DJ Handbook: Setups and Techniques of the Modern Performer* (Boston, MA: Course Technology, 2011)
Finney, John, Laurence, Felicity, *Masterclass in Music Education: Transforming Teaching and Learning* (London: Bloomsbury Academic, 2013)
Goodson, Ivor, *Studying Teachers' Lives* (London: Routledge, 1992)
Goodson, Ivor, *Professional Knowledge, Professional Lives* (Maidenhead: Open University, 2003)
Goodson, Ivor, *Investigating the Teacher's Life and Work* (Rotterdam: Sense, 2008)
Goodson, Ivor, Biesta, Gert JJ, Tedder, Michael, Adair, Norma, *Investigating the Teacher's Life and Work* (Abingdon: Routledge, 2010)
Green, Lucy, *Music, Informal Education and the School: A New Classroom Pedagogy* (Aldershot: Ashgate, 2008)
Holt, John, *How Children Fail* (Harmondsworth: Penguin, 1965)

Moore, Alex, *The Good Teacher: Dominant Discourses in Teaching and Teacher Education* (London: Routledge, 2004)

Moore, Alex, *Teaching and Learning: Pedagogy, Curriculum and Culture* (Abingdon: Routledge, 2012)

Regelski, Thomas A., Gates, Jerry T., *Music Education for Changing Times* (London: Springer, 2009)

Rimmer, Mark, 'Listening to the Monkey: Class, Youth and the Formation of a Musical Habitus', *Ethnography*, 11/2 (2010), 255–283.

Scott, David, *Reading Educational Research and Policy* (London: Routledge, 2000)

Scott, David, Usher, Robin, *Researching Education: Date, Methods and Theory in Educational Enquiry* (London: Continuum, 1999)

Thompson, Paul, 'An Empirical Study into the Learning Practices and Enculturation of DJs, Turntablists, Hip Hop and Dance Music Producers', *Journal of Music, Technology & Education*, 5/1 (2012), 43–58.

PART I
Engaging disaffected students

1
CURRICULUM TENSIONS

What to teach? It is a rather important question and, despite the increases in prescription faced by contemporary educators (in the UK's mainstream school system, at least), one which remains open – up to a point, at least. We will examine the UK's National Curriculum for Key Stage 3 in some detail in Chapter Seven below but for now, we can note the first stated aim of the current National Curriculum. According to this document, all students should 'perform, listen to, review and evaluate music across a range of historical periods, genres, styles and traditions, including the works of the great composers and musicians'. The statement is clear enough but, we should add, there is quite a bit of room to manoeuvre. *Which* 'great composers and musicians' should we listen to, review and evaluate? (Which of their works, come to that?) *What kind* of performing should we be aiming to encourage/develop/instigate? *How* do we best select 'periods, genres, styles and traditions' from the impossibly wide range of possible selections within this thing called 'the history of music'?

The music teacher has to make some decisions, in practice. Inevitably, this will include some exclusions. For a long time, including this author's years of secondary-level education (11–18 years of age, in the UK), popular music was the institutionally excluded other: twentieth-century music, in educational terms at that time, meant Bartok, Schoenberg, Britten, but certainly not Elvis, the Beatles or even Miles Davis. In the mid-1980s, when I was studying for my O-level, one might well have found some jazz and pop in the school orchestra's repertoire and one's school master might even be willing to encourage pupils to form rock bands. Such was the periphery, though, not the expected core of the curriculum. The O-level syllabus which I encountered between 1985 and 1987, for example, had one of Corelli's concerti grossi, Brahms' *Academic Festival Overture* and Bartok's *Concerto for Orchestra* as the core study pieces. One would sit at one's desk, gamely trying to follow the score (many of my classmates were even worse at this than

I was, which is saying something). Intermittently, the teacher would pull the needle out of the groove of a recorded rendition of the work and draw our attention to a specific bar or two, in order to tease out the significance of one cadence or another, or perhaps to ask a question relating to the composer's decisions in his employment of the resources of the orchestra.

I honestly enjoyed this work, up to a point at least: it was a challenge, but I learnt a great deal about harmony, timbre, the history of European art music and so forth. That said, I was near seventeen years of age (being an October-born child) when I sat the exam: my favourite bands, at that time, were probably Stiff Little Fingers and the Smiths. I would soon be listening to the likes of the Pixies and Sonic Youth – contemporary US 'indie rock' groups whose employment of dissonance seemed to me, then and now, to be a fascinating correlate of the experimentations with harmony, timbre and rhythm which had been undertaken by the twentieth-century composers I had learnt about in my O-level. The curriculum, then, was far too restricted. Most of the thirteen learners in my class of '87 were listening to heavy metal, if the truth be known. Although I may have been the least unenthusiastic about the Baroque music of Corelli within my class, I think it is fair to say that we were part of a whole generation who thought of 'music' as encompassing a considerably wider bracket than that which our curriculum covered.

Something had to shift at an institutional level and, in the UK at least, it began to do so thanks to two main factors. Firstly, the replacement of the O-level with the GCSE, from 1988 onwards. Secondly, and in the same year, the introduction of the National Curriculum. From a music education perspective, these brought an immense shift. The GCSE allowed students to compose relatively freely rather than simply to attempt to replicate the highly formal rules of counterpoint and SATB harmony; the listening paper could include popular and 'ethnic' music and was much less notation-focussed. These and other developments made the new qualification very different from the O-level which had preceded it, and allowed learners with less traditional musical skills to score higher grades. The National Curriculum, meanwhile, gave a crucial *entitlement* to practical/creative music-making in the classroom. Although actual music-making will doubtless have occurred in some classrooms prior to 1988, Gary Spruce has suggested that music education had for too long been 'dominated by passive listening and the didactic imparting of information' prior to the 'remarkable transformation' within which the introduction of a National Curriculum was a crucial component (Spruce 1996: 3).

Even with these improvements, though, the situation for music education remained imperfect. For example, Peter Dunbar-Hall argued in the mid-1990s that 'Popular music, despite its existence on syllabuses in various forms, is still a problem for many music teachers' (Dunbar-Hall in Spruce 1996: 216). In his view, the 'art music backgrounds of many music teachers act against an understanding of popular music' (ibid.). Within the same mid-1990s survey of music education, George Odam reports a students' view that 'most teachers … don't listen to pop music or understand it. Schools haven't got the right equipment or the right sort of rooms to work in' (Odam in Spruce 1996: 186). Bernarr Rainbow argues that disdain for popular music goes back at least to the beginning of the twentieth century when the likes of Arthur Somervell (HM Inspector of Music at that time) believed that 'an important part of their task was to wean their pupils away from "the raucous notes of coarse music-hall songs"' (Rainbow in Spruce 1996: 14).

Few, if any, who are *au fait* with the general state of play for music education in the UK would deny that this situation has improved in the twenty years since Spruce's *Teaching Music* was published. Today, many music teachers do have a good understanding of pop and rock and many have a background in making such music. Most schools, if not all of them, now have some suitable equipment for mainstream popular music: guitars, drums, electronic keyboards, software for recording and editing music and even for 'making beats' (although too few schools have DJ decks and too many music teachers lack the knowledge as to their use, unless I am sorely mistaken). With the increasingly common introduction of music-editing software, indeed, there has been at least some engagement with EDM (Finney and Burnard 2007). There is much room for improvement, however. For one thing, it remains the case that 'Teachers tend to use elaborated codes derived from Western European "elite" culture, whereas students use vernacular codes', as John Finney puts it (18). By elaborated code, Finney means musical values such as 'periodic phrasing, harmonic conventions, extended phrases, developmental variation and so on' – relied upon at least partly because 'teachers know that examiners also operate within elaborated codes and will negatively assess work that does not conform to the norms of the code'.

In my view, Finney's complaint is most astute: even if a teacher is sympathetic to the culturally-specific appeal of musical effects such as, for example, the repeatedly thumping bass and repetitively-delivered simple phrases found in happy hardcore EDM, the teacher is also likely to be conscious that an institutional preference is at large in music education. Many teachers, rightly or wrongly, assume that such music cannot be granted much if any value for assessment purposes. This institutional preference remains tied, as Finney highlights, to the elite art music which originated in Europe. Things have improved, certainly, with music education being much more likely to reflect the musical interests and passions of learners in the twenty-first century relative to the state of play even in the later decades of the twentieth. However, if popular music is now a fairly central plank within school-level music education, rather than existing at the periphery as it did for so long, it nevertheless remains the case that certain kinds of popular music are much more likely to receive coverage than others. 'Popular music', after all, is a hopelessly broad church: the term, in the last analysis, can be used to cover absolutely everything beyond the confines of European art music and, for this reason, the journal *Popular Music* has even gone as far as to ask 'Can We Get Rid of the "Popular" in Popular Music?'. Consequent to this terminological/categorisation problem, the acceptance of popular music in the classroom has, in practice, meant the acceptance of only the most central forms and types: the peripheries are less well served. Hardcore EDM, we can add, is arguably the least well-served area of contemporary music within the supposed broadening of the music curriculum which has been occurring for the last quarter of a century. (One could also note the poor fit of death/doom/screamo/ grindcore metal, avant-garde noise and other peripheral forms of so-called popular music with the preferences and tendencies of mainstream music education at the present time, but this would be beyond the scope of the present study.)

How far can we go, then, with the inclusive approach to music education? Is there a point where opening up the classroom to peripheral musics makes teaching itself untenable? Do we risk losing sight of the centre if we over-emphasise the peripheral (the very 'throwing the baby out with the bathwater' issue which would appear to have provoked the UK government to introduce the stipulation, mentioned at the top of the present chapter, that secondary-level music education should be 'including the works of the great composers and musicians')? Or might it be the case that 'Music is a universal language' (the first statement within the UK's current National Curriculum) and thus the study of *any* music will aid learning about *all* music? What about learner identity, furthermore – what are the advantages and disadvantages of teachers reflecting back to learners the music within which they are already enculturated? Would such a reflection constitute merely an empty gesture on the part of the teacher, or could it be highly valuable for those who are already socially 'marginal' and thus struggling to associate the academic experience with lived realities beyond the school gates? In order to address such questions, we need to move beyond a purely musical focus and introduce some broader pedagogical theories and debates, and some philosophical theories which I feel are of relevance to the questions at hand. I attempt to do this in the next section.

When is music not good music for the classroom? The inclusion debate

Most urgently within the queries just raised, we must dispel immediately the false idea that music is a universal language. In fact, there is no single element which can be located in everything which calls itself music everywhere. Take harmony, for example: we know that much popular music follows the functional tonality which was formalised within baroque and classical European art music, but at the same time much of it certainly does not. In any case, didn't the romantic music of the nineteenth century slowly unpick functional tonality until, to cut a long story short, we were left with atonality as a core element of musical modernism? Furthermore, popular music, particular after the ruptures of sixties rock, often relies upon a modal rather than a strictly functional tonality. Much punk, indie and post-punk music, as well as some metal, uses copious amounts of dissonance. In fact, it is not only the case that the harmonic rules which were established within 'the classical style' (Rosen 1998) are often a poor fit with popular music (Middleton 1990); it is also the case that art music itself has no universal harmonic language, at least from the outset of the twentieth century onwards. We can easily perform the same deconstruction on any musical element: the status of bar lines in African music is, at best, 'contested' (Agawu 2003: 56); many pieces of avant-garde music are devoid of rhythm and melody in the normal sense of those words; and so forth.

Music is also not a universal language because it is not a language at all: it is music. Music cannot say anything whatsoever in the denotative sense; and if it can *imply* certain things/feelings/sentiments, which doubtless it can, this is no more than the taste of food can do, or the sense of smell, neither of which are languages. Clearly, then, the first statement of the current National Curriculum is nonsense in musicological terms and is about as useful as saying that eating is a universal language. (Everybody eats, granted, but people eat such different things and in such radically different ways, around the world and even within one country, that the idea that there is something universal about eating, beyond the necessity to do it with at least some regularity, is obviously preposterous.) However, to attempt to be generous to the document in question, one can hope that a message of inclusion is intended. Let us note, then, that the statement under discussion leads directly to a demand that 'music education should engage and inspire pupils to develop a love of music and their talent as musicians, and so increase their self-confidence, creativity and sense of achievement'.

The important words, here, are 'develop' and 'increase', I would argue. To make the best of the requirements of the National Curriculum, teachers could do worse than to take wherever the learner is 'at' (in terms of both taste and knowledge) as the starting point and then to develop and increase this knowledge/experience base. I will say more about such learner-centred pedagogical strategies in Chapter Two, but from the standpoint of the 'what to teach' question, for now we can at least say that such will likely be a valuable starting point when deciding how to balance the classical, the popular and any other kind of music.

We know, from an immense literature built up over the last fifty years and more, that many young people start out from a position of enthusiasm for mainstream popular music. This, then, will certainly be a valuable starting point, in many cases, from which to build learners' 'self-confidence, creativity and sense of achievement' (as the National Curriculum puts it – see above). In my own practice, I very often encountered vocalists who arrived at secondary school already being reasonably adept at mimicking contemporary pop singers. I am confident, furthermore, that most secondary-level music teachers can say the same, in the UK and elsewhere. If, say, a youngster who has developed this skill then acquires extended vocal skills such that they can sing elements of harmony, or can vary the timbre of their voice, or extend their range, or can begin to make an association between actual melody and notes on paper, this is surely no bad thing from an educational point of view. There is every reason to think that such a pop-orientated youngster, if exposed to 'classical' (ie traditional, essentially) educational challenges, will gain the self-confidence and sense of achievement for which the National Curriculum calls, and doubtless this is to be applauded if it occurs.

Does the opposite apply? Randall Everett Allsup has offered a 'democratic vision' of the advantages to 'classical musicians' of developing popular music skills, particularly if those classically-trained musicians are to go on to become teachers themselves (Allsup 2011: 34). (My own experiences as mentor to PGCE trainees confirmed the need for this – on more than one occasion, I worked with ABRSM

Grade 8 pianists who were unable to busk a piano accompaniment for whole class singing; in practice, however, such is a vital skill for the typical classroom teacher today.) Lucy Green has also argued that, for example, it is beneficial for 'classical learners' to become aware that there is not a single 'correct' way of making music and that exposure to the 'informal learning' which is common within popular music contexts can therefore be valuable to such learners (Green 2008: 171).

By contrast, though, Robert Walker has argued that 'pressure from parents, teachers or peers' and/or 'media pressure' can make 'teenage students rate popular music more highly than classical'. In instances 'where no media or popular music pressure existed, and where classical music experiences were institutionally and culturally supported', by contrast, 'powerful emotional engagement with classical music was reported'. Walker concludes from this that 'where high quality music is institutionally and culturally embedded, it becomes important to young people' (Walker, 2005: 53). We can note Walker's problematic conflation of the classical with 'high quality music' (and thus his exclusion, by implication, of popular music from such a rating). Indeed, Walker is unambiguous in his dismissal of any worth in popular music: 'the elevation of pop singers not only denigrates the value which art stands for, but [also] supports an elevation to a spurious greatness with relativistic arguments which ignore the facts of musical content' (Walker 2007: 7). Nevertheless, perhaps there *is* an issue worth talking about here, at base. Perhaps the authors of the UK's current National Curriculum are justified in thinking there is now a need (after decades of pressure for popular music to be recognised as a valid component within music curricula) for music teachers to be reminded that young learners will benefit from exposure to 'great composers and musicians'. As mentioned above, do we not otherwise risk 'throwing out the baby with bath water' (as the saying goes)?

In practice, every student I taught at Key Stage 3 (11–14 years of age, the compulsory period of secondary education) heard the music of Bach, Beethoven, Brahms, Mozart and so forth, and most had a go at using notation in order to attempt to perform famous phrases such as the opening of Beethoven's fifth symphony. Clearly, then, I am in broad agreement that a diet which completely excludes 'the greats' would not be the best possible diet. In a school such as the one where I taught, indeed, there was a particularly great need to ensure that every learner at least gained some kind of sketch of basic historico-cultural facts which less socio-economically deprived learners might take for granted (more on this issue shortly). However, I cannot agree with Walker's implication that exposing learners to popular music will somehow infect their ability to rate classical music – years of teaching has shown me that it is perfectly possible for, say, the daughter of a bricklayer to develop a passion for both Mozart *and* Lady Gaga before their sixteenth birthday. Indeed, I would suggest (as Green and Allsup also imply) that rubbing classical music against the popular stuff benefits both sides of the (possibly illusory) great divide.

Is it as simple as that, though? Philosopher Alain Badiou has complained of 'the plurality of "music" – folklore, classicism, pop, exoticism, jazz and baroque reaction in the same festive bag' (2005: 89). I have critiqued Badiou's general hostility to popular music at length elsewhere (Dale 2016). Certainly his argument that contemporary music (by which he means, shall we say, post-Schoenberg concert music) is 'the only thing in the twentieth century which merited the name of "music" – if we grant that music is an art and not that which some minister subjects to the demands of gruelling festivals' (Badiou 2009: 81) is hard to swallow. (By 'gruelling festivals', I have argued that Badiou is clearly gesturing towards popular music – and I have shown that he demonstrates disdain for 'hard rock' and other forms of popular music elsewhere within his writing [Dale, 2016]). I *am* inclined, though, to think that the 'festive bag' of which Badiou complains can indeed be a problem for thinking (and teaching) about music. If music is not a universal language (and it certainly is not), each different kind of music needs to be respected for its differences, perhaps.

Let us divert here, for a moment, into certain issues which have preoccupied 'continental' philosophers such as Badiou in recent decades. The core issue at hand is arguably around the relation between self and other. Kathryn Jourdan has drawn valuably upon Levinas and Derrida in order to explore the educational problem of 'Making Sense of the Music of the Stranger' (Finney and Laurence 2013). As Jourdan notes, this boils down to a problem of *ethics*, at least in the sense that Levinas uses the word: the different music of the other, of the 'stranger', must be accepted as wholly other; it can never be fully dissolved into 'the same' music of the teacher, the school and the educational mainstream. Rather, the educational challenge for a Levinasian pedagogy would be to offer responsibility to the 'face' (Levinas uses the word literally, but we can argue that one shows one's face through music in a certain sense) of the other and, in that moment, to make present a certain 'collectivity that is not a communion' (Levinas 1979: 94). Badiou's ethics is at odds with that of Levinas and Derrida (Badiou 2001) in ways which are too complex to adumbrate here. The point, moreover, is that 'difference' and the ethical questions it throws forth have been an important area of enquiry amongst continental philosophers. How relevant (and how practically applicable) are such enquiries in a pedagogical context?

Certainly there are difficulties around practical application in the classroom of the theories of, in particular, Derrida, as I have shown elsewhere (Dale 2012: 142–3). Nevertheless, I maintain that an ethical imperative of the type outlined by Levinas and (in slightly different ways which we need not explore here) Derrida *is* pedagogically viable and valuable – and especially so in a music classroom. The trick, I suggest, is above all to keep in mind that other musics are not the same as ours: to keep this fact always in mind and thus, rather than seeking to make different musics conform to each other's value systems and 'logics' (as it were), to accept the radical difference as necessary, irreducible and worth respecting.

Is such acceptance of difference what occurred when 'popular music' eventually wormed its way into Britain's mainstream education scene at the very end of the twentieth century and the outset of the twenty first? Not exactly, if Lucy Green is to be believed. Green has noted that music teachers, due to their typical enculturation in classical music and its associated musical value system, have often prioritised 'classic' pop such as that of the Beatles or Queen. The problem, Green notes, is that such music 'is often, from pupils' perspectives, as far removed from their lives and identities as mainstream classical music or twentieth-century atonal music' (Green 2007: 12–13). The problem, in other words, is that this other music ('pop') was dissolved within the self-same musical values of the musical establishment such that only the popular music which most readily conformed to classical musical values was typically accepted. Marginal popular music, meanwhile, has continued to struggle to find a place in the classroom. Indeed, the kind of hardcore EDM enjoyed by many of the most disaffected pupils I taught was a particularly extreme example of such: many non-music-teaching colleagues told me that the perpetual thump of the music, not to mention the fairground-recalling melodic motifs, literally made them feel sick, sentiments which I occasionally shared myself, I have to admit. I am confident, therefore, that most music teachers will struggle to 'get their heads around' this stuff and, initially at least, to tolerate it in their classrooms.

That given, shouldn't the boys and girls (but particularly boys, I found) who enjoyed this music just be left to listen to it at home, where only their families and immediate neighbours might be troubled by the thumping bass, grating synths and dogged MCing? If I thought so, I would not be writing this book, obviously. What are the benefits to students, then, of bringing such wholly 'other' music into a mainstream music classroom? I will give my extended answer to this question in Chapters Three and Four below. For now, we can be content with the explanation of Alexandra Lamont: 'Children with a positive musical identity, as shown by their self-descriptions, are those who engage in more extra-curricular musical activities, show more positive attitudes towards school music and like their music teachers. In some cases', Lamont notes, 'this is also associated with a greater sense of identification with school in general.' (Lamont 2002: 59). A music teacher who welcomes, for example, hardcore EDM into their lesson time will feasibly be much more well-liked by some of the most 'difficult' (disaffected, that is) learners in their school, in other words; and those learners might well achieve higher and even identify more strongly with the school itself. I saw everything which Lamont describes, including unexpected engagement with extra-curricular activities, happen to disaffected learners I worked with in the North East of England (see Chapter Three for more on this).

My research beyond the North East has suggested that this had little if anything to do with some 'charisma' I may or may not personally possess (see the Introduction herein for more on the methodological question of charisma and educational research). Rather, learner identities were transformed because a little bit of the students' socially marginal culture had been recognised by the otherwise-alien school (or, more accurately, its music-teaching representative – me, in the case at hand). I did not need to pretend that I was the same as those students, let alone that my taste in music matched theirs; on the contrary, I openly admitted that my music tastes were wholly otherwise to theirs. However, this did not preclude me from showing a recognition that their music (though it might be wholly otherwise to the Beethoven, Beatles, Brubeck and Bhangra I would routinely play in class) *was* music and, therefore, was worthy of respect.

Wholly otherwise? I have repeated this couplet to link my ruminations here to the discussion of Levinas's and Derrida's theories as discussed above. However, as I will show later in the book, some of the greatest opportunities to encourage learning amongst the enthusiasts of hardcore EDM arose precisely because I could perform melodies from the hardcore 'tunes' on keyboards, transcribe the melodies on to a stave and then help the students to learn to play them themselves. Not every single element was other to the European musical 'language', then; and highlighting certain similarities enabled the 'collectivity that is not a communion' which Levinas encourages (see above), I would contend. Is there a significant semantic difference, here? Communion suggests a cohesion, the 'as-one' of the '*comme-une*'; a collectivity, by contrast, collects disparate elements but does not have to deny them their disparate character: this distinction, I am quite sure, is Levinas's essential point. At core, the happy hardcore my students enjoyed was other to the music I enjoy; and I don't think any of them took Dave Brubeck's music close to their hearts. Nevertheless, faced with each other in the classroom, a certain level of mutual respect was collected together: a respect for the otherness of each other.

Students' right to their own music

Before concluding the present chapter, I want to make some observations in relation to the educational question of 'Students' Right to Their Own Language' (SRTOL) in particular, and sociolinguistic issues in education more generally: to what extent can music education 'map on' to the debates around SRTOL (and their right to their own dialect, come to that)? Do students have a right to their own music, or should it be the role of schools in socio-economically deprived areas to give young learners a glimpse of the 'world outside of the manor' (or 'the 'hood', as African-Americans often put it), to quote Dizzee Rascal?

Debates around SRTOL have a long pedigree in the USA. First mooted by a committee within the Conference on College Composition and Communication (CCCC) in 1971, the SRTOL Resolution was eventually finalised in 1974. It seems to have quickly become 'one of the most controversial position statements passed in the history of CCCC' (Perryman-Clark, Kirkland and Jackson: 1). That said, the broad position resonates strongly with certain arguments already offered above: 'Students whose languages are valued in classrooms perform better in school and in life'. By contrast, 'students whose languages are devalued perform less well in school and in life' (5). Thus far, the argument is fairly uncontroversial. However, a proposal that, for example, 'Tests should not be focussed on whether students can think, speak or write in the institutional dialect, but on whether they can think, speak and write in their own dialects' (34) is rather more of a challenge. The book from which I have sourced these quotations is admirably even-handed in its presentation of arguments for and against SRTOL. For convenience, I shall focus on a single counter-argument against SRTOL, put together by Jeff Zorn (150–62).

Experienced as an English teacher in a 'Historically Black College in Alabama', Zorn begins by quoting from a female African-American teaching colleague.

At the time of the SRTOL Resolution in the 1970s, this teaching colleague had stated that 'With friends like these, black children hardly need enemies' (Perryman-Clark, Kirkland and Jackson: 5). Zorn's position, in brief (and in line with many who have argued against the SRTOL idea), has two main elements, on my reading. Firstly, that what is under discussion is not really a 'right' properly so-called and has no basis in pre-SRTOL educational practice: more accurately, he insists, the CCCC might have said 'We are now granting students a right that we just invented for them'. Secondly, by prioritising learners' 'own language'/dialect, the teacher loses the chance to develop linguistic skills and competences with standard English that, in practice, are rather important for enabling the socio-economically disadvantaged to improve their lot in life. In short, Zorn argues that SRTOL 'feeds into a reactionary politics of ethnic-cultural chauvinism': its advocates claim that non-SRTOL-inflected educational work aims (in Geneva Smitherman's words) 'to remake those on the margins in the image of the patriarch' (155–6). No enthusiast of the 'Black Power' idea, Zorn is (as are most if not all of those who have opposed SRTOL) essentially an integrationist who calls for 'the *same* standards whatever the individual's race and cultural style' (158–9, emphasis retained).

A vital turn within Zorn's argument, for our purposes, comes when he praises educational work which 'puts into doubt everything students think they know. If in the end students keep what they came with, it will be only after entertaining the live option of wholly different beliefs' (Perryman-Clark, Kirkland and Jackson: 159). How well does this map onto music educational work and its importance/potential/responsibility? The first thing to acknowledge is that the stakes, as a rule, are much lower with music education. A student from a socio-economically deprived background who thinks that Beethoven is a dog (as a frightening number of my students claimed to, apparently due to some Hollywood movie or other) is unlikely to find this becomes an impediment to employment later in life. Students who can only express themselves in their 'own language', by contrast, might face such a challenge, or at least are likely to struggle to find better-waged and/or non-manual employment.

That said, there will doubtless always be a large minority for whom music is the most important subject in the curriculum. This author and, I imagine, many readers can vouch for the possibility of such a preference. We might recall, furthermore, Lamont's argument that a 'positive musical identity' can have a significant impact on overall attainment in and identification with school (see above). If Lamont is right (and I am confident that she is), there is every reason to think that even a child with only a modest interest in music might benefit in significant educational ways by finding their 'own music' (the music which is popular in their non-school 'lifeworld') represented in music lessons. There is, then, perhaps more at stake here than meets the eye.

Do students have a right to their own music? Moreover, how prominent should the music in which students are already enculturated be in the classroom – at the centre, the periphery or perhaps even placed as the sole focus of study? Before attempting to answer these questions, let us briefly consider (primarily as a cross reference against the issues around SRTOL already discussed) the sociolinguistic-educational research of the likes of Peter Trudgill in the 1970s. In *The Social Differentiation of English in Norwich* (1974) Trudgill showed that sociolinguistics 'can shed light, for instance, on problems concerning the discreetness and continuity of social classes, on certain aspects of role and status, and on the class structure of the community generally'. Such illumination can 'be of use in pointing to some of the barriers that exist in the way of social and educational advancement for many members of our society' (Trudgill 1974: 5). Subsequently, in *Accent, Dialect and the School* (1975), Trudgill detailed the nature of some of these barriers. Of particular interest, for our purposes, is his proposal of 'a conflict between the language of teachers and the school, on the one hand, and the language of many children, on the other' (1975: 46). Noting that the issue at hand is 'greater for children from working-class backgrounds than for middle-class children' (47), Trudgill proposes some ways that the problem at hand can be redressed. For example, 'if a London child pronounces *our* the same as *are*, he is reading correctly [due to his particular accent], and his reading should not be "corrected"' (49, emphasis retained).

Due to such concrete problems in the way that English was being taught at this time (problems which, it is fair to say, remain at the core of the British school system today), Trudgill suggests that 'we should aim for … a society free from dialect prejudice, where everybody can use their own dialect without fear of ridicule or correction' (1975: 69). The similarity to the SRTOL position should be obvious. Interestingly, though, Trudgill goes on to ask 'are there any reasons why we should continue to teach standard English in schools … at the same time as trying to cultivate dialect tolerance? (71). He notes again, as he had in *The Social Differentiation of English*, that 'standard English is a variety which is symbolic of membership of a particular social group' and thus 'to speak standard English is, at least to a certain extent, to align yourself with this social group' (78). Consequently, 'the only legitimate motive for teaching children to speak standard English as a second dialect is to prevent them from being discriminated against for speaking socially stigmatised dialects'; but even then 'We would be much better advised, for example, to concentrate on producing dialect tolerance and linguistic security' (79). This applies specifically to *speaking*, Trudgill insists, but much less so to *writing*, for one thing because 'Writing is a very different kind of activity from speaking' (80). In the case of writing, for pragmatic reasons which are very similar to those who have made counter-arguments against SRTOL (ie employment opportunities, above all), Standard English 'can be taught for certain types of written work' although 'we must also hope for a future in which dialect tolerance will be extended even to the written language' (83).

Broadly correlative to all this, I am strongly inclined to suggest that, although marginal musics such as hardcore EDM certainly require inclusion in the curriculum wherever there is interest in them amongst learners, it would be hasty to focus upon them to the exclusion of all other musics. For one thing, as implied above, there are benefits to gaining cultural knowledge and experience which may have pragmatic utility for, say, getting a job. Additionally, knowing at least something about, for example, European art music may save the school-leaver from avoidable embarrassment. It helps, in life, if you are aware that Beethoven was the name of a famous German composer prior to providing the name for a dog in a movie; or, to give another concrete example, if you know how to pronounce Dvořák. (An unusually bright and slightly eccentric young student who had been listening to records from the collection of his 'Nana' [grandmother] mentioned the Czech composer's name to me one day, but made the error – unforgiveable in certain bourgeois environments, one imagines – of prominently sounding out the 'D' and pronouncing the 'ř' as if it were an 'r'. One supposes I could have left his error unremarked upon, in order to avoid 'stigmatising' him; it is hard to imagine that I would therefore have been doing the young man any favour in life, though.)

There is more to the matter than just this. As Zorn points out (see above), it is arguable that education can and should put into doubt *all* that the learner thinks they know. If that learner then decides to 'keep what they came with' – for example, if they carry on preferring the hardcore EDM which, in my teaching practice, was the music of choice for many parents, uncles, aunties and siblings of some of the most socio-economically-deprived learners – we can at least say that a choice has been made. Without exposure to other musics, by contrast, no choice might have been available to the learner. In practice, furthermore, I found that learners who had seen their 'own music' welcomed in the music classroom gained an increased respect not only for more mainstream forms of popular music but also folk music and even classical music. On one occasion, for example, I had to persuade an MC from the lower school to leave the school hall where I was rehearsing traditional Christmas Carols with the school band (the word 'orchestra' would be far too grand for the ensemble we were able to put together). The student in question had absconded from a lesson but seemed to quite enjoy listening to the music we were making and, indeed, made a point of telling me so. (I am confident that he was sincere and not 'taking the piss', as they say in England.) On another occasion, I persuaded a small, bottom stream class of very low-attaining students (mostly boys) to sing folk songs on the proviso that they would be allowed to do some DJing and MCing next lesson. I was pleased and slightly surprised to see that the boys took to the singing with marked enthusiasm; they even had some fun re-writing the words to the traditional and local song 'Dance Ti Thy Daddy'. (The lines 'now I've smoked me baccy' quickly became 'smoked me wacky baccy', the boys in question being far more streetwise than one could wish a twelve-year-old to be.)

Assuming that the reader is willing to accept that a mixture of differing musics will be valuable to the mainstream music classroom, then, the question remains as to how the balance should be struck. On this question, I am sure that no hard and fast rule can be established. Factors which we might want to keep in mind, though, certainly include the make-up of the class. The bottom set class just mentioned featured a majority who loved happy hardcore music, and this in itself made it wise to allow the DJ decks and microphones to be used in class more often than might have been fair in another class. Where a smaller number of DJs and MCs were in the class, correlatively less time 'on the decks' would be allowed. If one or two pupils found the music hard to bear (which often was the case), I would typically allow them to do different work in a separate practice room (particularly in classes where the MCs and DJs were more numerous and thus the decks were more often used, for obvious reasons of fair balance). If there were only one or two DJs or MCs, I would sometimes allow them to work on the decks in a practice room. With the same class, on other days, I might also allow the anomalous DJ or MC to 'be the teacher' for a lesson or two: after all, if a child has a passion for and/or a skill in any area of music-making, an effective music teacher should surely embrace this.

What of the distinction Trudgill casts between speaking and listening – can we make a similar distinction in regards to, say, practical and theoretical aspects of teaching and learning in music? In practical terms, I believe that, for example, an MC is very likely to benefit from varying the pitch of their voice through more conventional vocal work (ie singing). That said, to tell an MC that rapping was/is somehow wrong or inadequate would surely risk replication of the 'correction' of a London dialect-speaking child who renders 'our' and 'are' as homophones (see above). The trick, then, is to offer opportunities for the learner to explore music-making beyond that which they are already practising but, ideally, to centre such opportunities around learner interests, needs and wants (see the next chapter for more on learner-centred pedagogical strategies and issues). Certainly a learner should never be told that any element of the music they make or listen to is wrong or incorrect. Music has no right or wrong; or at least, there is no logical reason why a musical detail could be shown to be wrong purely by comparison with the way that musical detail would be handled by other musics, for each music carries its own paradigmatic logic, in a sense. (Take graded exams on traditional instruments: if a student chooses to enter this game, it is fair to tell a violinist, for example, that their lack of vibrato where the notation demands it is 'wrong'; however, it would be quite inappropriate to say that a self-taught folk fiddler is a poor player because she never uses vibrato. Parallel fifths are 'wrong' for a Bach chorale, but they are very 'right' in the popular song 'Paranoid' – unless innumerable Black Sabbath fans are 'wrong', that is.)

Comparably to an MC, a DJ who explores, say, the djembe drums (commonly found in music classrooms, currently in the UK at least) might well advance their sensitivity to rhythms beyond the 'four-on-the-floor' of hardcore EDM. If music-making with this instrument is undertaken, the DJ might acquire theoretical knowledge about bar lines, rests, syncopation and other European-derived concepts which can be helpful to musical discourse and understanding. If, however, the learning is imposed as an obligation rather than being selected as an option, problems certainly abound (again, see the next chapter). We need, then, classrooms where other musics are made available – but not force-fed to learners who lack an appetite for the unfamiliar. In many ways, indeed, the teacher's first task is to stimulate such an appetite; and the level of success in this regard will largely determine the balance of, shall we say, other musics relative to the music which learners might claim as their own.

Conclusion

What kind of music belongs in the classroom? In the first instance, whatever kind the learners are interested in, I would assert. (I once said just this to a class of students in a 'critical thinking'-based music class at Oxford Brookes university, to find that the group burst into laughter as one; what was funny remains a mystery to me, however, for I certainly maintain faith in such a principle.) What other musics should be introduced? Again, the initial basis for answering this question should be *whatever other musics the learners are curious about*. A successful classroom, on my view, would be one where learners are hungry to discover new musics. I won't pretend that my classroom always enjoyed such success, but there were certainly times when an appetite for new discoveries arose in class (including music which the learners introduced to me).

What if conservatism prevails such that the learners react against music beyond a narrow range with which they are already familiar? As a teaching practitioner, I was always a pragmatist and I doubt that many educators in schools which are comparable to the one where I taught (ie in areas of stark socio-economic deprivation) could survive without balancing their ideals against pragmatic compromises. In practice, then, it might make sense to insist that, say, some African pop, or some Irish fiddle-playing, or even some 'works of the great composers and musicians' are studied in class sometimes. I won't pretend, furthermore, that I was above using the DJ decks as something of a carrot-on-the-string incentive if I needed a class (or, more often, specific learners) to undertake some specific piece of work which the National Curriculum demanded (listening to 'great composers', for example, to quote again the current specification).

That said, I am convinced that a classroom which welcomes whatever music its learners enjoy, no matter how marginal or indeed unpleasant to the less-attuned ear, will thereby encourage open-mindedness about unfamiliar musics including, say, classical music. My own practice leads me to draw this conclusion, as does a whole host of educational and philosophic theory some of which I have drawn upon in the present chapter. Today, classical music is wholly otherwise to the taste and preferences (and, moreover, the listening experience) of the average school-aged child; so is much jazz, folk, 'ethnic' music and even a good deal of pop and rock in some contexts (the typical inner-city context, for example). In a successful music classroom, however, such otherness need not be an impediment to engendering a certain collectivity, mutuality and, most fundamentally, respect. The trick, in the last analysis, is to face up to what is not the same as one's self and accept that this otherness can, impossibly enough, make a level of justice in the classroom feel possible.

References

Agawu, Kofi, *Contesting African Music: Postcolonial Notes, Queries, Positions* (London: Routledge, 2003)

Allsup, Randall Everett, 'Popular Music and Classical Musicians: Strategies and Perspectives', *Music Educators Journal*, 97/3 (2011), 30–4

Badiou, Alain, *Handbook of Inaesthetics* (Stanford: Stanford University Press, 2005)
Badiou, Alain, *Logics of Worlds* (London: Continuum, 2009)
Dale, Pete, 'Derridean Justice and the DJ: A Classroom Impossibility?', *Philosophy of Music Education Review*, 20/2 (2012), 135–53
Dale, Pete, *Popular Music and the Politics of Novelty* (London: Bloomsbury, 2016)
Finney, John, Burnard, Pamela (eds.), *Music Education with Digital Technology* (London: Continuum, 2007)
Finney, John, Laurence, Felicity, *Masterclass in Music Education: Transforming Teaching and Learning* (London: Bloomsbury Academic, 2013)
Green, Lucy, *Music, Informal Learning and the School: A New Classroom Pedagogy* (Farnham: Ashgate, 2008)
International Advisory Editors, 'Can We Get Rid of the "Popular" in Popular Music? A Virtual Symposium with Contributions from the International Advisory Editors of "Popular Music"', *Popular Music* 24/1 (2005), 133–45
Levinas, Emmanuel, *Time and the Other* (Pittsburgh: Duquesne, 1979)
Perryman-Clark, Staci, Kirkland, David E., Jackson, Austin, *Students' Right to Their Own Language* (Illinois: Bedford/St. Martin's, 2015)
Rosen, Charles, *The Classical Style: Haydn, Mozart, Beethoven* (New York: Norton, 1998)
Spruce, Gary (ed.), *Teaching Music* (London: Routledge, 1996)
Trudgill, Peter, *The Social Differentiation of English in Norwich* (London: Cambridge University Press, 1974)
Trudgill, Peter, *Accent, Dialect and the School* (London: Arnold, 1975)
Walker, Robert, 'Classical versus Pop in Music Education', *Bulletin of the Council for Research in Music Education* 163 (2005), 53–60
Walker, Robert, *Music Education: Cultural Values, Social Change and Innovation* (Illinois: Thomas, 2007)

2
CHILD-CENTRED LEARNING

During a brief stint as a primary school teacher in the early 2000s, I was amazed by a remark made by the Head Teacher of the particular Catholic school where I was working. Halfway through a staff meeting, the Head exclaimed that 'we need to make sure that the LEA [Local Education Authority] understands that it's the children who are the problem and not us'. Several members of staff exchanged shocked glances at this bald statement. To me, this was as much as to say 'this school would be outstanding if it weren't for all the pupils getting in the way of our teaching'.

In 1967, the *Plowden Report* declared that 'at the heart of the educational process lies the child', as we noted in the introduction of the present book. To some, however, the child-centred ethos of *Plowden* and the pedagogical efforts which grew exponentially in that era were a huge mistake for the educational scene. The heart of education, many today seem to believe, ought rather to be providing enough workers with the skills which society and/or business interests require. For others, meanwhile, the centre of the education process ought to be the provision of greater 'employability' for disadvantaged children. The latter position commonly is taken irrespective of the fact that ever increasing numbers of socio-economically deprived children are in fact voting with their feet by becoming 'school refusers'. 'We know what's good for them, even if they don't' is the effective faith of the 'employability' position; 'childhood must conform to the requirements of an adult society' is the central tenet of the skills-based educational principle.

What are schools *for*? The typical answers we hear today would imply that music can have little justification for inclusion in the curriculum. Schools are for training the young for a life of work; for acquiring, above all, key skills in reading, writing and arithmetic as well as, we are frequently reminded, science. The arts might offer 'enrichment' for the learner but they are explicitly excluded from the 'Core' of the UK's National Curriculum, instead being hived off amongst the 'Foundation subjects'. On the 4th of April 2012, a *Daily Mail* columnist insisted that 'If, as we are often told, the key to recovery is research and development, we must not hesitate in ditching child-centred nonsense for knowledge-centred excellence.' One can feel confident that the 'research and development' the columnist has in mind is not musicology or art history: given that 'putting our children in touch with their feelings will not earn them, or their country, lasting success', it is evident that the 'knowledge-centred excellence' in question is of an essentially scientific type. 'Feelings'? These, the *Daily Mail* columnist seems to believe, are not educationally valuable: 'the purpose of genuine education is to replace subjective emotion with rational objectivity', he insists, as if all emotion is intrinsically irrational. Without emotion, though, how can you have art? It is hard to see how such polemical opponents of child-centred education can justify schools being used for the making of and appreciation of artworks (pieces of music, for example): isn't to encourage children to paint and make music to risk bringing 'subjective emotion' in to the classroom?

It is the premise of my book that bringing DJ decks into classrooms and encouraging children to MC over EDM, if that is their 'thing', is an intrinsically good idea precisely because it provides a space in which children can centre their musical learning, in the first instance at least, around music with which they identify. By starting with what the child knows, one can open a window onto a wider world; not necessarily in order to take them away from the world in which they are encultured, but rather to widen their palette in regards to musical possibilities, differing traditions and the relationship between the music they love best relative to the rest. What, though, are the pedagogical issues around child-centred learning and the principle of placing the interests of the child/children at the centre of one's teaching? Clearly there are some who vehemently oppose child-centred methods: the *Daily Mail* columnist is merely one commentator amongst many contemporary voices against 'progressive methods'. Mainstream commentators on the topic of child-centred teaching almost invariably offer fact-free polemic against such methods, typically being individuals who have little or no experience of actual teaching. Beyond this, though, we also now have a large corpus of reflective research and commentaries in relation to the perceived 'progressive era' of, essentially, the 1960s and 1970s. Not all of this literature is entirely affirmative of the value of progressive and child-centred methods and, that given, we should explore some of the critical reflection which is currently available. I begin, however, by outlining the arguments of some key theorists of the era in question.

How Children Fail

In the past, in jovial conversation, I have argued that John Holt's *How Children Fail* ought to be given out to trainee teachers like free milk. It's worth remembering, that said, that the era of free milk in British schools was brought to an abrupt halt in the 1970s thanks to Prime Minister Heath's Secretary of State for Education, a certain Margaret Thatcher. Much the same can be said of Thatcher's relationship to the era of child-centred and progressive idealism in UK education, but we should start our story at the beginning rather than the end.

It would be a mistake to claim Holt as the first of the child-centred progressives: he was not, for the lineage goes back, via Dewey and A.S. Neill (amongst many others), to Rousseau and beyond (Darling 1994: 6). Writing in the late 1950s and early

1960s, however, Holt brought a particular (and particularly inspiring) attitude to the educational scene: a clarion voice noting that, in short, children were not so much learning to *think* as learning to (or developing strategies to) *give the teacher what he/she wanted*, namely 'the right answer'. Our *Daily Mail* columnist might want to know how getting the right answer could be a bad thing. In itself, one supposes, it is a good thing: if a learner can recall, say, that the second degree of D# major is E# (not F) whilst the third degree is F## (not G), this could be valuable to the learner in subsequent music-making. Just how much practical utility does this information *really* have, though? And how much, as a music teacher, should we worry about the overwhelming tendency of young musicians (especially guitar players, I find) who refer to the major third of D# as 'G' instead of F##?

Holt shows, with non-musical examples (mostly mathematical ones, as it happens), that learners who struggle to *understand* the rationale behind agreed facts may be able to produce the 'right answer'; they will, however, struggle to hold on to their knowledge. Such learners, Holt argues, will typically feel adrift in the classroom and, in an overwhelming number of cases, will prefer to fail than to maintain their struggle with learning. His descriptions – of the way children attempt to read the face of their teacher in order to calculate what the right answer is, for example – are marvellously written; intelligence and human sympathy shine from *How Children Fail* like a beacon in the dark. I repeat, therefore, that young teachers should read this book despite the half century which has elapsed since it was published: whatever you are teaching, Holt will illuminate the problematic power relationship you are trapped in within a classroom situation. The trick, as Holt also shows, is to listen to what the child says and to search for the logic behind it: by centring your teaching upon the learning which is or could be taking place before you, you can adapt and modify your methods and, as if by magic, confusion can be coaxed into knowledge and understanding.

If, by contrast, you say that 'the children are the problem because they are not learning properly', it is not only the children who must fail. A lightbulb factory will not be able to stay in business if the filaments are so volatile that the lightbulbs malfunction as soon as they get out into the 'real world' beyond the factory gates. At present, of course, educational disaffection remains broadly within socially manageable levels; it would be an optimistic individual, however, who presumed that there is no near or present risk of a return to the dystopian rioting seen in the UK in the summer of 2011. I have argued elsewhere that improved creative opportunities in schools, certainly including working on DJ decks and encouraging MCing in classrooms, could help to discourage such a return (Dale 2013).

Holt is a great writer and educationalist, then, but we will look more critically at his later (and more anti-educational) work towards the end of the present chapter. First, though, I want to note that the 'progressives' of the 1960s and 1970s (amongst whom Holt was certainly a key figure) were preceded by numerous critical and experimental thinkers on childhood and education in earlier decades of the twentieth century. These are too numerous to explore individually in any depth here, but it should be obvious that, for example, Maria Montessori's prescription that 'the child must shape *himself*' (1975: 50, emphasis retained) leads logically towards the child-centred idea. A.S. Neill, we can add, was concerned in his writings of the 1930s, 1940s and beyond with the 'moulded, conditioned, disciplined, repressed child' who 'lives in every corner of the world' (1968: 95). There was, it is fair to say, a groundswell of critical thinking in regards to education in the period between the Wars and immediately after the Second World War.

What did the later progressives have to add to this, in the 1950s, 1960s and 1970s? To some extent, here, we need to disambiguate the merely child-centred impetus from the child-centred and *progressive* tendency. The latter moved towards an educational critique so radical that 'deschooling' became the order of the day. The former impetus did not go quite so far: the *Plowden Report* suggested new approaches in the classroom in order to prioritise the interests and immediate needs of the child; it did not go so far as to suggest that schools should actually be abolished and replaced with a radical alternative, however.

Which of these two orientations is more pertinent for pedagogical purposes when we bring DJ decks, MCing and EDM into the contemporary mainstream music classroom? In order to attempt a satisfactory answer to this question, we need to learn something more of what the more radical progressives were proposing. Beyond Holt, Paul Goodman's work is a significant indicator of a certain tendency which was growing rapidly from the late 1950s onwards. Initially renowned for his 1960 classic *Growing Up Absurd*, Goodman insists in *Compulsory Miseducation* that 'we already have too much formal school and ... the more we get the less education we will get' (1971: 11). Writing these words in the early 1960s, the author was pushing towards an idea that compulsory schooling was *per se* a bad thing: a child-centric pedagogy was required which would be so complete that the very choice to attend or not to attend would be left to the child. A.S. Neill had pioneered, some decades earlier, the idea that a child should be able to choose not to attend classes. Goodman and others of his generation were prepared to go somewhat further, however: for them, the very existence of such an institution as a school was up for debate and teaching itself was not necessarily necessary. On his view, 'the attempt to control *prevents* learning': as with teaching a child to ride a bicycle, 'the more you try the more he fails. The best one can do is to provide him a bicycle, allay his anxiety, tell him to keep going, and *not* to try to balance' (78, emphasis retained).

Goodman's arguments retain a radical shock value even fifty years since their first publication. An English teacher in a twenty-first-century British school would likely find himself out of a job if he informed an Ofsted inspector that he simply intended to step back and leave the child to learn to read of their own accord, just as one would do if the child were learning to ride a bike. Perhaps a music teacher can take more risks than an English teacher, given that an inability to play music is unlikely to ruin a person's employment prospects. Being able to read and write is more important (arguably, at least). What is certain, in any case, is that the radical critique of the 'deschoolers' has little currency today.

Does all this mean that using child-centred methods for music teaching with DJ decks is necessarily a 'blind alley', given the current climate in education? To make such a conclusion at this point would be to foreclose prematurely the discussion at hand: we need to see, firstly, what is at stake and what may or may not seem to be possible in the current situation, rather than immediately admitting defeat based upon the dominant (anti-child-centric) trend in education at present.

I will pass over the excellent and extremely important work of Paulo Freire by quoting a single argumentation: 'analysis of the teacher-student relationship, inside or outside the school, reveals its fundamentally *narrative* character'; 'Education', Freire goes on, 'is suffering from narration sickness' (1996: 52, emphasis retained). The work of Freire's close associate Ivan Illich will be dealt with in a little more detail, however, for I find more to query in his work. On Illich's view, 'the inverse of school is possible'; that is, 'we can depend on self-motivated learning instead of employing teachers to bribe or compel the student to find the time and the will to learn'. Furthermore, 'we can provide the learner with new links to the world instead of continuing to funnel all educational programs through the teacher' (1971: 73). The title of the book from which these comments are sourced, *Deschooling Society*, gave not only a collective name for the radical theorists ('deschoolers', as they are commonly known) but also something of a manifesto. On Illich's view, 'to hope for fundamental change in the school system as an effect of conventionally conceived social or economic change is … an illusion. Moreover, this illusion grants the school – the reproductive organ of a consumer society – almost unquestioned immunity' (74). In other words, we have to change the school system *before* we can change the society, it seems: the Marxist idea (namely that, 'come the glorious day', institutions such as schools will be radically transformed along with the rest of society) is anathema to Illich.

What is there to query, here? In short, I am not convinced that the argument is not putting the 'cart before the horse', as we say in Britain. It is reasonable enough that Illich should wish for 'an Age of Leisure (*schole*) as opposed to an economy dominated by service industries' (1971: viii), I think, but I am not convinced that deschooling could *precede* such a radical transformation of society. 'Workers of the world … relax', seems to be Illich's unspoken motto. One can wish for such an opportunity for the proletariat, however, without necessarily agreeing that this can be *spontaneously* achieved. Similarly, one might agree that 'public education would profit from the deschooling of society, just as family life, politics, security, faith, and communication would profit from an analogous process' (2). The question, however, is whether the 'analogous process' in question is actually *imminent*; if not, one can argue that it is in fact the children of working class families who would suffer from deschooling. Yes, 'The poor have always been socially powerless', and perhaps it is also the case that an 'increasing reliance on institutional care adds a new dimension to their helplessness: psychological impotence, the inability to fend for themselves' (3). If such helplessness has already arisen, though, will it really help the impotent poor if we simply sweep away the institutional care which is embodied by the schools? One could argue that, where Illich should be turning to Marx, he instead gropes towards Nietzsche (ie his assumption that an ability to 'fend for themselves' can be summoned through the raw power of human will, rather than being nurtured, with the aid of a class conscious leadership, towards collective empowerment).

Illich is very much what Marxists will call a 'voluntarist', then. It may well be the case that 'most people acquire most of their knowledge outside school, and in school only insofar as school, in a few rich countries, has become their place of confinement during an increasing part of their lives' (Illich 1971: 12). It is also fair to suggest that 'Most learning happens casually, and even most intentional learning is not the result of programmed instruction' (ibid.). However, if we are to 'break the spell of this economy and shape a new one' (51), deschooling surely could not occur in isolation: rather, it would need to be one element within a whole pattern of dissent and conscious struggle, considered seriously. Perhaps, in the early 1970s context in which his text was published, dissent and consciousness *did* seem to be gathering in strength. Even then, though, I am inclined to think that the proposal of spontaneous deschooling was hasty and, frankly, folly on the part of a surprising number of otherwise excellent minds. Of course, we can agree with the desire for a future society wherein 'the educational path of each student would be his own to follow' (99). A more sober estimation of the likelihood of imminently moving towards such a society would probably have been wise, though.

At times, that said, Illich is remarkably prescient. If the idea of knowledge as a 'commodity' does not change, he proposes that in the future 'Pedagogical therapists will drug their pupils more in order to teach them better', whilst 'students will drug themselves more to gain relief from the pressures of teachers and the race for certificates. Increasingly larger numbers of bureaucrats will presume to pose as teachers' (Illich 1971: 50). In the decades since Illich wrote these words, Ritalin and other drugs of this type have reached epidemic levels in the West. Meanwhile, recreational drugs have been more and more prevalent in schools and universities. Successive Governments have been more and more confident to instruct teachers about what and how they should teach, despite the Ministers' typical ignorance about educational realities 'at the chalkface'. Government meddling since at least the 1980s has unquestionably interfered with the prestige of teaching as a profession to the extent that, today, some 'teaching' reduces to little more than rubber stamping bureaucratically-decided policies. (I write as someone who has taught 'Citizenship' lessons. Probably a good idea in principle, I felt these lessons were pitiful primarily because I was delivering a subject which I had not been trained to teach and which had been pushed into the curriculum very much by the 'bureaucrats [who] presume to pose as teachers' of which Illich writes.)

Also remarkably prescient is Illich's proposal that 'it should be possible, at any time, for any potential client to consult with other experienced clients of a professional about their satisfaction with him [sic] by means of another peer network easily set up by computer' (1971: 96). With the arrival of the Internet, we have gained precisely such a situation, have we not? However, the Internet alone, as it currently stands, is hardly an adequate substitute for the educational experience which is typically gained in school. Most readers will agree, for example, that the Internet's facility for 'peer networks' such as Ratedpeople.com does not quite ensure that we can source reliable professionals to work with or employ in day-to-day contexts. Some of Illich's 'blue skies thinking', then, has proven to be dubious: we now know that a computer can help us to learn, but few would claim that it renders obsolete the benefit of learning directly from (or, perhaps better, with) another immediately-present person. (One can probably learn from the Internet something about the way one should hold a violin bow, but the computer cannot look at one's hand and make a judgement as to how well one is actually holding this musical tool.)

The greatest problem with *Deschooling Society*, on my view, is its all-or-nothing approach. To 'encourage school reform', Illich insists, equates to striving for 'less poisonous automobiles' (1971: 50). Perhaps so, of course, and perhaps we would be better off if cars were banned immediately everywhere. Until such a thing occurs, though, even the sympathetic commentator might feel that less poisonous automobiles (eg 'cleaner' emissions and so forth) are pragmatic. We might say much the same about the existence of schools, furthermore.

In any case, I would argue that the book is not watertight in theoretical terms. Take Illich's proposal for 'a "bank" for skill exchange. Each citizen would be given a basic credit with which to acquire fundamental skills' (1971: 90). 'Beyond that minimum', he suggests, 'further credits would go to those who earned them by teaching, whether they served as models in organized skills centers or did so privately at home or on the playground.' However, 'Only those who had taught others for an equivalent amount of time would have a claim on the time of more advanced teachers.' How convincing is this as a theoretical proposal? Illich admits himself that such a system would be at risk of ceding 'further advantage to the privileged classes'. Similarly he admits that his idea of 'educational vouchers' through which 'The "teacher" could even be paid according to the number of pupils he could attract for any full two-hour period' could be 'abused for exploitative and immoral purposes' (94). He parries that 'Concern about the dangers of the system should not make us lose sight of its far greater benefits' (50). Is such making-do-despite-problems not precisely a *reformist* attitude by any other name, however? One assumes Illich had not consulted Marx's *The Poverty of Philosophy* (1847/1975), with its devastating attack on Proudhon; arguably the 'bank' idea outlined above is even more 'schoolboyish' (Marx 1975: 183) than Proudhon's proposals for an alternative to capitalist methods of exchanging labour time. Indeed, as Illich himself essentially admits in the quotations just offered, the bourgeois 'privileged classes' might well gain more than they lose from his proposals.

Not long after he had published *Deschooling Society*, Illich became significantly more circumspect in his prescriptions: 'For all its vices, school cannot be simply and rashly eliminated; in the present situation it performs certain important negative functions' (1974/1981: 38). He adds that 'graduates' of alternatives such as 'free schools' had been 'rendered impotent for life in a society that bears little resemblance to the protected gardens in which they have been cultivated' (43). In this later text, *After Deschooling, What?*, Illich even goes as far as to admit that 'The rash and uncritical disestablishment of school could lead to a free-for-all in the production and consumption of more vulgar learning, acquired for immediate utility or eventual prestige' (44). Consequently, we need to proceed by 'ruling out not only schools but [also] all other ritual screening' such as that which ensures 'employment, promotion, or access to tools'; unless we do this, 'deschooling means driving out the devil with Beelzebub' (47).

The edition of *After Deschooling, What?* from which I have sourced the above quotations features an introductory essay by Ian Lister which extends our impression that, as the 1970s progressed, the progressive educationalists came to doubt the coherency of some of their former anti-school arguments. I would not say that Lister is exactly humble: he maintains a (fairly astonishing, I would think) opinion that Illich's work is 'more critical and more radical' than Marxism (Illich 1974/1981: 6–7). However, he does yield to a 'sobering thought, that in western society, deschooling and alternatives were features of an economic boom rather an economic crisis' (7). This, I think, is a likely story: that the radicalism of the progressive, child-centred era was a product of the (economically booming) 1960s rather than being some kind of vanguard creator of the fabled 'swinging sixties'. Lister is hinting, in other words, that economic factors may have encouraged the remarkable spread of radical ideas in the 1960s more than the radical thinking in itself providing the causative factor.

By the mid-to-late 1970s, things looked very different: boom had turned towards bust, economically speaking. 'Today educational reformers of all varieties have gone quiet. The spate of radical literature … has come to an end', Lister writes in September 1976 (Illich 1974/1981: 27). The date is telling: the following month, Prime Minister Callaghan (a Labour PM, significantly enough) would make perhaps the most decisive move in post-war British educational history. In short, Callaghan decried the state of the nation's schools at that moment in time and thus, by implication, denounced the child-centred philosophy which had taken centre stage, in the UK at least, since the *Plowden Report* of 1967.

Look back in anger – or in intrigue?

I have consciously criticised Ivan Illich's work herein because I feel that there are definitely problems with his thinking (as, it seems, Illich himself came to realise). There is a great deal to applaud in the child-centred and progressive tradition, however, which is why I would suggest that many of the associated pedagogical principles can be successfully applied when DJ decks are used in the twenty-first-century classroom. What, then, should we keep from the ideas of the progressives, and which ideas should we jettison? Might music make a good fit with child-centred methods? These are the key questions for the present section of this chapter. I begin by looking at some reflective studies of the era in general before exploring more music-specific work on child-centred teaching methods. In the conclusion I circle back to John Holt's later work which, I contend, has much merit as well as some ideas which I will query.

Roy Lowe's *The Death of Progressive Education*, it is fair to say, is both exceptionally well-informed and highly pessimistic about the past, present and future of child-centred and progressive education. The pessimism of his closing sentence – 'I see little prospect of the major redirection of our education system which I believe is needed' – renders questionable my contention that child-centred methods retain some validity in the twenty-first century, perhaps (2007: 161). Naturally, in regard to the past, he acknowledges the pivotal role of Callaghan in the effective closure of the child-centred progressive era. Lowe's take on the infamous Ruskin speech is markedly bleak. 'The precedent set by Callaghan ... of side-stepping both Parliament and the DES, was to be copied by both Thatcher and Blair, although in 1976 it was clearly a new departure', he suggests (70). Nevertheless, 'much that was said in October 1976 [by Callaghan and a wide range of other commentators both before and after his Ruskin speech] on the subject of educational policymaking was already to some degree foreseeable and even preordained'. 'It was', Lowe adds, 'by October 1976, in many ways, inevitable that power would now be exercised more directly by central government' (77–8).

Why was this (definitively reactionary) shift 'inevitable'? According to Lowe the 1960s and 1970s were actually a 'period of partial and timid reform which ... carried with it the seeds of its own undoing'. 'By the mid-seventies', as a result, 'everything was in place for the next swing of the pendulum' (Lowe 2007: 60). The metaphor of the educational pendulum 'which swings back and forth between prescription and freedom, formal teaching and discovery learning, between trusting teachers and telling them exactly what to do' (a *TES* correspondent quoted in Lowe: 152–3) is one which older teachers can very often be heard to remark upon in informal conversations in the staffroom, in my experience. However, if Lowe is to be believed (along with most other well-informed reflective accounts of the post-war period in education I have encountered), the pendulum idea masks a more bald truth: the short-lived progressive era actually had limited impact and has been followed by a fairly continuous flow away from progressivism and towards formal, prescriptive, competition-centred education.

Lowe is unambiguous that 'The child-centred approach, though it had become the established theoretical orthodoxy [in the 1960s and 1970s], had clearly failed to percolate down to the grassroots level of education' (2007: 97). There has, he insists, been a 'slow retreat from progressive education' (1). 'Virtually at a stroke, teachers were made answerable to their political masters' after the 1988 Education Reform Act (3). 1988, as a result, provided 'a step-change which transformed permanently the way in which curriculum reform was approached in modern Britain' (91). Indeed, from the time of Callaghan's Ruskin speech onwards there has been a 'semi-permanent shift to the right in the grounds of educational debate in modern Britain' (74). 'There is no sign of any administration in the foreseeable future which would turn the clock back', Lowe suggests (3).

A reader who is unfamiliar with the arguments around child-centred methods would be entitled to wonder if the contemporary educational scene is really as devoid of child-centric teaching as Lowe insists. We should certainly note that a rhetoric can be found in current discourses around respecting differing 'learning styles' and remembering that 'every child matters'. According to James Avis, however, such rhetoric is merely 'an appropriation of progressive education … reflected in the concern with a student-centred, activity-based education…. This progressivism, which presents itself as radical, is in fact deeply conservative' (quoted in Lowe 2007: 94).

Perhaps the most decisive period in the UK's drift away from child-centred methods, according to Lowe and many other commentators, is the era in which Chris Woodhead was in charge of Ofsted (late 1990s). As opposed to child-centred education, Woodhead was in favour of 'didactic, teacher-centred methods', Lowe argues (2007: 122). The description is reasonable, in so far as Woodhead complained explicitly about 'progressive teaching methods whereby children are expected to learn by discovery and are never told anything' (125). Woodhead's statement is a distortion of the working methods of most progressive educators, in fact. If a learner requests information, the progressive 'teacher' (a word which is often given scare quotes by progressives) can provide it; but discovery by the learner, driven by her/his individual interests and needs, should always be given priority over the interests and needs of teachers, politicians or the society at large.

Much of the polemic against child-centred education which Lowe reports is shocking in its naked hostility and distant relationship with the facts. Observe, for example, the following complaint from *The Spectator*: 'the state sector includes the worst schools in the land. The private sector includes the best…. The reason? Teaching-training colleges … are staffed by Marxists who peddle an irrelevant, damaging, outdated ideology of anti-elitism' (Lowe 2007: 122). *The Daily Express*, meanwhile, attacks 'Trendies in class who harm pupils' and ex-Prime Minister Blair is quoted in regard to 'a culture that tolerates low ambitions, rejects excellence and treats poverty as an excuse for failure' (146). A *TES* correspondent comments upon the 'reluctance of those involved in primary education to renounce the doctrine of Plowden altogether and view their task with objective clarity *untainted by ideology*' (157, emphasis added). However, opposition to an 'ideology of anti-elitism' would be a counter-ideology, logically; and such pro-elitism may or may not be a good thing but it can hardly be claimed to be truly untainted by ideology therefore.

Such journalism barely merits discussion, of course: an argument that ideology is a condition from which others suffer whilst the journalist himself is untainted by bias is obviously extremely weak. Much the same can be said of Blair's idea of a conscious rejection of 'excellence' (as if it is an excess of success in the classroom which spurred the progressives to make their disapproving critiques). We can observe, though, that *The Spectator*'s idea that success in the private sector and problems in the state sector are purely a result of ideological biases in teacher training (rather than having anything to do with, say, funding and class sizes) has been fairly recently echoed by *Standpoint* magazine. Writing in *Standpoint* in June 2012, Matthew Hunter asserts that the difference between his own private education and 'Britain's abundant failing state schools' is not a consequence of 'material deprivation': 'Instead it was a deprivation of effective teaching methods' which was/is the problem. State funding per pupil, according to Hunter, is broadly equivalent to 'a good private day school'.

Again, the journalism hardly merits comment. (Hunter asserts that it is 'hard to imagine' the child of a lorry driver attaining high level academic success today, and yet I saw several pupils from similar working class backgrounds leave the school where I taught to attend 'Russell Group' universities in order to study Law, Medicine and Sciences. Clearly, then, *Standpoint* is happy to publish evidence-free and factually inaccurate assertions in its pages.) Disappointingly, however, it has to be acknowledged that at least one contemporary academic, who one might otherwise assume to be a friend of progressive ideals, shares comparable views. The scholar in question is Guy Claxton and, at face, his work chimes with child-centred methods. He encourages, for example, 'groups researching self-chosen projects', 'collaboration and discussion' and 'self-organisation' (2008: vii). He thinks, as did A.S. Neill, that a happy child will be an effective learner (13–15) and that there is no such thing as a child who is not motivated to learn (89). He is also of the opinion that 'school learning is, in many ways, a rather odd kind of learning which may not recur' in adult life; 'interesting kinds of out-of-school learning' (such as learning to DJ or MC, we might posit) are worthy of educational attention (126). One is not surprised, therefore, that Claxton hints at a sympathy for the 1960s progressives (186–7), except in that he goes no further than a hint (with none of the giants of the child-centred tradition we have mentioned so far in the present chapter earning a name check in Claxton's book, disappointingly).

What, then, is my criticism of Claxton's position (beyond the fact that he writes as if the impetuses mentioned in the last paragraph are a new idea where they are in fact part of a long-held tradition)? First, I feel that his proposals are too modest; second, and more critically, Claxton effectively lays the blame for ineffective teaching and learning at the hands of *teachers* rather than acknowledging that the *education system* has forced a teacher-centred pedagogy on a largely unwilling teaching community. As to the modesty issue, Claxton suggests, for example, that school assemblies should include a 'round of applause for Best Question of the Week' from a particular pupil (2008: 149); 'Do students get to nominate each other for Improvement in Learning Awards, or is it down to the teacher? (150). These are good suggestions but are hardly radical; a 'swearbox' to be used in class to discourage teachers from using the word 'work' (158) hardly compares with the kind of re-drawing of the educational map which the progressives demanded in the 1960s and 1970s. (We can note, on this topic, that the child-centred progressives *did* successfully influence the educational mainstream in the UK and beyond during the later decades of the twentieth century. For all the fury against their 'ideology', we now have primary school children clustered around rectangular tables rather than sitting in rows facing the teacher as was *de rigueur* in the 1940s and 1950s and before. Even the UK's current Conservative government are not proposing to reverse this innovation – not yet, at least.)

Claxton's most problematic argument is that 'The key to educational reform does not lie in grand structural changes'; rather, we need to adjust 'teachers' daily habits' so that 'teachers pay closer attention to students' achievements' (2008: 167). The implication that the latter would not be a normal habit for teachers is somewhat insulting; and the idea that the educational structure is adequate as it stands makes the kind of (actually child-centred) ideals which Claxton promotes hard to implement for the mainstream teacher. After all, the current head of Ofsted has explicitly attacked the 1960s 'ideology which ruined the lives of generations of children at that time' on the grounds that 'it was unstructured, it wasn't teacher led', according to the *Daily Telegraph* report on 21 March 2014. If Ofsted demands 'to see teacher-led activities, we want to see structured learning, we want to see teaching in more formal settings' (ibid.), it is hard to see how a teacher could actually implement key ideals which Claxton holds. Only a structural change (such as, most pressingly, replacing the leadership of Ofsted) could enable a more child-centred educational scene in the UK, therefore.

Instead, Claxton states that 'parents need to be confident explorers' (2008: 170) which, though obviously a fine aspiration, is not too helpful for the teacher in the kind of inner city school where I worked. Parents of young people I taught included alcoholics, the mentally ill (named and effectively lampooned for her problem by a local newspaper, in one particular case), heroin addicts and/or convicted prisoners. What if mum and dad are both in prison for drug-related offences (something which I was aware of in one particular case, the child of their union being in fact a very decent and pleasant young man in the 'top set')? Is it fair, in that case, for the likes of Tony Blair to insist that schools are to blame for having low expectations, if and when they base their curriculum around the child's specific needs? Is the 'time out card', which so many troubled young people are given by staff in the desperate attempt to help them to cope in school, just a cop-out for teachers who refuse to 'aim high' on behalf of their learners? Or is there something more broadly 'rotten in the state of Denmark'?

'Government reforms of class size' are less important than the 'classroom ethos and methods', Claxton claims (2008: 186). As should be clear by now, I find this a dangerous idea because, as with the journalism of *Standpoint* and *The Spectator*, it implies that the small class sizes and extra funds which are available to the privately-educated child give no significant advantage. The problem with the state sector, according to the journalists quoted above, is merely the child-centred ethos and methods which an allegedly Marxist teacher-training establishment have foisted upon teachers. Claxton's arguments do too little to challenge such nonsense and do too much to place the blame for unsuccessful learning on the heads of teachers working within a state-controlled education system which has been chronically interfered with by ill-informed and ideologically-driven politicians. He is quite correct that 'There are many teachers who do not believe that Learning to Learn could make a real difference for the disaffected students they have to deal with every day' (189). In my case, this disbelief was driven by the fact that I was instructed, along with the rest of the teaching staff (and without any consultation), to teach 'L2L' for one hour per fortnight with my tutor group. Amongst my group of predominantly 'bottom set' 15- to 16-year-olds, very few could read, write and add up well enough to be predicted to achieve five 'good' (ie grade C or above) GCSE passes. Several were regularly in fairly serious trouble with the law; it was common for the Police to deliver one particular tutee to school after they had caught him roaming the local area whilst truanting. Another tutee was already working every night in his uncle's Indian restaurant, biding his time until he could legally stop coming to school. What would have 'made a difference' with these learners, to at least some extent, would have been the opportunity to self-direct their learning by, for example, using DJ decks (which more than one student in the group was passionate about) for that one hour per fortnight. Instead, they had to 'Learn 2 Learn' (L2L) with a teacher who had been given little or no training for delivering a tightly prescribed curriculum based on insultingly simple and utterly uninspiring worksheets and 'Powerpoint' presentations. The head and deputy head were the only individuals whom I ever heard voicing any enthusiasm whatsoever for the dry L2L sessions: teachers and students were of the opinion that it was a serious drag.

I am in favour, then, of child-centred approaches such as the idea that 'there may be alternative ways of experiencing life and telling stories than those legitimised by the teacher, the school, the National Curriculum and the public examinations' (Moore 2012: 95). The classroom practitioner who is persuaded that such methods are wise, however, has to face up to the fact that institutional pressures (primarily the government and Ofsted, in the UK, but also a prejudiced and primarily right wing media) militate against such the practice of such methods. I will say more, in Part Two herein, about the varying ways that child-centred methods can be slipped into a music teacher's work without too much risk of disapproval by such institutional pressures.

It certainly is important to be aware, though, that ambiguities abound in the contemporary scene. Alex Moore has shown, for example, that the UK's National Curriculum 'continues to promote individualism and competition at the same time as ... it encourages collaboration and inclusion', with such contradictions and ambiguities even being embedded within key policy initiatives such as the *Every Child Matters* policy of 2003 (2012: 167). There is plenty of enthusiasm for child-centred learning amongst university-based researchers today but very little progressivism amongst daily practising teachers, I would contend. This is hardly surprising, of course: the HMI and, latterly, Ofsted must 'judge schools, and therefore headteachers'; they 'do not confine their attention to individual teachers'. In the 1960s, this meant that government reports such as *Plowden* strongly encouraged a 'child-centred philosophy [which] effectively created a new and powerful definition of good teaching' (Darling 1994: 45). Today, the opposite applies: the current Ofsted chief is emphatic that teacher-centred education is the best policy, and a head teacher who wants to hang on to his hat had better follow this prescription, without doubt. For the reasons just outlined, this ideology at the top has to filter down to classrooms and certainly will influence (and, in my experience, actively damage) relationships between teachers and learners.

What can one do, then, as music teacher? One option, of course, is to get out of the game, which this author did after ten years in which the teacher-centred ideologues tightened their grip on the UK's educational system to the point where I personally felt it had become a stranglehold. I am not the only teacher (labelled as 'outstanding' by Ofsted, I suppose it is worth repeating) who has found such a move necessary in recent years. It is hard to justify contributing to a school system which is institutionally determined to turn children away from that which they are interested in (the UK's EBacc 'performance measure' certainly meaning that senior staff actively discourage individual children who are passionate about music from taking the subject in question, as I directly observed). As music teacher, one is teaching a subject with very little esteem afforded to it by the modern education system. The educationalist who has perhaps done the most to rubbish the child-centred approach, R.S. Peters, offers a philosophy which 'even if the argument worked for science, it would do nothing to establish the value of music' (Darling 1994: 65).

All this said, I would nevertheless maintain that attempting to deliver child-centred music teaching *is* worth the effort. The best music-specific overview that I am aware of regarding such efforts is John Finney's superb *Music Education in England 1950–2010* (2010). Finney notes Peter Aston and John Paynter's ground-breaking insistence, *circa* 1970, that learners should be granted 'the freedom to explore chosen materials. As far as possible this work should not be controlled by a teacher. His [sic] role is to set off trains of thought and help the pupil develop his own critical powers and perceptions' (53). Finney goes on to reveal that he received in-service training from Paynter in which 'We were exhorted to give up the idea of the music teacher as guardian of the sacred flame of tradition in the form of inert knowledge separated from practical application' (54). Paynter was explicitly opposed to 'Music for the Minority', believing that all children could develop imagination, creativity and musicality in classrooms (57). Consequent to his training by Paynter, Finney suggests that 'Music was now pouring from the children and not into them and I learnt how to accept and value their music' (55).

Such corresponds closely to my own experience of attempting child-centred work in secondary level music: by starting with the child's interest, a level of engagement and development became possible which more prescriptive 'learning objective'-centred work had failed to yield. We should note, though, that Finney is no uncritical advocate of child-centred methods in music education: 'In fact the whole progressive movement falls as being insufficiently grounded', he argues, suggesting that Keith Swanwick is important (relative to Paynter) precisely because he 'provided music teachers with an easily comprehensible scheme, rather than a philosophical argument' (2010: 60). In any case (and despite all the 'progressive thinking within music education of the 1970s and 1980s'), the 'model of the music teacher as co-composer, co-adventurer' which Paynter and others had espoused remained 'by no means common' at the end of that period (70). This is partly because it was 'an ideal requiring a range of skills that few teachers possessed or were motivated to acquire'. The risk was 'leaving the pupil to "flap like a butterfly" just at the point where teacher support and intervention was crucial' (ibid.).

Again, my experience as a teaching practitioner tallies with this argument: I was no blind advocate of child-centred methods and, if and when I felt it would be profitable in a concrete situation, I would certainly intervene rather than allow a learner to be left flapping. Finney argues that such a pragmatic *modus operandi* was always the tendency: 'Music in school, even in its most progressive form, *was* regulated' (2010: 76, emphasis added). This led him to research 'a non-school rock band', with some interesting findings: for example, that his role was, initially at least, 'as "caretaker", the person who showed a little interest in them, the person who loaned equipment and locked up after their meeting' (77). Finney was prepared, in this research, to take seriously a teenage punk band influenced by Crass and Conflict (80) – the latter two groups being no less aggressive and harsh than the happy hardcore music which my students enjoyed. (It is worth adding that both hardcore punk and happy hardcore EDM are essentially only aggressive on the surface: underneath all that harshness, there *is* interesting musicality at work, to varying extents.) What happens though, when the music teacher shows that little bit of interest? The possibility, I would argue, is for a child-centred classroom in which mutual respect between teacher and learner becomes significantly more thinkable.

Finney critiques the 2000 text *Music Teaching in the Secondary School* (written, he pointedly informs us, by an Ofsted inspector) for its closed preoccupation with musical facts (such as the appearance of ninths in a twelve bar blues or the names of the notes in chords I, IV and V) over and above emotional responses to the music. 'There is no mention of musical qualities, of human interest or of felt experience', he ruefully remarks (2010: 94). There is every reason, then, to think that Finney is critical of the currently dominant ideologies in the broad educational scene. If, though, Ofsted and the exam boards and the other institutions which dominate the educational field are predisposed against learner interest/experience, the practising teacher will naturally want to be wary when introducing child-centred work into the classroom.

What is the way forwards today, then? Perhaps that 'The music teacher would become a community musician, a generalist able to draw upon and harness diverse resources' (Finney 2010: 99). If such a thing occurred, 'Pupils would be able to engage with music at their own pace and, in their own way, and be released from pre-specified learning outcomes', Finney suggests (ibid.). Whether this would satisfy Ofsted, and the head teachers who answer to them, is open to debate: music teachers are effectively 'required to choose how best to perform, for which audiences and for what purposes', Finney admits, and to that extent we have to tread carefully (140). Nevertheless, I am inclined to state that the risk to the teacher's prestige (in terms of evaluation by Ofsted and so forth) is worth the trade-off (namely, a potentially huge boost to learner engagement with and enjoyment of music lessons).

Interestingly enough, 'the potential for DJ-ing' is mentioned but Finney suggests that 'The resource implications are formidable' (104). This is less the case of late, I think, with educational catalogues offering DJ-orientated equipment at ever-lower prices. It is probably worth adding that my own classroom work with hardcore EDM began with pupils bringing cassette tapes into class and simply MC rapping over the top of them: the only resource I required for this was a tape player. The learner who brought in the first cassette was a difficult and troubled young man, but he performed for the class with a marked level of seriousness, intensity and – I believe this is the right word – professionalism. This, in short, is the potential of child-centred work in music classrooms: turn on, tune in and watch the disaffected learners get seriously engaged.

Conclusion

The child-centred progressive era of the 1960s and 1970s is best eyed critically, with 'important caveats' existing if we are to avoid 'chaos rather than continuity' in the classroom (Sugrue 1997: 21). In practice, most teachers mix formal (ie traditional and instructional) methods with informal (ie child-centred) strategies (24). Although I have argued in this chapter that much of the rhetoric against child-centred and progressive education is markedly right wing, I certainly support the broad refusal to allow 'inner-city children' to be 'underestimated by their teachers' (31). Indeed, I value highly Ciaran Sugrue's argument (based on actual classroom practice during the progressive era of the 1970s, importantly) that 'too much of what was valuable from traditional teaching had been sacrificed in a spirit of reforming zeal' (32). For this reason, Sugrue proposes that we look back in *reflection*, not anger or envy: whilst we can approve of the *Plowden Report*'s placement of the child at the centre of the educational process, 'the head, heart and guiding hand of the teacher needs to be reinscribed in that process also' (227).

In any case, and as I have attempted to show here, the music teacher who wants to keep her/his job ought best to show balance. The balance in question will be between any enthusiasm she or he might feel for child-centred learning, on the one hand, against the top-down demands of the educational establishment for a formal, teacher-centred approach in which learning objectives are placed at the heart of the educational process, on the other hand.

We can note, incidentally, that Ivan Illich's closest co-conspirator Everett Reimer refers in the sub-title to *School is Dead* (his 1971 text which is widely perceived as a companion text for *Deschooling Society*) to 'alternatives *in* education' rather than alternatives *to* education. Perhaps, then, the deschooling tendency which embodied the most extreme end of the child-centred progressive movement was always a bit less anti-educational than it appeared at face. That said, the rhetoric against schools clearly influenced the later thinking of John Holt (whose early work I prioritised in the present chapter). Holt's *Instead of Education* (1976) retains the sensitivity and practical utility which marks out his *How Children Fail* as a classic educational text. Here, however, we can ascertain a strong influence from Illich which is recognisable throughout the book and sometimes explicitly so (Holt 1976: 110-1). Certainly worth reading, the book is full of practical suggestions as to how a teacher (as opposed to a capital t 'T-eacher') can attempt to avoid dominating the learner and instead can work with them in order help them to do things they want to do *better*. As promised, though, I want to conclude with some critical remarks about the Holt of *Instead of Education*.

The first thing we should note is that Holt, here, writes explicitly with a view to 'a society that does not exist' (1976: 9) and encourages 'a different view of human beings' (212) in this future society. He aims to 'attack the legitimacy of compulsory education and schooling' (12) and argues that 'education – compulsory schooling, compulsory learning – is a tyranny and against the human mind and spirit' (226). His late 1970s position, then, is a fairly extreme one wherein nothing of value can be seen in the presently existing (capital s) 'S-chools' and any improvements are for the future. Even more worrying, on my reading, is his declaration that 'None of [his proposals are] very likely to happen in the next ten years or so' (214): the big change, in other words, is not even particularly imminent. With the benefit of hindsight, we can add that things were actually set to get a good deal worse for child-centred and progressive methods in the decade(s) after Holt wrote this book.

Does this mean that we should just give up and go home, forget schools and those who have to work in them (teachers and learners, who are arguably both trapped in a system over which they little or no control)? Such a decision would, I feel strongly, be a step too far. I have made no secret, in the present chapter, of my personal disdain for certain dominant tendencies in contemporary education and my unwillingness to continue working as a secondary-level teacher in an inner-city school. I will add that my own attempts to place the child at the centre of the curriculum were less fully realised than I would have liked. However, I am quite certain that not everything which I did, nor everything which happened within the school more widely, amounted to a tyranny against the children's minds and spirit: some of the children, indeed, showed signs of enjoying school and all benefitted to at least some extent from it, I would assert.

Within my own practice, providing the opportunity for 'sessions' of DJing and MCing in my classroom certainly brought forth the most successful child-centred moments in my school teaching career. Kathy Kiddle, writing about educational work with 'Traveller' children, remarks that 'there is a desperate need for the children of these minority groups to have a way of finding an identity and a voice' (in John 1996: 79). 'Denigrated by the public at large', she insists that 'there has to be some way for them to develop a positive self-image'. Some of the children I worked with were indeed Travellers, but a good many more besides these (most if not all of whom would be labelled as 'chavs' by many within the UK) were desperately in need of positive self-images. I am convinced that, by bringing their low-esteemed (by society, in general) happy hardcore music into a mainstream educational environment, a significant number of children were able to move towards such positivity: suddenly, even if only for a moment, their 'other' music was at the centre of the curriculum. In the next chapter I shall say more as to how this shift within the classroom directly influenced and developed the learners' self-image in positively important ways.

References

Claxton, Guy, *What's The Point of School?: Rediscovering the Heart of Education* (Oxford: Oneworld, 2008)

Dale, Pete, 'Remember the Riots in 1991?: The Very Specific Context of Newcastle on Tyne', invited speaker at the Subcultures Network's one-day symposium 'Re-telling the Riots! Music, Community and Civic Unrest', Bristol, 18 October 2013.

Darling, John, *Child-Centred Education and Its Critics* (London: Paul Chapman, 1994)

Finney, John, *Music Education in England 1950–2010: The Child-Centred Progressive Tradition* (Aldershot: Ashgate 2010)

Freire, Paulo, *Pedagogy of the Oppressed* (London: Penguin, 1970)

Goodman, Paul, *Compulsory Miseducation* (Harmondsworth: Penguin, 1971)

Holt, John, *How Children Fail* (London: Pitman, 1965)

Holt, John, *Instead of Education: Ways to Help People Do Things Better* (New York: Penguin, 1976)

Illich, Ivan D., *Deschooling Society* (London: Calder and Boyars, 1971)

Illich, Ivan, *After Deschooling, What?* (London: Writers and Readers Publishing Cooperative, 1974/1981)

John, Mary, *Children in Charge: The Child's Right to a Fair Hearing* (London: Jessica Kingsley, 1996)

Lowe, Roy, *The Death of Progressive Education: How Teachers Lost Control of the Classroom* (Abingdon: Routledge, 2007)

Montessori, Maria, *The Child in the Family* (London: Pan, 1975)

Moore, Alex, *Teaching and Learning: Pedagogy, Curriculum and Culture* (Abingdon: Routledge, 2012)

Neill, A.S., *Summerhill* (Harmondsworth: Penguin, 1968)

Reimer, Everett, *School Is Dead: An Essay on Alternatives in Education* (Harmondsworth: Penguin, 1971)

Sugrue, Ciaran, *Complexities of Teaching: Child-Centred Perspectives* (London: Falmer, 1997)

3
UNDERSTANDING STUDENTS

I have asserted that DJ decks in classrooms can seriously aid the re-engagement of disaffected learners for music lessons. How and why does this happen? In short, how it can happen (if it happens, which will not always be the case in every school let alone with every class) is that a learner who may have refused to even participate in lessons in a particularly meaningful way suddenly leads the class and demonstrates musical skills which even the teacher lacks. Why this happens, putting it briefly again, is because the learner has been honing his (sometimes hers, but typically his – see below for detail on this issue) skills in private but did not anticipate his form of music-making being recognised as valid in a school environment.

When I brought DJ decks in to my teaching, it turned the classroom upside down; not quite literally, but very often symbolically. One particular pupil, whom I shall refer to as 'Johnny', had refused to open his mouth to sing since arriving in Year 7 (11 years old and rising). It made no difference if I cajoled him, berated him, threatened detentions; I am confident that even a financial bribe would have had to be seriously large to get this boy to sing. In practical work on keyboards or percussion, he was belligerent to a point beyond obstreperousness: a PGCE trainee whom I was mentoring regularly had to send him out of the class because the boy simply refused to do anything, in addition to disrupting the rest of his (bottom stream, ie Special Needs-orientated) class. On a 'parents evening', his mum told me that it was just her and him in the flat and, on more than one occasion, she had had to lock herself in the bathroom for protection whilst using a mobile to call for help from the police. Johnny was not a happy young man, then: I don't recall ever seeing him smile.

However, it turned out that Johnny was in fact a budding DJ with his own decks upon which he was practising with a furious passion every night after school. This came to light when I first acquired two second-hand decks and a mixer for my classroom. Johnny was one of several nascent DJs and MCs in his (numerically small class, by now in Year 8) and thus there was much excitement when the decks arrived in the classroom. However, we lacked suitable vinyl to play upon them.

Johnny, much to my surprise, offered to bring in some vinyl and a spare needle (stylus) to substitute for the damaged one which we had initially been trying to use. When he did so, it turned out that he had exceptional skill at, in particular, seamlessly blending one 'tune' into another. I remember very vividly the amazement one of his classmates displayed after a particularly impressive blend from the 'build up' of one record into the 'kick off' of another: the classmate pointed at the mixer in mute amazement before asking 'did you hear that, Sir?'

I did hear, and I saw it too: skill, in a word; real skill which I struggled to develop for myself in the coming months and years. I came to realise that some of these young people had abilities on the decks which, like many of my student violinists and all of the brass and woodwind players (I have never been good with instruments you have to blow into), went well beyond anything I would ever achieve on the particular musical equipment at hand.

Johnny would be dead before reaching the age of 20, sadly: I was told by a colleague that he drank himself to death, but it is likely that drugs will also have featured prominently in the period leading up to his demise. He had been permanently excluded from school in Year 10, although he did return the following year to shout at staff and students at the school gates at 'home time', refusing to leave until the Police came to take him away. His life, as far as I could tell, was fairly nasty, brutish and short. However, that day in Year 8 I saw a flash of something genuinely positive: Johnny, for once, was the envy of other learners and was undoubtedly proud of himself. As he collected his vinyl at the end of the hour-long lesson, he looked up at me and raised a thumb, saying 'thanks for that, reet Sir?' 'Reet' is a particular word in the North East: it implies, as does the word 'alright' from which it obviously derives, that all is well. Maybe for just a moment in his young life, all was well for Johnny; maybe, furthermore, if he had experienced more moments like that then he might not have caused so much trouble in and out of school, might not have been permanently excluded, might not have died.

Johnny's death was mentioned in passing during a staff briefing. However, as a student who all teachers will have remembered as, at best, 'difficult', his death did not attract the kind of remorse and discussion and demonstrations of emotion which one might otherwise expect when a recent alumnus dies before completing their teenage years. Another pupil (roughly the same age) lost his life fighting in the British Army in Afghanistan, a tragedy which earned several mentions in staff briefings and several teachers appearing at the funeral. Somehow, this didn't seem evenly handled and the death of Johnny played on my mind for some time. In large part, indeed, Johnny's death spurred me to write this book. There were many students over the years who were similar to him: difficult, troubled, disruptive but incredibly passionate about happy hardcore EDM and the DJ decks (or the MCing which is the classic bedfellow of this form of music-making). They deserve a chance to freely express themselves whilst they are young; that chance might never come again. My overarching hope is that the present book will encourage more music teachers to consider using such music and modes of music-making in their classroom: this is life and death stuff, I would assert; what, after all, is life for if not for expressing oneself?

In the first half of the chapter I focus upon my own teaching experiences and the effect that lessons based around the DJ decks had upon learners. In the second half, I try to problematize this positive element by examining thorny questions around crime, drugs, race and gender. In this second half I introduce some data generated in my researches not only in the North East but also in Oxfordshire and the North West of England, as well as drawing on some secondary sources.

Pure lethal on the decks

The North East of England is a unique place. Not only the accent and dialect of the region is distinctive: the whole way of behaving, interacting, looking at the world, is somewhat different from any other part of the UK, I would argue. The 'Geordies' of Newcastle/Gateshead (and 'Maccams' of Sunderland, Teesiders of Middlesbrough and so forth) are certainly a proud people, but they are also very creative – a fact which comes through very strongly in their speech. One of the statements I would often hear, and which I never tired of repeating in a plummy, Southern accent, was that such and such a pupil was 'pure lethal on the decks' or at MCing. 'Purely lethal? What could be better than that?', I would ask myself.

There were quite a few things beyond 'lethal' skills on the DJ decks for which the pupils in my classes often wanted: parents who weren't in prison, someone to read them a bedtime story when they had been small, a clean and safe and calm place to live, even just some decent food on the table in some cases. As a teacher, one would hear of severe neglect and abuse, sometimes on a 'need to know basis' from other staff and sometimes by joining the dots between things one had been told by children. (I will never forget the embarrassed explanation of a boy who couldn't do his Tenor Horn lesson because he was unable to comfortably lift and hold the instrument the day after carrying countless crates of beer into the storage room of his local pub; his mum was able to get a couple of free drinks in exchange for his services. By the time he was taken into council care, some years later, his childhood had already been effectively robbed from him.)

Neglect and abuse were as common as one might expect in an inner-city school on the 97th percentile for Fischer Family Trust national measures of socio-economic deprivation, with an inevitable knock-on effect upon behaviour. According to the Save the Children/CRSP's joint report on *Britain's Poorest Children*, the specific category of 'severely poor children' are eight times more likely to be suspended from school than 'non-severely poor' children (Adelman, Middleton and Ashworth 2003: 43). We need to bear in mind, here, that Ofsted can punitively place a school in 'special measures' if too many suspensions and exclusions take place. Given that, it is fair to assume that instances of challenging/disruptive behaviour are far more than eight times as common in schools with large numbers of severely poor children as compared with schools which are populated with children from more comfortable and/or affluent families. One is not supposed to argue that this situation has a negative impact upon the educational prospects of a school: to say so is supposedly to make 'excuses' for low ambitions with regards to the poor.

If a child cannot make progress on a musical instrument due to neglect and/or other forms of abuse at home, though, how is a music teacher supposed to achieve results which are comparable to those attained in schools where most if not all of the children have secure and safe home lives? (I have already mentioned the Tenor Horn incident. Other cases include innumerable parents who simply did not want the 'noise' of their child practising an instrument or singing – 'I keep telling him to pack it in!', one mother told me earnestly at a parent's evening – and boys getting beaten up primarily because they were carrying an instrument.) The playing field is not level, in fact, and when one works in a school with overwhelming numbers of severely poor children, one has to just be proud to be doing something positive for the young people: a teacher who holds her/his breath for supportive feedback from Ofsted runs a serious risk of asphyxiation, I would suggest.

For me, then, the job of music teacher was simultaneously emotionally rewarding and emotionally draining. It was never easy, and many of the traditional tasks – maintaining a school choir and orchestra, arranging instrumental tuition timetables, putting on school concerts – were a real challenge. As a matter of fact, I always managed to have a respectable choir, a ramshackle school band (featuring brass, woodwind and strings) and concerts once or twice a year; and these were a great leveller wherein the most academically capable would rub shoulders with the least able. I couldn't help but notice, that said, that far more of the children who opted into musical activities (with the possible exception of the choir) were from the top sets: musically-gifted children with weaknesses in literacy and numeracy rarely stuck at instrumental lessons for long; I just couldn't seem to convince them that it was worth the effort.

It was also obvious that very few boys – almost none, in fact – would participate in these traditional musical activities. Music, in the school where I worked (as with many, many other schools, of course), was perceived as essentially a girls' subject. The academic literature on this topic is too vast to even recount; rightly or wrongly (wrongly, as regards the way things ought to be at least, obviously), this is the common perception. For whatever reason, though, a small but significant minority of the boys I taught chose to pour hours of their post-school free time into rehearsing mixing, cutting, scratching and, for the MCs, rhyming techniques. This, I discovered, was the way to bring on the boys (or at least some of them) with music: by allowing them to DJ and MC in the classroom, my relationship with specific learners was transformed. In many cases – the likes of Johnny, for example (see above) – the most troublesome, disruptive and hostile young men in the school demonstrated a degree of willingness to work hard, follow discipline and even to interact positively with myself and other staff.

For example, it became a tradition at the school to celebrate the annual (BBC-led) Children in Need day by replacing the normal school curriculum with a whole day of fun, fund-raising activities. All the staff (including the Head) and a large number of children would arrive at school in fancy dress. Naturally enough, this created an environment in which teacher–student relations were a little different than one might normally expect. Even given this context, though, the environment which developed in my classroom on these annual Children in Need days provoked amazement from senior staff including the Head. Within hour-long workshops, some of the most disruptive boys in the school, some of whom were known to have bullying tendencies, would patiently and kindly assist younger boys in developing DJing skills on the decks. Boys who could barely string a sentence together in conversation, let alone read and write, would be MCing freely on the mics. Positive behaviour was displayed by learners (girls and boys, it is worth noting) who would more typically display immensely negative/challenging behaviour.

This positivity could quite often be seen when the DJ decks were being used (or when the promise of using them was in the offing) – not only on the Children in Need days. Why was the transformation occurring, then? Obviously part of the answer is that the children were allowed to do something which they themselves wanted to do: the child-centred principle (as discussed in the last chapter herein) in action. This, though, is only part of it, I think. What we need to bear in mind is the (low) social status of hardcore EDM: these 'tunes', many non-enthusiasts will insist, are melodically hideous; the 'beats' are thuggish and an insult to the ear, some will say. What happens, though, when the flowers are pulled from the dustbin, as it were, and given nourishing water and light? Sometimes – to stretch the metaphor – the flowers can bloom to a surprising extent, I would suggest.

To support this claim, I want to offer some comments from young DJs and MCs which were recorded during formal interviews with myself and my fellow researcher Garth Stahl on 13 May 2011. 'Happy. Just makes us [feel] better. Cheers us up' ('Connor', Year 9; the word 'us' equates to the word 'me' here, it should be noted); 'sometimes I feel down in the dumps after stuff and that, and it doesn't make me feel powerful. When I'm, like, happy I feel powerful … Keep learning and you'll get better.' Connor was a boy who was being given strong 'medication' to make it more viable for him to get through a day at school. The medicine, it was hoped, would help him with his Special Educational Needs: it was not unusual to hear of him literally running out of lessons when things became difficult and, therefore, his positive attitude here is highly notable.

'Glyn' (Year 11), like Connor, was not given to positivity regarding his educational experience: asked by my fellow researcher Garth 'what interests you in school?', Glyn responded 'nothing really – I don't like school', adding that he resents it 'when you get wronged [reprimanded] for something you ain't done'. Regarding DJing and MCing, however, Glyn suggests that 'it makes you feel betta'; 'it's, like, good to get into it. Keeps you off the streets and that, really. Like, keeps you occupied.' It is notable, I think, that Glyn is specifying here not only that he *prefers* to stay out of trouble in and out of school but also that he particularly resents what he perceives as the injustice of the classroom. As with Connor, Glyn expresses a willingness to work at the acquisition of his musical skills: 'sometimes you're just like practicing the mixes – you do them over and over again – then you can just do them.' As with the majority of the learners Garth and I interviewed (who, we should note, had been selected for interview primarily because they were the most enthusiastic DJs and MCs in the school, as far as I was aware at least), Glyn was not predicted to attain five 'good' GCSE (ie Grade C or above) passes that year. He was not known as a hard-working or 'academically-inclined' student, it is fair to say. It seems, however, that he *was* willing to persist in his acquisition of skills – but only if the learning related to his actual interests and passions.

Regrettably, Glyn had no option to take music after the age of fourteen: the school had decided that only the more 'academic' half of each year group (the 'X stream', as opposed to the 'Y stream') should be given the option to continue with music. This decision had been made on the basis of staffing pressures: with only one music teacher (me), this was argued to be unavoidable. (There were three art teachers we can note, but for some reason music was not staffed to a comparable extent.) Given that Glyn and innumerable other 'low-ability' disaffected learners had demonstrable skills in MCing and DJing, such a situation is very much to be regretted. 'Like, you start at a point and you get frustrated – like, 'cause I couldn't do it at first but I kept trying and trying', Glyn told us. He would, he said, 'work with me mates' after school until 8pm each evening, topping this up with an hour of further practice 'at night'; this was preferable to 'mischief on the streets'. Fortunately, there was some provision in the locality, at that time, for youths such as Glyn to practice DJing and MCing outside of their homes in the evenings. That said, 'you have to book because there's only like one place' – consequently, the opportunity to DJ and MC in school (at lunchtimes or after school, once per week) was very much appreciated by the young people in question.

Two things are particularly notable about these extra-curricular sessions which I ran for several years. Firstly, there was at least one 'persistent absentee' pupil who turned up to school, in Year 11, on only one day per week: Wednesdays, when I would run the lunchtime session for DJs and MCs. On the day of my PhD *viva*, for example, I realised on the day that the timing of the oral examination would prevent me from running the weekly lunchtime DJing session. That morning, when I informed one young man of this problem, he exclaimed 'but Kyle' – the aforementioned persistent absentee – 'has come into school especially!'. Given that high levels of absenteeism can trigger an Ofsted inspection, such a situation is worth talking about: perhaps the use of EDM music and DJ decks in inner-city schools, and in schools in general, could contribute significantly to the fight against persistent absenteeism, at least in the case of some (highly disaffected) learners.

The second notable thing I want to mention in regards to these extra-curricular sessions on the DJ decks is that some of the most challenging boys in the school, to the amazement of several colleagues, would choose to stay after school to participate in an activity. Prior to this, most if not all of the boys could be seen staying back after school for detentions, certainly, but for them to voluntarily remain and participate in a guided activity – well, it was a great surprise to me as well as my colleagues. When I managed to arrange a whole morning of DJing and MCing in my classroom, with a large group of boys being granted time 'off timetable' to participate, I insisted that parental permission slips would need to be completed if the boys were to take part. These slips were essential for ethical reasons, because I planned to film the boys making music and then show it at the School of Education in Cambridge University at a seminar presentation I had been invited to give. Again, colleagues expressed amazement that the boys actually managed to take the paper home, get it signed and bring it back to me. Readers who have not worked in inner-city schools with overwhelming quantities of severely poor children might not be aware of it, but learners of a certain social character (shall we say) are not known for their diligence when it comes to home–school relations. Many of the parents were ex-pupils, indeed, and were actively hostile to the school: it may well have taken some persuasion, in some of the households, to get the slip signed; in some cases, indeed, it may have been difficult even to locate a pen. The thing is, though, the boys were desperately keen to be in the music-making session.

One thing which helped a great deal with generating an appropriate environment for this music-making was the economic climate of the period (pre-2008): enough money was available in the school budget to pay for a guest DJ to come in to school for an hour per week. This DJ, who we will call Tim, was quite open, in private conversations with me, that he was not from the kind of severely deprived background which was typical of the young people we were working with. Indeed, the happy hardcore EDM which they loved was not central to his own listening preferences, by any means. However, like me, he could see that this was the passion of the young people and, more broadly, that this was the music which was central to the lives of many of the denizens of the locality of the school: it was their music, and had been for many years. For this reason, Tim and I recognised the social power of welcoming this (perceived by many to be anti-social) music into the classroom: the young people, in a sense, felt barely legal, but if we embraced their music, it felt as if we were accepting their chosen identity and thus accepting them as people.

Tim's expertise was greatly admired by the learners. I also learned a great deal about DJing skills from him: beat-matching, elements of scratching and so forth (see Chapter Eight for more on these and other DJing skills). One thing which was really notable, from my point of view, is that the learners would exhibit a level of respect for Tim which they rarely if ever offered me. This was quite natural, of course: if a teacher is going to let you do something you want to do, that's all well and good, but exhibiting too much respect for a direct representative of the school would be, as it were, *infra dig*. Tim, however, wore a cap and a t-shirt, understood the music and had skills which the learners lacked but desperately wanted: these things made him very different from me.

Early in Tim's tenure as visiting tutor in DJing skills, the whole arrangement nearly fell to pieces in a manner which is worth describing here. Initially, the Head Teacher was very supportive of the plan for the after-school sessions, agreeing to fund them and meeting with Tim and the boys in his office to make it clear that, for example, alcohol must not be brought on to the school premises. He was emphatic that Tim must show an 'enhanced disclosured' Criminal Records Bureau (CRB) certificate to evidence his suitability to work with children, naturally enough. Tim 'forgot' to bring it to the first session, but things were sufficiently lax in British schools at that time that the session could run anyway. (In the coming years, the CRB checks required of any individual coming into contact with children in schools were seriously tightened and, today, the session would not have been allowed to run without Tim producing a certificate. Things were different, then, however; and it's worth adding that, in any case, many of the learners' parents were in prison or had been in prison, thus rendering the question around protecting school children from criminality somewhat moot.) At the end of the session, Tim confided in me that his police check had two counts of possession of drugs recorded on it.

Naturally I immediately spoke to the Head about this, who initially was minded to pull the plug on the whole plan. It is to his immense credit, I feel, that instead he spoke with Tim and, thereafter, was satisfied that these offences were sufficiently far in the past that he could take Tim at his word that dealing in drugs was no longer part of his lifestyle. (Again, the legal procedures are different today, and it is doubtful that the Head could make such a judgment call in the present climate.) Why is this relevant for our purposes? I think, in short, that there is a vital question around drugs, school and EDM which is perhaps not quite as it might otherwise appear. In the next section, I want to explore some questions around, in the first instance, criminality and drugs. I will also briefly examine issues around gender and race specifically in regards to student experience (that being our central topic of interest in the present chapter). In order to explore some of these broader issues, I now move somewhat away from discussing my own experiences as a school teacher in a particular school to look at some findings I have generated through my own broader research and through secondary reading.

Different strokes

We must protect children from drugs. It's obvious – and therefore it's the kind of thing which a serious scholar ought to be willing to query, but I happen to agree wholeheartedly with this prescription. Drugs are not good for children, including alcohol: the effect upon them can be devastating, as I have seen. That said, young people today, across the UK as with other countries in the West, are experimenting with drink and drugs. Sometimes this is happening on a daily basis, and it is certainly particularly predominant in inner-city areas. The picture is not entirely simple, therefore. In one instance, for example, it was an openly held opinion between the Police, the School and the local population that the mother of one of our most challenging pupils was a medium-level drug dealer. The idea is a bit dubious, therefore, that in order to protect learners from access to drugs, we needed to keep Tim (the aforementioned DJing tutor and, it is worth repeating, *reformed* drug-offender) outside of the school gates. In impoverished inner-city areas, drugs are rife today; we need to keep them out of schools as much as possible, but there is no point in being pretentious about it.

On the topic of music and crime, I want to mention some research by Ornette Clennon (2013) in a pilot study of music interventions in the criminal youth justice sector. Clennon draws on a range of existing studies which, like his own work, suggest that 'reducing offending' through music-making is thinkable (125). In Clennon's research, music-making 'seemed to have had a direct impact on

[the] attitudes towards "Anticipation of future offending"' amongst a case sample of 'young people who were either at risk of offending or had received Penalty Notices for Disorder (PND) between the ages of 9 and 18 years' (104). He also notes an improvement in 'attitudes towards "victim empathy"' (125). Consequently, Clennon stresses the importance of 'participatory music-making' for its potentially 'far-reaching implications in terms of building Social Capital' (125–6).

It is not unusual to hear claims of this order, sometimes from the famous and successful: for example, Dead Kennedys' vocalist Jello Biafra has argued that 'In all honesty, without punk rock, I would be dead' (quoted in Arnold 1993: 19). Johan Söderman, meanwhile, reports a respondent's remark that hip hop had kept him out of prison: 'Without the music and my girlfriend, I would have been in jail serving a bloody long prison sentence' (2015: 24). The effects on children in a school environment might not be quite as extreme (although there is every reason to think they could be: it was certainly not unknown for alumni of the school I worked in to end up dead or in prison, for example, as I have indicated already). They are still worth talking about, however.

How big, potentially, could the effect upon learners be if we made our schools more open to various forms of EDM/urban music? It is hard to say; moreover, we will never find out if we do not begin to open the doors of music classrooms to EDM in its various forms. David Kirkland has suggested that 'If we hope to transform society into a better place for everyone and equip students with the academic competencies needed to improve their qualities of life, then we must also take notice and learn with and from students in their postmodern and, dare I say, hip-hop situations' (2008: 73). A starting point, in other words, can be to notice the students' 'situations' (their music tastes, for example) and learn from them.

Kirkland's principal interest is largely 'blackness' or, more specifically in the paper from which this quote is sourced, 'postmodern blackness'. Happy hardcore EDM, which was preferred by so many of the mostly white young people I worked with in the North East of England, is arguably the ultimate in postmodern blackness, in the sense that it relies upon 'black' signifiers (the DJ decks, rapping, graffiti and so forth) but is performed, with an arguably blank irony, by 'whites'. Despite white skins, though, these young people could hardly be said to own much if any privilege over and above any other contemporary urban poor in the post-industrial West; 'niggers' by any other name, some might therefore say. When Kirkland speaks of 'Shawn, the most vocal and least academically successful of the group, [who] reads all the time', I immediately think of numerous similar individuals I worked with: 'He reads hip-hop, which fed his friends and him a steady diet of words-language laced with tight beats, rhymes, and rhythms. Hip-hop also gave them poetry to read, such as the poems featured in the book of slain hip-hop icon Tupac Shakur' (2008: 68). For Kirkland, the core question is 'Beyond using hip-hop to trick students into reading the canon, a more salient question is, why aren't we using hip-hop anyway to help students make sense of the world and make meaning of their lived situations?' (74). This, I think, is a great argument; but it is not one which has to be contingent upon the skin colour of different sections of the proletariat, in practice, I would maintain.

I realise that I am risking, here, the fury of a range of readers. I should perhaps clarify, then, that I recognise that the historical treatment of the UK's industrial working class in the nineteenth century (frequently brutal and inhumane though it certainly was) does not equate to the horrors of the slave trade. We should also note that opening a music classroom up to a range of EDM can certainly produce tensions and difficulties around race which require careful treatment. I want to openly acknowledge, therefore, that I occasionally had to instruct MCs not to use certain racist words, not to use sexist words and not to mention drugs. Tim informed me that he would also have to interrupt MCs for similar reasons: there were certainly racist tendencies amongst some of the milieu in which we were working. It is worth remembering, though, a possibility which is raised by Michael T. Putnam in relation to a 'growing tendency of right-wing terminology and ideology in mainstream music' in Germany: such material can provide 'an excellent resource to stimulate in-class discussions pertaining to the feelings and opinions of young Germans and their relationship with Germany's past' (2006: 74).

In relation to race, it is worth mentioning a session which I ran in a school we will call St. John's on the east side of Oxford. With many learners facing somewhat challenging socio-economic conditions, I had selected this school for a one-off workshop in order to get a feel for music tastes in the South of England: I suspected that they might differ from the tastes of the predominantly white population of the North East region in which I had previously worked. Would the greater racial diversity be reflected within the musical preferences of the learners? If so, I wondered how many of my existing strategies for working with DJ decks in classrooms would work in a different part of the country. I was also interested as to the effect that the music-making equipment and the engagement with urban music might have on disaffected learners, and thus requested that less able and 'difficult' individuals should be included in the group. To support my argument, I will be quoting some remarks from Jaz Wharmby, written in a piece of coursework which she submitted as part of an undergraduate study into music and education which I supervised at Oxford Brookes University. Jaz, who had a keen interest in the topic and went on to teach music at Ambitious About Autism in London, accompanied me on the visit to St. John's. Her notes, which she included in her essay, remark that 'At the end of the workshop a young boy (John) volunteered to MC. His peers filmed him on their mobile phones and demonstrated their clear support and admiration for his talent and bravery.' Jaz goes on to suggest that she 'could see his confidence building as this support increased. After the workshop, I heard a teacher talking about John and his disengagement within school, which was not obvious within the workshop.' From Jaz's point of view, indeed, 'John appeared to be an enthusiastic and eager pupil.'

Was this result purely the result of some kind of mystical or hard-to-identify 'charisma' which I may or may not possess? I think not: John and his classmates had not met me before and, therefore, I would have to be a seriously charismatic individual to be able to transform his attitude so quickly and effectively. Rather, I would argue, John was showing enthusiasm and eagerness precisely because he was actually being allowed to express himself in the manner which he chose to: MCing or, in John's case, rapping. What is the difference? In the North East, the MCs would offer 'shout outs' and would rap rhythmically across 16 bars in recognisable phrases, but they themselves would distinguish between what they called rap and their own vocal performances which they called MC. [There is a scene for rap in the North East of England, we should note, about which the interested reader can glean some insight from Bennett (1999).]

This distinction between rap and MC has some racial undertones which are of particular interest for present purposes. What was notable, from my point of view, was that the happy hardcore vinyl which I had used in the North East was considered more or less a joke in Oxford: the ethnically diverse group (as opposed to the white working class young people which I had taught in the North East) had no empathy for it. Fortunately I had purchased some 'dubstep' records especially for the visit, which did seem to be more to the taste of the class. When I engaged them in discussion about MCing and rapping, however, John was emphatic that he could not rap over dubstep. I searched through my bag and found a Dead Presidents disc which I had actually bought for my own listening use back in the 1990s. I knew the song had no rapping on the b-side: instead, just the backing track was available, with a laidback, 'classic' hip hop groove offering the possibility for about three minutes of freestyle rapping. John listened to the whole song through, whilst standing in the centre of the classroom with his eyes shut. He then instructed me to spin it a second time from the beginning, proceeding to rap fluently (using some decent rhymes, as far as I recall) across the whole three minutes. Jaz's description of the atmosphere in the room tallies with my own recollection: John had shown that he could do something, and by doing it well he gained the admiration of his peers.

This session could have gone quite differently if I had not happened to have thrown a hip hop disc into my bag that day, however: any good teacher will tell you that if you are not well prepared, you are prepared to fail, and my 'antennae' (before John started rapping) told me that the class was becoming restless. Hip hop, as it happens, is an area of EDM for which I have much higher levels of personal enthusiasm than happy hardcore: I have several hip hop albums at home and very much enjoy listening to them, whereas my children and others have expressed astonishment when they have occasionally caught me listening to hardcore. The truth is that listening to hardcore at home was research for me, pure and simple: I don't really enjoy it as music. It interests me, though, that a middle-aged, middle class white man listening to happy hardcore is such an astonishing thing. Is this thuggish music? My guess is that the boys I worked with in the North East would shrug it off if they were described as thugs; and, indeed, I think there is something brutal about both the 'tunes' and, in particular, the MCing. For those who are enculturated into happy hardcore, that said, I believe there certainly is beauty here; and even I can see it sometimes (especially, indeed, when I see troubled young people using it for expressive release).

This brings me to the final issue I want to discuss in this section: gender. It is well known that women can make great MCs: the famous names are too numerous for me to list here, although it is worth adding that the quantity of famous male rappers certainly exceeds that of the females. There have also been growing numbers of female DJs over the years (Katz 2007). The hardcore EDM which was enjoyed by the young people I worked with in the North East, however, was uniformly accompanied by male MCs: I did not encounter a single female MC in nine years of classroom practice in the North East. There was one fairly skilful female DJ, who was encouraged by the boys to a pleasing extent, and girls would explore the decks, on occasion, during whole class sessions. It is fair to say, though, that happy hardcore is perceived as boys' music, broadly speaking, at least in practical terms (MCing and DJing, that is).

How significant is this problem? On this question, it is worth consulting an assertion from Glenda McGregor and Martin Mills: 'an inclusive music curriculum would foreground issues to do with gender. It would explore women's experiences of music, both positive and negative, and would ensure that boys understand the processes that have marginalised women and girls within the fields of classical and popular music' (2006: 228). I agree with this wholeheartedly, but I also think that an inclusive music curriculum needs to foreground young men's experiences of and tastes in music: we need to wonder why boys are so often reluctant to sing and why boys get beaten up for the 'poofy' act of carrying a musical instrument. I feel anxious writing these words: I am aware that the concept of 'inverse sexism' is deeply problematic. However, I found the sight of a group of boys passionately MCing, eyes closed, brows furrowed with concentration, to be a very beautiful thing; I was conscious, furthermore, that many girls very much enjoyed seeing some of the toughest boys in the school doing something creative, physical and passionate. One can say much the same about the DJs: one of the best turntablists I encountered, who we will call Sean, once bled on my shirt after I got between him and another lad who were trying to fight. He was not the kind of boy who would normally be described as poofy: like most of the DJs and MCs in the school, he performed an overtly 'tough' masculinity and appeared ready to fight at all times. Nevertheless, when spinning discs, he was able to show a creative side which one might otherwise have thought he did not possess.

'We are supportive of attempts to make curricula more connected to students' interests', suggest McGregor and Mills; 'However, there is a danger here when this entails reinforcing traditional constructions of gender' (2006: 230). Again, I am inclined to agree, but only with the caveat that male-dominated spaces, if they are also creative spaces, are not quite replicating the dominant gender constructions of a school such as the one in which I worked. Music, there and in many other schools, was perceived to be for the girls: simply by vocalising over a beat, or by mixing tunes, these boys were breaking certain boundaries. We should encourage girls to DJ and MC, if that is what they want to do: I certainly tried to so do and, as I have hinted above, some of the male DJs and MCs did much the same. If it is a 'danger' – in terms of race, gender or potential glamorisation of borderline criminality – to encourage this form of music-making in classrooms, however, I would suggest that the risk is worth taking: the positives, as far as I can see, far outweigh the negatives in the case at hand.

Conclusion

Imagine a school PE department in which the boys never got the chance to kick a ball around. Suppose that playing football was considered by many to be an anti-social nuisance, with a socially-demonstrable link to drink and drug abuse. Consider the possibility that a large minority of boys within this school, unbeknownst to the PE teachers, had nevertheless been rigorously practising their football skills. It would be reasonable to suppose that the PE staff, in this fictional school, would actively embrace the enthusiasm if they uncovered it, would it not? Football, after all, is a kind of sport; and happy hardcore, furthermore, is a type of music. Any links between these pastimes and drink/drugs/violence are indirect; there is no necessary link between these problematic behaviours and the music or sport in question.

When I threw open my classroom to hardcore EDM and other forms of dance music, my working life was improved to a drastic extent: lessons which had previously tended towards a combative atmosphere became productive, educational (for me as well as for the children), even enjoyable. Discussions with others who have brought urban musics into classrooms have indicated that similar results can be achieved elsewhere. I have mentioned some such work in this chapter and will mention more in the next. Essentially, of course, what I am suggesting is simply a particular practical case: there is theory behind it, however – child-centred learning, as discussed in the last chapter. In my own case, I could not over-estimate the importance of DJing and MCing in my classroom. Some classes had no enthusiasts of such music-making, and in those classes I would rarely draw the learners' attention to the presence of the decks in the room. Where there was an appetite for it, however, I took great pleasure in feeding the learners with opportunities to MC and DJ, as well as the chance to reflect on the history and context of electronic dance music (see Part Two for detail as to the content of such reflective lessons).

This is not to say that there were never issues to be confronted. As I have indicated, there were occasions when borderline and even outright racism needed to be challenged. There was also a need (which, on reflection, I think I could have better fulfilled) to encourage the learners to consider the actual African-American and Jamaican heritage which the essentially 'white' happy hardcore music, by dint of its use of DJ decks and MCing, had significantly grown from. In regards to gender, meanwhile, there were certainly some very positive elements to the form of masculinity which came to be engendered in my classroom (for more on this, see Stahl and Dale 2013). Having said this, there were also some improvements which perhaps could have been and certainly should be sought as regards the encouragement of girls to participate in MCing and DJing.

As regards drugs and criminality, meanwhile, I was always conscious that (as the Head Teacher put it to me) 'there is a drug culture around this kind of music'.

However, we might just as well say that there is a drug culture around these young people. Moreover, this was their music: bringing it into the classroom made them feel more welcomed, I am very confident to say. I am not naïve enough to imagine that children never bring illegal substances into inner-city schools – indeed, I was aware of punitive measures, including permanent exclusion, occurring for precisely this reason during my tenure at the school. Nevertheless, I am also absolutely confident that, in the main at least, the hardcore sessions which happened in my classroom featured sober young people who just loved the music. Indeed, I recall a particular moment when an MC, with severely delayed literacy and a general lack of social awareness, mentioned 'E' (Ecstacy, also known as MDMA) in a rap. Quite quickly, the other boys (who were a bit more savvy, although they were also on the Special Needs register for non-behavioural reasons) started telling him to pack it in whilst nodding at 'the Sir' (me, that is).

What does this demonstrate? To my mind, it suggests that the boys had a good general sense that drugs and school are incompatible. It also indicates, I think, that their eagerness to work on the decks, combined with a degree of respect for me after I had allowed such music-making in my classroom, meant that moderation of behaviour was something the boys were willing to concede. In sum, we can say that the chance to MC and DJ made the boys want to work hard and behave better. This, I would suggest, is as good a reason as any for bringing this form of music-making into the classroom.

References

Adelman, Laura, Middleton, Sue, Ashworth, Karl, *Britain's Poorest Children: Severe and Persistent Poverty and Social Exclusion* (London: Save the Children, 2003)

Arnold, Gina, *Route 666: On the Road to Nirvana* (New York: St. Martin's Press, 1993)

Bennett, Andy, 'Rappin' on the Tyne: White Hip Hop Culture in Northeast England – an Ethnographic Study', *Sociological Review* 47/1 (1999), 1–24

Clennon, Ornette, 'How Effective Are Music Interventions in the Criminal Youth Justice Sector? Community Music Making and Its Potential for Community and Social Transformation: A Pilot Study', *Journal of Music, Technology & Education* 6/1 (2013), 103–30

Katz, Mark, 'Men, Women, and Turntables: Gender and the DJ Battle', *Musical Quarterly* 89/4 (2007), 580–99

Kirkland, David, '"The Rose That Grew from Concrete": Postmodern Blackness and New English Education', *The English Journal* 97/5 (2008), 69–75

McGregor, Glenda, Mills, Martin, 'Boys and Music Education: RMXing the Curriculum', *Pedagogy, Culture and Society* 14/2 (2006), 221–33

Putnam, Michael T., 'Teaching Controversal Topics in Contemporary German Culture through Hip-Hop', *Die Unterrichtspraxis / Teaching German* 39/1 (2006), 69–79

Rimmer, Mark, 'Listening to the Monkey: Class, Youth and the Formation of a Musical Habitus', *Ethnography*, 11/2 (2010), 255–283.

Söderman, Johan, 'Hip-Hop Academicus: Examples of Bourdieusian Field Effects within Two Hip-Hop Spaces', in Burnard, Pamela, Trulsson, Ylva Hofvander, Söderman, Johan, *Bourdieu and the Sociology of Music Education* (Farnham: Ashgate, 2015), 13–27

Stahl, Garth, Dale, Pete, 'Success on the Decks: Working-Class Boys, Education and Turning the Tables on Perceptions of Failure', *Gender and Education* 25/3 (2013), 357–72

4
INCLUSION

Excluding children from school is an expensive business; it's almost as costly as putting them in prison when they are adults, and it is well known that the former often leads directly or indirectly to the latter. How can we reverse this trend, and keep 'at risk' young people in mainstream schools? Our concern with DJ decks may offer a clue to this question, and this is my broad topic in the present chapter. DJ equipment, I will argue, is far more likely to be on offer in PRUs and youth centres than in mainstream schools. It is difficult to find a music classroom with vinyl or CD decks, or to find boys rapping over hardcore EDM in the music department. We can note, for example, that Lucy Green found no use of 'twin decks', ie DJ decks, within the schools she worked with in her influential *Music, Informal Education and the School* study (2008: 48). You might find some hip hop rapping occurring if and when it demonstrates some musical restraint and/or 'good taste', but the really ugly, harsh, thuggish stuff (so beloved of so many at-risk youngsters) is nearly always assumed to be *infra dig*, I would suggest.

Why, then, does it get permitted in PRUs and other non-mainstream educational settings? What makes it OK there but not OK in the ordinary music department? The answer, I think, is that the PRUs, pathways for NEETs and suchlike are looking for anything which will keep the troubled youngster engaged and in attendance: the harsh music seems to be less of a worry because there are few if any 'high achievers' who might be musically corrupted by the unpleasant sound. (I am not placing the word unpleasant in scare quotes because I think many sounds found in hardcore EDM *are* markedly unpleasant for timbral reasons which are readily identifiable. Those who assume I am being pejorative might want to think about whether it is acceptable to talk about 'distorted' guitars, given that a distortion is strictly an infidelity of a certain kind.) The PRU, you could say, is the desperate last effort for an educational system which has utterly failed a consistently large minority of young people. Just keeping 'bums on seats' and minimising outbursts of violence might be an achievement.

What actually happens when the DJ decks and other equipment commonly used to make EDM are brought into the PRU and other non-mainstream educational situations? In this chapter, I discuss just this: case studies of educational settings where DJing, MCing and EDM/urban music have very successfully been used to engage young people, giving them an outlet for creativity and self-expression and, indeed, an opportunity to have some fun whilst actually learning new skills. In the first two sections, the case studies are based on primary research of my own. The third case relies largely upon Sam Seidel's book on the High School for Recording Arts in Minnesota. Finally I offer a short discussion on inclusion and a conclusion to Part One.

Groove Noise

I begin with the case of a DJing tutor, Spencer Hickson, who I interviewed on 25 November 2015. Based in Cheshire (North West England), Spencer has a personal background as a DJ and electronic music producer. Latterly, he has been providing DJing sessions in non-formal educational settings, finding similarly transformative effects upon disaffected learners as I had found in the North East.

At the age of eighteen, in 1990, Spencer had become fully enculturated in what was then a fairly new form of music known by most as 'acid house': 'I just remember the vibe; y'know, "wow, what is this sound", y'know', he reflected during our conversation. Prior to this, Spencer had little or no background in making music: 'I wasn't really interested that much in music at school'. After discovering acid house, however, he began 'to think, well, I want to be able to play this music that I'm listening to'. Consequently, 'I got in to DJing, I got some decks, I got some vinyl'. However, he 'didn't know anybody that did it [so] I just painstakingly spent days, months, trying to work out beatmatching'. This, he found, was 'very difficult' – more difficult for a beginner in the early 1990s than it is today, it is fair to say, given that the contemporary enthusiast can learn a great deal from YouTube. Through perseverance, however, Spencer learned on his own to 'tune your ear in to the beat rather than, y'know, any other, sort of, effects or any other, y'know, tonal things'.

To cut a long and interesting story short, Spencer now has over twenty years of experience in the dance music scene. He has been involved in tracks which were played regularly on BBC Radio 1, he has worked professionally as a DJ, he has successfully run his own independent label for many years and, since 2012, he has provided DJ-orientated workshops for young people. It is the latter work which is of particular interest for us, of course. Interestingly, Spencer fell into it almost by accident: a friend of his who worked at a local branch of Total People suggested that the young people with whom she worked would benefit from a workshop on making dance music. Financed partly through the European Social Fund, Total People is, according to their website, 'one of the largest suppliers of work-based learning in the North West of England'. In Spencer's words 'their funding is reliant on them getting [clients] back into the education system or workplace'. I asked Spencer whether there was an element of the music workshops being a 'carrot on the stick' incentive to get the young people to attend and perhaps to indirectly develop 'key skills' such as basic literacy. He replied 'that's the level of the child's ... that they were being sent, y'know'; asked whether the young people were sometimes barely literate, he replied 'absolutely'.

In his words, Spencer's friend at Total People 'was struggling to keep them there because, obviously, if they leave, one, they [the young people] don't get any money and, two, they [Total People] don't get any money'. Ruminating on the invitation, Spencer (with no background in education beyond his own schooling in the 1980s) thought 'DJing has got to be better than music production because, y'know, it's so hard to get your head around [music production]'. Subsequently, 'when I met [the young people] I was blown away by how – they'd all have smart phones, for instance, and they might not be able to read and spell but they can work phones, and jump on to different sites and download ...' On realising that 'this is the digital generation', he came up with a plan for his workshops. Spencer was aware that 'the DJing now, y'know, is not so much decks – it's still deck format but it's a midi controller', so he decided to place midi controllers at the heart of his sessions. He has now run innumerable workshops in a wide range of educational settings and 'there's always at least one [participant] who'll say, "oh, I've got a DJ software app or package at home and I've been having a play", but they haven't got the money to buy these controllers'.

Regarding that first workshop, Spencer says that 'it was a strange experience for me because I'd never done anything like that'. However, 'the people that run, y'know, their, kind of, courses there were blown away because [the young people] were smiling, they were wanting to get on'. This was achieved with a laptop, only one midi console – Spencer's own – and some speakers. Despite these limited resources, 'they were really engaged by just looking at it'.

In regards to his pedagogical approach, a clearly child-centred approach was taken: 'I show them the basics and then stand back'. Initially, the learners 'weren't really interested in the ins-and-outs of beatmatching and mixing techniques – they just want to play, they want to scratch, they want to play with the effects'. Consequently, 'you hear some strange things'. I mentioned my interest in child-centred methods and Spencer suggested that 'if I was showing somebody how to do it, I'd start with, y'know, a couple of 4/4 beat loops, y'know, and it'd be very boring – it'd just be those two loops and we'd play around with them for, y'know, for an hour'. However, 'they're not interested in that – they're interested in "oh right, so that does that and that does that and that does that", and they just go! They play music.' The results were not always displeasing, he suggested: 'some of the things you hear, it's ... it's different, I would never do that [laughs] but then...'. He suggested, for example, that these novices might 'chop a loop right up into, y'know, an eighth or sixteenth, and it's repeating like that, and then they'll put some effects on it and they'll play some other track' with a result that is 'kind of out of key but it kind of works'.

Spencer mentioned one particular young man of about sixteen years of age with whom he had worked: 'they said, "you won't get him off [sic], he's heavily autistic", [but] I didn't experience him in any negative way'. Rather, 'I had a positive experience because he was so. ... The way he touched every knob and fader was just, y'know, meticulous.' On Spencer's view 'it was beautiful to see how he did it – you could watch this guy and, if he'd learnt a bit about how to do it …'. Interested by this positivity where regular staff had anticipated hopeless negative, I asked Spencer to clarify his view and his experiences. 'Well', he began cautiously, 'I meet these kids on a blank canvas, I don't know [them], the staff work with them'; however, he went on to say that 'I kind of find them [the staff] a bit judgmental, y'know'. He clarified that the staff will 'give me this overview from their experience [but] I never experience [the young people] like that'. This, he added, was because 'I'm giving them something that's colourful and vibrant and loud and different'.

When I asked Spencer 'not just with this one particular autistic boy, but in general have you had people saying "oh, I'm surprised at how engaged such-and-such a pupil was because he's normally really difficult", have you had stuff like that?', he replied 'oh yeah. Absolutely. Every time, yeah.' I decided to triple check that I was understanding him correctly: '*Everywhere* you go, that happens – someone who normally is supposed to be really "difficult" actually engages really well?' Spencer was emphatic that such was occurring: 'absolutely', he repeated.

Given his immediate success in engaging disaffected learners with music, Spencer made a successful bid for approximately £1,500 to Cheshire East council for funding to buy equipment and extend his work beyond Total People. Amongst other work, this led him to a project with slightly more mature young people at the YMCA. The more mature cohort was 'really good', Spencer suggested, because some were capable at MCing whilst others were making 'all sorts of weird and wonderful mixes … without me, kind of, directing it'. Referring back to an issue which I raised in the last chapter, we can note that Spencer observed that at least some of his participants here were used to 'a smoking environment': 'they were of that age [where] I could, y'know, kind of smell that vibe from them'. However, there was nothing to suggest that Spencer was surprised by this situation (the implication of cannabis smoking, that is): only the very naïve observer would be surprised to hear that vulnerable young people who are at risk of homelessness (as many who are supported by organisations such as the YMCA will obviously be) are sometimes cannabis smokers.

Spencer's educational activities, which operate as an arm of his broader 'Groove Noise' organisation, have grown primarily through word of mouth. Even with little or no advertising, however, the requests for his services have been consistent. That said, these have always been in 'summer schools' and special units separate from mainstream classroom or in projects 'run by the police to keep these kids, just, off the street, y'know'. In school-based contexts, Spencer found that the learners had to be chased out at lunch time because they want to stay and continue mixing music – an experience which tallies very closely with my own experience of bringing this kind of musical mixing equipment into classrooms. Overall, indeed, it was overwhelmingly evident that Spencer's workshops replicated, in his region, many of the same successes I had previously happened upon in my own teaching work in the North East of England.

Ark T

In the Spring of 2013, I spoke at length with Brett Gordon who, at the time, was co-running a Youth Music–funded project within the Ark T Centre in South East Oxford. Located within the grounds of the John Bunyan Baptist Church and not far from the notorious Blackbird Leys estate, Ark T provides opportunities for its local community (dance, drama, a café). It also provides, via the Youth Music Project, opportunities for rapping, music production and other music-making for a range of participants including excluded learners and/or learners at risk of exclusion/disaffection. Brett and his co-worker Rory 'Rawz' Campbell, who I also interviewed, talked to me about their work and I was particularly interested to know more about their relationship with local schools. Rawz is primarily an MC and, prior to his employment at Ark T, had a project called the Urban Music Foundation which involved him doing 'lyrics workshops' in schools, youth clubs and other contexts involving young people. Brett's expertise was in production as well as, it is worth mentioning, composition which he was studying at MA level at Oxford Brookes University at the time I spoke with him.

Ark T works with local schools to combat disaffection in a range of ways. For example, Brett told me of an arrangement they had with one local school where every Monday a small group of boys from Years 8 and 9 would come to Ark T to do music-related work. Brett confirmed that this was being done, essentially, because the boys had been causing trouble at school. 'Some of the girls and some of the boys that come up here are not interested', he explained, 'but others have got really bang into it' to the extent that they would perform at evening performance events which Ark T would host in central Oxford. I attended one of these as part of my research and was impressed with the quality of the performances, the enthusiasm of the performers and the pleasing level of support from friends and family in the audience.

One might assume that local schools would seize the opportunity for outreach workshops from Ark T but in fact this did not seem to be the case. 'Me and Rawz wrote to all the local schools', Brett stated, but there were 'only two schools we heard anything back from'. One of these 'didn't happen' because the school 'didn't follow it through basically', Brett explained: the same indifference I received when I emailed numerous Oxfordshire schools in 2013 offering free workshops involving DJ decks. The other school, however, had 'a learning support unit really, um, for some of the kids that are there and they send us every week'. Again, though, the provision was only for disaffected students and only off-site: Brett was not invited to do workshops within the school's normal music curriculum.

Rawz, meanwhile, had experienced much the same thing prior to his work with Ark T when he ran the Urban Music Foundation. Although he had higher success levels at being invited into school, 'mainly it was, kind of, the kind of ones that are on the edge of being excluded or not really engaging with the mainstream school' with whom he would be asked to work. 'If I were to approach a school in a more upper class/middle class area', he claimed, 'they were, kind of, "oh, no-one raps here'". Rawz's Urban Music Foundation workshops entailed 'mainly poetry and lyric writing but also a bit of beat making and stuff like that'. His motivation for doing this had a philanthropic element: 'growing up, I really found, kind of, writing lyrics down and making music really helped me through some tough times and kind of helped me to get my head straight, if you see what I mean'. He hoped 'to pass that on to the younger generation; also I saw that there was possibly a career in it as well'.

In addition to being put to work with pupils at risk of exclusion, Rawz's workshops seemed typically to be hosted by the English department rather than the music department. Engagement levels would seem to have been impressive, though: 'I always ask, "has anyone ever tried writing their own lyrics or any poetry or anything before?", um, and to be honest the initial response is normally maybe one or two people'; however, 'as the session carries on, they start feeling a bit more comfortable'. At this point, Rawz claimed, 'they start admitting that they actually have been doing it' with 'maybe ten or fifteen in a class that have actually admitted to have tried writing their own lyrics before'. Part of this success may have been enabled by Rawz's streetwise character, of course: 'I've been that kid, so I can really relate to where they're coming from'. Because 'I'm not just their English teacher who's just decided that today were going to do rap' but, rather, someone who is 'more in touch with that kind of culture', the workshops were largely successful. 'I'm coming from the outside', Rawz told me, 'to work on this subject that possibly they didn't even know was classed as a subject before'.

Clearly, then, an element of legitimation is important here: the English staff (although sadly not so many of the music teachers, it seems), by inviting Rawz into their classrooms, give academic credibility to creative work which is normally assumed (by learners, at least, if Rawz is correct) to be *infra dig* from a school point of view. On Rawz's view, 'a school in a city [sic], they're definitely a lot more keen to, kind of, want their kids to engage with it – they can see more of a need for [workshops involving rap and urban music]', as compared with schools in affluent areas. When I asked if he had ever needed to censor the content of raps which pupils created, he replied that 'I believe that they should be able to say whatever they want, whatever is in their heart I think they should be able to say it. Let them say it; let them get it out.' However, he added that 'I have worked in circumstances where it's not allowed' and acknowledged that 'trying to think of a different way to get across the same message' sometimes 'works better than with swearing – "do you need to swear there?"'. He also accepted that 'with drugs and violence, it's a bit harder. Especially if it's coming from an experience that they have actually had: it feels wrong to say you can't talk about that experience you've had.' Nevertheless, he accepted that there could be a need for certain forms of censorship given the school context.

As with Spencer Hickson, then, Brett and Rawz of Ark T/Urban Music Foundation had significant levels of success in encouraging inclusion of disaffected learners – but almost always at the peripheries of mainstream education. Our next case is of much the same character but, additionally, provides a comparative case from across the Atlantic Ocean.

Hip Hop Genius

Sam Seidel's *Hip Hop Genius: Remixing High School Education* (2011) is primarily focussed upon the world's first 'hip hop high school' – the High School for Recording Arts (HSRA) of St. Paul, Minnesota. Interested readers can consult Seidel's fascinating book for a more detailed discussion of the school than I am able to offer here, of course. My main interest in the school, for present purposes, is its success at encouraging inclusion of students who otherwise might be at risk of exclusion (and, of course, at risk of the subsequent difficulties in later life which so often follow in the wake of exclusion from school).

According to HSRA's own website (www.hsra.org), the school grew from a pilot programme in 1996, developing into an independent school in 1998. Minnesota's Department of Education has repeatedly renewed the school's charter in the ensuing years, with school enrolment stabilised at around 200. Judging by Seidel's account, the school certainly has faced a range of difficulties including being labelled as a 'persistently low-achieving school' by the Minnesota Department of Education (Seidel 2011: 108). However, a commitment amongst both staff and students to the school's Mission ('to provide youth the opportunity to achieve a high school diploma through the exploration and operation of the music business and other creative endeavors', as the HSRA's website puts it) has brought success on a number of levels. It has been 'lauded around the country and internationally', becoming a mentor school for the Coalition of Essential Schools and a model school for the EdVisions network (134). More importantly, if Seidel is to be believed, it has positively influenced the lives of innumerable young people.

The citations Seidel (2011) offers are emphatic. 'In HSRA I saw a school that could reach and retain the young people that few other schools wanted or knew how to serve', remarks the Director of the Black Alliance for Educational Options Small Schools Initiative (2). Buki, a student at HSRA at the time of Seidel's writing, came to the school (after being 'kicked out' of another school) wanting to be a rapper but soon decided that 'helping other people handle their business' was what she preferred to do (23). According to the school's education director, HSRA is 'one of the few places in Minnesota where African American culture is dominant' (24) – in other words, where the socio-economically deprived (speaking generally, of course) are, in a sense, allowed to prioritise their own voice(s). In Seidel's own view, the school fosters 'respect for the brilliance and resilience of young people – especially kids from the 'hood': the students 'are not seen as problems to be solved or empty vessels waiting to be filled' but rather 'are valued as thinkers, artists and entrepreneurs – survivors and thrivers' (22).

How crucial to this success is the emphasis upon 'recording arts' (as mentioned in the school's name) in general and hip hop music in particular? 'The chance to explore musical production and other passions are a big part of the draw', Seidel proposes; however, 'in the end, what matters most to many students is not whether they have access to beat machines and microphones, it is whether the school is *theirs*' (2011: 47, emphasis added). The question as to 'whether they love and belong to [the school] and whether it loves and belongs to [the students]' (ibid.) is the nub, in other words.

It is an important question: how pivotal is the music itself for the inclusivity which, in this chapter, I have proposed can be kindled through the use of contemporary urban music in the classroom? Seidel suggests that there is a tendency for some teachers and schools to 'view hip-hop as a negative influence' which 'promotes violence, misogyny, homophobia, hypercapitalist consumption and – to add insult to injury for the English teachers – bad grammar' (2011: 117). If this is correct (and I think it broadly is, in some cases at least), it would be fair to complain that the teacher or school has failed to see, as it were, the diamond in the rough. Doubtless there is some urban music which glorifies violence, which denigrates women to a misogynistic extent, which is homophobic and so forth (Seidel hints as much himself, 145). The point, however, is that not all urban music has these faults (far from it) and, in any case, such music (even at its most offensive) always does a bit more than promoting violence, misogyny and so forth. It doesn't matter whether a music teacher or whoever else thinks this music is 'good' music: from the point of view of students who are enculturated in hip hop and other forms of contemporary urban music, this is *their* music; to reject it is to reject them, they might well feel.

The problem with this logic is that the music, according to the above argument, seems to become merely an emblem: by embracing the music, one symbolically embraces the child, but the music itself is nothing more than a placeholder for a broader recognition that the young person *has a culture*, a fact which should be respected in itself. I have already offered my own general position on this question, in Chapter One herein: with Levinas and Derrida, one can perhaps suggest that the otherness of the other should remain wholly otherwise; just this, perhaps, can make justice feel possible. I recognise, however, Seidel's caution against the 'carrot on the stick' approach (as it is often known in the UK) which he calls 'the peanut butter and the pill' and, in a rather striking phrase, 'the Tupac-Shakespeare bump and switch' (2011: 119-20). In short, the risk here is precisely the use of some strand or other of pop culture to engage the learner in material which is supposed to be of a more appropriate nature for the classroom: a trade-off wherein the subaltern's culture is never properly valued *on its own terms*. I recognise Seidel's concern but note his description of Tony Simmons (Executive Director at HSRA) unmistakeably using a carrot and stick method with a particular student in order to get her to complete some crucial course work: a 'timeline' which, Seidel quotes Simmons as saying, 'could open up some opportunities for you' once completed (56–7). We can also note that Seidel reports, without any critical comment, the *Hip-Hop Education Guidebook*'s encouragement of using rap to get students 'hooked' so that they might develop 'academic literacy'. As someone with years of practical experience teaching in an inner-city school, I am not in the least surprised by this information: when one works with troubled young people and/or those facing socio-economic disadvantage, it is often very difficult to see any option other than subtle coercion. I point out the apparent contradiction merely to emphasise that, in practice, pop culture is likely to provide something of a 'sugared pill' when conventional academic requirements are lurking in the shadows.

What about this urban music itself, though – the hip hop which preoccupies Seidel, and the hardcore EDM upon which I have primarily focused herein? With Seidel, I would suggest that it *is* intrinsically valuable: there is a great risk, he is right to point out, of an educational 'obsession with literary skills over all other forms of intelligence' (2011: 119) and, therefore, we should see 'music production as an end in itself' (123). However, we should also pay close attention to the revelation from Young Menace (an alumnus of HSRA) that 'I wasn't an angel, but when music was integrated, I was motivated' (33). The remark is telling, I would suggest. For all the school's inclusive rhetoric and efforts toward hearing the student voice, the whole project might well collapse were it not for the music itself, judging by Young Menace's comment. The use of urban music, indeed, will only engender greater inclusion to the extent that there are young people for whom the music is important and who are at risk of exclusion: 'Just because a student is a sixteen-year-old black male who lives in an urban community doesn't [necessarily] mean he listens to rap music', Seidel wisely warns (120).

The music teacher who aspires to an inclusive curriculum, therefore, must learn *from his students* what music is of interest to them. In Seidel's view, such a teacher would best avoid a 'position of authority' when working with urban music such as hip hop (and we can reasonably assume that he would say the same of hardcore EDM): after all, this would be 'a peculiar position when studying something of which students often have more knowledge than their instructors' (3). It should be obvious that this way of thinking tallies with my general trajectory thus far in this book. The only thing I would query about Seidel's thinking is the idea that much of what he finds positive in HSRA could not be achieved in a mainstream school. In the discussion section which follows, I begin by querying precisely this idea before, thereafter, reflecting on certain inclusion-related themes in the other cases discussed earlier in the chapter.

Discussion on inclusion

At one point in *Hip Hop Genius*, Sam Seidel describes an observation he has made of a student handling a mobile device during a mathematics session. (HSRA provides a curriculum which covers what are known in the UK as the 'core' subjects – Maths, English and, one assumes, Science although the latter is not specifically mentioned in Seidel's book – as well as the 'recording arts'-specific work which is the more distinctive aspect of the school.) 'It would be easy for [the instructors] to assume [the student] was using the MP3 player to DJ for himself during Concentrated Math', Seidel points out (2011: 62). As it turns out, though, the student was demonstrably using the calculator function on the device for legitimate purposes. Any teacher worth their pay should agree that the instructors made a good call here.

'Many schools – both traditional and alternative – have policies instructing teachers to confiscate such items from students without pausing to consider how they are being used or how they could be used to further the student's education', Seidel goes on to assert (2011: 62). In regards to the confiscation policy, he is quite correct. However, is it really the case that this has been done without pause for reflection? I am far from convinced that such is the case and am happy to report that, in the school where I worked, it was not difficult to negotiate an exemption from the school's ban on mobile phones so that children could play me (and play each other) MP3s of particular music at particular moments for particular reasons. Given that I knew next to nothing about happy hardcore, which was the music of choice for a very large minority within the school, this was essential for the purpose of inclusion because the large minority in question included many of the most disaffected young people in the school. (Indeed, numerous other functions of modern mobile phones, such as recording snippets of sound and providing frequencies for tuning guitars, can be a great aid to music teaching, as is noted by Baxter [2007]. Mobile phones can also be a great disruption to quotidian teaching and learning, however, and thus a flexible school policy is probably the ideal solution here, I would argue.)

In brief, then, I am inclined to think that Seidel is over-pessimistic in regards to the possibility for key aspects of HSRA's success to be replicated in mainstream schools. It is right, of course, that 'educators must encourage, extend and learn from students' ingenuity and resourcefulness' (Seidel 2011: 145) and doubtless HSRA has done a good deal to ensure that this occurs within their establishment. To suggest that 'this *cannot* happen in a reality confined by rows of desks, textbooks, lockers, and bells that ring every forty-five minutes' (ibid., emphasis added) is to overstate the restriction which the mainstream school places upon the would-be progressive teacher. The fact that a school has lockers and numerous sets of textbooks (or, come to that, sets of calculators so that students don't need to reach for a mobile phone in order to electronically aid a calculation) does not remove all possibilities for progressive methods to be attempted. Yes, rows of desks can be problematic, as the child-centred progressive tradition pointed out fifty years ago. Seidel may even be right that now is the 'time to call into question not only what happens within classrooms but also whether classrooms are needed at all' (129). *If* the time is right for a new attempt to re-think education from top to bottom, however, I would think it crucial that we learn from the errors of haste and overstatement which I critiqued in Chapter Two herein. Without such reflection, any attempt to radically re-think education risks repeating history as farce. The greatest victims of such an error might well be the students in inner-city schools, who are at the greatest risk of exclusion and of the range of problems which almost invariably follow in the wake of exclusion. Regrettably, Seidel's aside as regards 'whether classrooms are needed at all' stands alone. This being the case, it would probably be better if he had not made the comment at all.

I am also unconvinced by Seidel's tendency to assume that effective teachers need to be from similar backgrounds to the learners. 'David "TC" Ellis is a great school leader', Seidel argues, 'not *despite* the academic struggles he went through but *because* of them' (2011: 78, emphasis retained). In the section which follows this, he repeatedly emphasises the street credentials and industry connections of 'TC' – an impressive-sounding character who seems to be worthy of admiration on several levels, we should add. Without affording a lot of space to an argument which is somewhat peripheral to our main concerns herein, though, it seems highly problematic to assume that only those who are, as they say, 'from the 'hood' are capable of supporting and successfully working with troubled youngsters. Moreover, we need to think about successful strategies and methods for inclusion which can be exported to *any* school: not every teacher, after all, has a personal relationship with the artist formerly known as Prince (whereas 'TC' reportedly did).

Again, though, Seidel's pessimism about more ordinary schools renders such an export difficult. He is right, of course, that 'Many teachers in traditional schools see different cohorts of students every day' (2011: 41). He is probably even underestimating when he adds that 'teachers commonly work with anywhere from one hundred to three hundred students in a single year' (ibid.). (Personally, I commonly taught eighteen different classes per week with typical class sizes of nearly thirty students. Therefore, with a tutor group and extra-curricular clubs such as choir and school band, I would have close to 500 children passing through my classroom each week.) 'In such a context, how can one be expected to notice, remember and build curriculum around Chantel's passion for singing?', Seidel asks. My response is that, if a child displayed any passion for singing, I would strive to notice it and I did find it possible to remember which children were passionate about which songs or types of songs, much of the time. (More than once colleagues expressed amazement that I could remember the names of every child I taught. However, this was not through some magical trick or exceptional talent with memory: rather, I could recall the names of children because my child-centred methods meant that I was always learning about individual children's individual tastes and preferences.)

HSRA is a special school with a tiny number of students. Much of what it does is excellent, judging by Seidel's account. He admits that his book is 'not an objective study' (2011: 150), but we can learn a great deal about what to do in our music classrooms from his work. If the small cohort (less than half the number which one would find in even the smallest UK secondary school and about one tenth of the size of a large secondary school) means that closer relationships with individuals was/is possible, doubtless this is great for the HSRA. However, the purpose of the present book is not to suggest improvements which could arise if we had smaller class sizes in the UK (one would be ill-advised to hold one's breath waiting for this to occur). Rather, I would contend that greater engagement with DJ decks and/or MC-orientated musics could do an enormous amount to improve inclusion in almost any mainstream school but particularly those (commonly found in inner-city contexts) which have exceptionally large numbers of students at risk of exclusion.

It is no surprise to hear that Seidel's background is in youth work with 'those in and transitioning out of juvenile prison, group homes and foster care'

(2011:149). These are the young people who are most likely to gain socially-funded opportunities to DJ, MC or take part in 'making beats' and other forms of EDM-related music production. We can see this in the other cases discussed above. Note, for example, that Rawz and Brett of Ark T offered their services to schools in their region but received little or no interest, other than the opportunity to work with the 'difficult' pupils at the margins. Much the same can be recognised in Spencer's case: it was a worker at Total People who hatched the idea of the DJ-orientated workshops, precisely because she could see that there was a link there with the interests and passions of the young people (predominantly NEETs, as far as I can tell) with whom she was struggling to engage. Elsewhere, Spencer has found significant demand to the extent that, as noted above, he has barely needed to advertise his services. The participants in his workshops seem to have found the experience overwhelmingly positive, with consistently high levels of engagement from students who were normally viewed as being devoid of potential for positive behaviour.

If this potential is/was there, why is it not being recognised/developed within mainstream classrooms? We will return to certain elements of the case studies discussed above later in the book, for they raise a number of important questions relating to actual pedagogical process. (How far, for example, can one get in a classroom situation if one only has one pair of DJ decks or only one of the launch pads which Spencer uses? This is a vital question to which we will return in Part Two.) The question as to the possibility to maximise inclusion in mainstream education is our core area of interest in the present chapter, however. Could the use of DJing equipment and/or lessons about contemporary urban music and EDM be some magical solution for mainstream secondary school music teachers who are struggling to engage disaffected and/or uninterested pupils?

I am sure there is no magical solution, here, and the value of the DJ decks will doubtless vary from school to school and from class to class. Even in a school where there is little or no interest in DJing, MCing and EDM/urban music, however, there is reason to think that thought-provoking and exciting lessons could be put together. If we assume that Rawz is talking with fidelity to his experience in regards to his dealing with 'schools in a more upper class/middle class area' (who, he alleges, told him that there was no appetite for 'rap' in their schools), does it follow that learning about contemporary urban music *as music* will be a waste of time? I think not. In my recent teaching of music in universities, I have had classes featuring alumni of top UK private schools including, for example, Charterhouse. These privately-educated young people seem to typically love EDM and 'clubbing' just as much as other undergrads from state schools. Why shouldn't they be learning in school about this music, and how it is made, then? Why would Beethoven or even the Beatles be more relevant for a contemporary musical education than the currently highest selling category of popular music in the USA (EDM, that is)? Moreover, why can't we study all of that and more music besides?

Meanwhile, one has the kind of young person I so often encountered in my own teaching work and who, it seems, engages so strongly with options such as Ark T, Groove Noise's workshops and the HSRA in Minneapolis. The kind of young person, that is, who loves listening to and making 'tunes', who wants to make music but doesn't necessarily know how (or wants to extend their knowledge), who isn't 'an angel, but when music was integrated, I was motivated'. One also, without doubt, has the marginal cases: those who doubt that they would ever produce any musical work of serious worth but who get a creative pleasure out of exploring sonic possibilities on equipment which, even used by a complete novice, can produce sounds which are interesting and which, as Spencer Hickson puts it, 'kind of works'. Aren't all of these people rather worthy of our attention, as music teachers? Shouldn't exploratory, messy, noisy and perhaps even nasty music-making be an option for those who haven't (or haven't yet) been excluded from mainstream school?

Conclusion

It is no secret which (stereo)types of young people are most likely to be particularly keen on hardcore EDM and other DJ-orientated forms of contemporary urban music. Consider, for example, the proposal of DJ Experience (a London-based business start-up who pitched to Virgin Media for funding as part of the Pitch to Rich scheme in 2015) that their workshops are ideal 'for pupils who may struggle with conventional subjects or who are confined within the current curriculum' (www.virginmediabusiness.co.uk/pitch-to-rich/new-things/dj-experience/). Meanwhile DJ Workshops Ltd (an established and, it seems, very successful company providing EDM-orientated workshops across the UK) report that 'we have worked with over 10,000 young people in over 150 schools and youth clubs as well as the youth offending teams, secure units and immigration centres' (www.djworkshopsltd.co.uk/). Then there is DJ School UK, which promises 'to increase engagement, attainment, school attendance and reduce re-offending rates' (http://djschooluk.org.uk/our-policies/mission-statement/).

Low-attaining students, youth offenders, young people in secure units, school refusers: these, it seems to be crystal clear, are the people most likely to enjoy DJ-orientated workshops. Once they have been excluded from school or have been in serious trouble with the police, my findings suggest that they have a higher chance of getting some educational exposure to DJ decks and so forth. What, though, if the music teacher has the proactive sense to bring some such equipment into the classroom *before* such drastic problems have arisen? Might it be possible to combat disaffection and even to keep a certain number of young people in the mainstream school system [where, statistics suggest, they have the greatest chance of avoiding a path towards prison and worse (Kim, Losen and Hewitt 2010)]?

It would seem obvious that, at least in some cases, broadening the music curriculum to reflect late twentieth- and twenty-first-century modes of music-making in popular music (eg DJing and MCing) will allow greater engagement in music lessons: why else would 'youth offending teams, secure units and immigration centres' (see above) be paying for specialists to deliver DJ-orientated workshops? It is thinkable in some cases, furthermore, that just this could break the cycle of alienation and hostility to school which so often results in permanent exclusion for at risk individuals. Less dramatically, though, will DJ-orientated lessons not be rather valuable to any music teacher who has faced disaffection in his lessons? It is, if nothing else, something a bit different, is it not? The very nature of EDM (being technologically-aided), furthermore, raises interesting questions about what music is (or could be) and how important (or otherwise) technical skill on a traditional instrument might be before one is entitled to describe oneself as a 'musician'. Such questions should be embraced by the effective music teacher, for a crisis in the ontological status of the object of enquiry is always an exciting starting point for any lesson or project.

What, though, should the music teacher actually *do* with this stuff? What might a lesson look like at Key Stage 3, when pupils are fresh out of the cosier environment of the primary school? How different might it be at Key Stage 4, when pupils have selected music as a subject they actively *want* to study? How do you keep a whole class engaged, and for how long should one seek to do so? What are the advanced skills involved in DJing, and to what extent are they codified and agreed upon? Should we have grades in DJing and MCing, as we do for playing the violin and so forth? How do we balance the rise of new technologies for music-making against the more traditional instruments which most music teachers are nearly always more used to? These are vital questions for Part Two, where I attempt to develop practical suggestions and strategies without losing sight of the pedagogic-theoretical questions which have been raised in the book so far.

References

Baxter, Alex, 'The Mobile Phone and Class Music: A Teacher's Perspective' in Burnard, Pamela, Finney, John, *Music Education with Digital Technology* (London: Continuum, 2007), 52–62

Green, Lucy, *Music, Informal Education and the School: A New Classroom Pedagogy* (Aldershot: Ashgate, 2008)

Kim, Catherine Y., Losen, Daniel J., Hewitt, Damon T., *The School-to-Prison Pipeline: Structuring Legal Reform* (London: New York University Press, 2010)

Seidel, Sam, *Hip Hop Genius: Remixing High School Education* (Maryland: Rowman and Littlefield, 2011)

PART II
Working with students and whole classes

5
CLASSROOM MANAGEMENT

It's not 'rocket science' to suggest this, but I am quite sure that Colin Lever is correct that 'if the work is repeatedly unstimulating… then disaffection and conflict are going to ensue' in the classroom (Lever 2011: 74). Lever's *Understanding Challenging Behaviour in Inclusive Classrooms* is less of a weighty research text than it is a 'nuts and bolts' handbook for teachers facing behaviour management difficulties in the classroom. His ideas fit well, nevertheless, with my overall argument herein. 'If a teacher is respectful of the children, they are more than likely to reciprocate', he asserts with good reason. 'If a teacher produces lessons that are interesting and motivating, the children will look forward to the lessons and are less likely to misbehave as a result', he adds. It is not a matter of teachers developing 'magical powers to control the "seething masses" or individuals hell-bent on causing mayhem'. Rather, the teacher who desires an inclusive classroom in which challenging behaviour is both understood and effectively combatted should strive for 'that elusive "empathy" built on mutual respect' (74).

For the music teacher, engaging with EDM and urban music can be one very effective method of generating a sense of mutual respect in classrooms – particularly inner-city classrooms where hardcore EDM is especially likely to hold popularity with young people, but also in pretty much any classroom today, given the popularity of such urban music in the current era. How, though, should the music teacher go about the classroom management which is required to make lessons relating to this music *effective*? This question is my main focus within the present chapter, with a particular emphasis upon the practical need, in mainstream classrooms, to keep a whole class engaged and learning.

I do this in three sections. Firstly, I explore pedagogical questions around whole class engagement, methods of interaction and the institutional pressure to keep the learners occupied and demonstrably advancing their capabilities. Can one set of DJ decks be enough to 'keep them going' if (as almost all UK teachers do) we fear negative appraisal by Ofsted? I suggest that a single set of such music-making equipment *can* be adequate for the purpose in question, but I acknowledge that the current situation with government inspection in the UK means that the wise teacher will tread carefully. With the latter situation in mind, the second section provides a detailed focus upon time management in the classroom whilst the third offers a brief consideration of the management of classroom space.

Before entering into the first section, I want to explore a particular case which crops up in Burnard and Finney's *Music Education with Digital Technology* (2007). In 'The DJ Factor: Teaching Performance and Composition from Back to Front', Mike Challis makes many remarks which support my findings in Part One of this book. He states, for example, 'there is a gender imbalance: while boys tend to be keen to use decks, girls are usually more reluctant, often not even trying when boys are present' (Burnard and Finney 2007: 69). We should not be surprised to hear that the research took place in a PRU (65): as far as I can tell, EDM- and DJ-orientated music-making is not too uncommon in PRUs, at least compared with mainstream schools where it is far rarer. It is also not surprising, from the point of view of my argument so far, to hear that Challis's three years of research consistently reflected that, 'Because of the nature of the PRU and the current trends in youth culture, the majority of students at Key Stage 4' enjoy urban music and EDM of differing kinds (65–6). By 'the nature of the PRU', Challis probably means that the learners were disaffected and/or disruptive. We can guess that he also likely means that it was in an area of socio-economic deprivation: my researches suggest that hardcore EDM is particularly likely to be at the heart of the popular music culture of the last quarter of a century or so in such areas.

This music-making, Challis informs us, 'does wonders for their self-esteem' (Burnard and Finney 2007: 66). Given that 'Most of the students at the PRU suffer from acute lack of self-esteem, and this cannot be underestimated as one of the key factors in their lack of achievement', this boost is crucial: 'one of the primary objectives of the music programme at the unit', indeed (70). I asserted in the Introduction that learners at risk of disaffection and exclusion from school are often likely to identify with 'underground' EDM rather than mainstream popular music: Challis's research strongly supports this claim (67). MCing, meanwhile, 'is an integral method for expressing their identity' (68) and could 'be supported as creative writing by the English department' (ibid.). In any case, this music-making acts 'as a strong motivator and its effects may be felt far beyond the music department' (ibid.): again, this supports my argument that engagement with this form of music-making can support many learners who are at risk of disaffection and exclusion. As with my own work, yet again, Challis found that the students themselves provide a vital resource, as it were: 'In buying [vinyl] for the project I am guided by the students themselves and helpful record shops' (ibid.). (Which record shops should one go to? I simply asked the students in order to find this out; I could tell that middle-aged men in suits were not the typical customer, but I found the staff most helpful I must say.)

Should a music teacher be excused from using DJ decks if they are not enculturated in such music-making and the EDM/urban music which this equipment is normally used for? Challis suggests that 'Facilitation and encouragement on the part of the teacher is [sic] more important than flashy DJing techniques' (Burnard and Finney 2007: 72). I very much agree with this: you don't need to be a 'flashy' DJ to bring this equipment into your classroom and demonstrate some basic techniques with it. However, Challis also proposes that if 'working with larger groups, other set-ups may be necessary' beyond vinyl decks (ibid.). 'A CD mixing set-up could be used along with computers', for example; 'this would remove the need to learn the art of beat matching' (72–3). CD set-ups and computer-based work can be helpful, I agree (see Chapter Nine for more on this), but I am not sure that beatmatching skills should be sidelined so hastily (see Chapter Eight for more detail on this question). I am also convinced that, although Challis's work may have been 'aided by the small numbers involved at any one time' (66), this kind of work can be undertaken by whole classes in mainstream schools. How can the teacher deliver this effectively, however? This, in short, is my core question in the present chapter.

The whole class challenge

Hardman, Smith and Wall have found that 'since the introduction of the NLS [National Literacy Strategy] there has been an increase of whole class teaching which is dominated by teacher-led recitation' (2003: 212). 'Far from encouraging and extending pupil contributions to promote higher levels of interaction and cognitive engagement', Hardman, Smith and Wall assert that 'the majority of the time teachers' questions are closed and often require convergent factual answers and pupil display of (presumably) known information'. Obviously this is a problem for effective teaching and learning: the approach in question 'seeks predictable correct answers and only rarely are teachers' questions used to assist pupils to more complete or elaborated ideas' (ibid.).

It is fair to say that the tendency in question has not been restricted to the NLS (although certainly the strategy in question, in combination with the NNS [National Numeracy Strategy] of the same era, was pivotal to the overall shift in educational tendencies as the 1990s gave way to the 'noughties'). Overall, I would maintain, the teach-to-the-test/regurgitation-of-facts pedagogical ideology has become entirely dominant in the new century: we noted in Chapter Two, for example, the current head of Ofsted's demand that the inspectorate should 'see teacher-led activities, we want to see structured learning, we want to see teaching in more formal settings'. As Hardman, Smith and Wall point out, however, this 'emphasis on directive forms of teaching … goes against the widely accepted social constructivist theory of learning' whereby it is assumed that 'classroom discourse is not effective unless pupils play an active part in their learning' (2003: 212). According to social constructivist theory, they clarify, 'our most important learning takes place when we relate new information, new experiences, and new ways of understanding to our existing understanding of the matter in hand'.

Assuming a teacher is willing to risk the disapproval of Ofsted by creating a classroom wherein 'pupils are given the opportunity to assume greater control over their own learning by initiating ideas and responses which consequently promote articulate thinking', what should that teacher actually do therein? 'One of the most important ways of working on this understanding is through talk', Hardman, Smith and Wall argue (2007: 212). 'If the pupil is allowed to contribute to the shaping of the verbal agenda in this way', they go on, 'the discourse is more effective in developing the pupil's own cognitive framework' (212–3). However, 'if teachers are to modify their practice in order to encourage reciprocal interactive teaching, they need unambiguous guidelines or the opportunity to identify and work through the contradictions between official guidelines and their own educational beliefs' (213–4).

Are such guidelines likely to arise, given the current climate? It is hard to be optimistic on this question. That said, I am convinced that teaching which includes the kind of reciprocity (in short, the *talk*) which is encouraged by Hardman, Smith and Wall (amongst countless other specialists in pedagogy) will pay dividends for the music teacher who aspires to engaging disaffected learners as well as promoting actual diversity and musical sensitivity within the classroom and beyond. We need, then, not only to talk to the classes but, pivotally, to listen to the learners talking and to encourage them to talk to each other. Contemporary urban music in general and hardcore EDM in particular are great ways to get a class talking. We need to be careful, though: in a separate study of the then-important NLS and NNS, Smith, Hardman, Wall and Mroz found that 'teachers spent the majority of their time either explaining or using highly structured question and answer sequences' (2004: 408). 'Far from encouraging and extending pupil contributions to promote higher levels of interaction and cognitive engagement', therefore, 'most of the questions asked were of a low cognitive level designed to funnel pupils' response towards a required answer'. By contrast, however, 'interactive styles of teaching encouraging more active pupil involvement can produce significant gains in learning' (410).

Let us assume that there is some truth in this, and let us presume that the reciprocity and interaction in question will not immediately result in too much disapproval by Ofsted of the contemporary music teacher. What, then, do we do in our music lessons? As stated, we need to get them talking – and therefore we need to stimulate them with something worth talking about. For this, vinyl DJ decks can be an excellent tool. I will explore specific approaches I developed within my own teaching work in the next chapter. For now, let us consider the example offered by Pitts and Kwami in response to the question 'Does music technology open up the subject to pupils who might not normally be interested in it?' Pitts and Kwami report a Head of Music, self-proclaimed as a middle-aged and 'very traditional musician' who 'thought I'd probably never need to touch a computer in my life', stating that 'I would say to anyone just "try it"… the results are so much better than I ever could have anticipated. They are amazing' (2006: 66).

Clearly, then, unfamiliar and untraditional music-making modes can 'get them going' in important ways. Pitts and Kwami emphasise that this very much includes students who are normally less motivated.[1] That said, the prime focus of Pitts and Kwami's research is upon practical composition work rather than the kind of analytical discussion which, I would propose, *can* be valuable in music lessons in mainstream schools. So, it is certainly relevant to hear of 'larger groups of pupils [needing] to share a computer workstation' (Pitts and Kwami 2006: 65) and 'single stand-alone machines for whole class use in their departments' (64): the limited availability of equipment seems not to have made alternative, technologically-driven modes of music teaching unthinkable at the time this research was published (2002). On the basis of this, we might well propose that a music department possessing only one set of DJ decks should not necessarily conclude that practical DJing work is unthinkable. If one computer could be shared, presumably in some form of rotation across the class, when computers were more scarce in the 1990s and early 2000s, the same should be possible for DJ decks. Moreover, though, I would contend that practical work need not provide the 'be all and end all' of the 'work' which we undertake in a musical classroom. Is talking about music also not rather valuable for young people who, in all probability, have less fixed ideas about what music is (or could be) as compared with a middle-aged, classically-trained teacher?

This may be to challenge a general (and arguably problematic) trend: writing in 2004, Tim Cain argued that 'Now, more and more, pupils [in music lessons] are working either in pairs or as individuals, each with a workstation and a set of headphones' (2004: 217). More than a decade later, I would suggest that this trend has only increased. It is not unusual, today, for a music lesson to be delivered in an ICT suite one week, on keyboards the next, with the syllabus rarely if ever requiring individual learners to actually make music in real time with other persons, let alone listening to and talking about music. Cain fears that this could mean throwing the baby out with the bathwater, as it were: a legitimate concern, I would say, given that not every aspect of the traditional modes of music education is necessarily illegitimate (needless to say, one hopes). One of these traditional modes was listening to and analysing music. Would it be a return to 'the bad old days' if we were to include such an activity in the contemporary classroom? If this included the kinds of contemporary urban music which, in truth, are rarely discussed in depth in a school classroom, and if talk were prioritised over writing, this would certainly not be a purely reactionary move. (If, furthermore, such music was featured within a listening diet which also included classical music, rock, mainstream pop, neo-tonal experimentalism and so forth, I am inclined to think that listening could provide a radical opportunity for a greater level of diversity, plurality and mutual respect in the music classroom.)

With a view to non-music-specific pedagogical questions around keeping the 'interactive' disambiguated from the 'inactive' classroom, Burns and Myhill have enquired 'about "interaction" as a process in learning in whole class situations, which will enable [teachers] to better promote children's learning in a whole class setting' (2004: 48). 'It is with the interplay between the pupils' talk and their learning needs and the teachers' use of the differing forms and functions of language to enable children to think and explore their learning through a *real dialogue* that teachers should be concerned', they suggest (emphasis added). This does not mean that all closed questions are intrinsically inappropriate at all times: 'There will always be times where closed questions, or a quick-fire hail of questions, or a well-paced recap are appropriate'. However, 'the imbalance in classroom discourse through an emphasis on the pedagogical use of questions and explanation needs redressing' (ibid.). This can be done, they suggest (drawing on prior research by Hughes and Westgate), by placing 'At the heart of whole class talk… sensitive teacher-led but not teacher-dominated discourse'. The difference lies in being 'attentive to what children's responses reveal about their understandings or misunderstandings'; we might add, from a child-centred point of view, that we need to be attentive to what children's responses reveal about their *interests* (musical and otherwise, assuming the music teacher retains some interest in 'teaching the whole child' as they say).

In keeping with the Hardman, Smith and Wall research discussed above, Burns and Myhill insist that 'The focus of whole class teaching should be on creating reciprocal opportunities for talk to allow children to develop independent voices in discussion' (2004: 48). All well and good, one might respond, but what will Ofsted say? As noted above, the current leadership can give us little cause for optimism. It is worth noting, that said, some comments from Janet Mills and Andy Murray in regards to Ofsted's evaluation of ICT usage in music lessons. All practising teachers are aware that governmental and Ofsted directives change at a frightening pace, such that a piece of research from 2000 may have limited value today. Nevertheless, I would argue, some of what Mills and Murray reveal is of interest for us, I think.

The first thing we can note is a cautiously positive tone in regards to 'how ICT resources are increasing pupils' motivation' in music classrooms (Mills and Murray 2000: 132). Given that the DJ decks are a form of technology and that certain modern developments with the making of EDM (such as Ejay and GarageBand, which will be discussed in Chapter Nine herein) are ICT-orientated, this positivity is notable. That said, Mills and Murray also warn that 'The presence of a dazzling array of ICT equipment in a music lesson is clearly not a guarantee of success: like all other resources ICT needs to be used effectively' (131). What, then, do Ofsted consider to be effective and 'good' teaching of music when (modern) technology is employed? Mills and Murray, on the basis of inspectors' reports, suggest that good teaching will involve six key elements. First, taking the use of ICT in music seriously. Second, being knowledgeable about the resources in use. Third, planning such that the equipment will 'promote progress'. Fourth, efficient time management for the class, including time-efficient management of resources as well as pupils. Fifth, encouragement of 'pupils to use their initiative, and to think about what they were doing'. Sixth, making sure that 'the lesson was clearly a music lesson'.

These proposals are troublesome for many of my arguments in this book. I would say, for example, that being 'knowledgeable' about DJ decks *is* important for the music teacher who would use such technology in class but, having said that, the teacher does not need to be an absolute expert. Rather, the teacher needs to have sufficient knowledge to explain something of what is occurring at a technical level when a DJ mixes 'tunes'. If, however, an enthusiastic pupil corrects the teacher's usage of the vernacular term 'needle' by mentioning that the technical name is 'stylus' (as once happened to me), I personally would not panic if, for example, this occurred during an Ofsted inspection. After all, can we not 'promote progress' amongst the rest of the class by allowing the enthusiast to share his or her advanced knowledge? Clearly, furthermore, the learner has 'used his initiative' by acquiring such terminological knowledge. Moreover, I would not think that an interjection such as the one I have just described would indicate that the music teacher had failed to take music and technology 'seriously'. Rather, I should think, the teacher had provided an opportunity for an enthusiastic student to display advanced knowledge ('you spotted my deliberate mistake' being one of the oldest lines in the book for teachers who have been corrected by learners, as inevitably will happen for all teachers on occasion).

Actually, the two riskiest elements for the music teacher who would like to bring DJ decks into a lesson, from amongst the list provided by Mills and Murray, are probably the insistence that 'the lesson was clearly a music lesson' and the question of time management. On the first of these, there is not much the teacher can do. The truth is that there is a social bias, in at least some quarters, against urban music in general and hardcore EDM in particular: Motorhead vocalist Lemmy's widely-reported criticisms of hip hop ('I don't call that music', he is reputed to have told the *Atlantic City Weekly*) would only be one example of this attitude. Whether the inspector has any sympathy with such music is possibly the 'luck of the draw', in large part, and perhaps the best one can do – at present, at least – is hope that this music is recognised *as* music. Beyond this, I will suggest teaching methods below that I have employed which assume that music should not be treated as a discrete phenomenon unrelated to cultural life but, rather, that music is best understood as an integral and illuminative component of a broader cultural and social environment. Will the inspector accept such a rationale? Many will, I contend, but certainly there is an element of risk here. The best I can say, on that question, is that the more music teachers base their work upon the principle of music as a socio-cultural phenomenon rather than as an 'autonomous artform', the better chance we have of Ofsted and other 'powers-that-be' in education accepting our methods/principles.

There is a good deal more we, as teachers, can do about the time question, however. I turn to this question now.

Time management

As a matter of fact, I am in full agreement with inspectors who insist on carefully planned time management of technological resources and pupils' activity: when resources are limited, it is particularly crucial that students are not left 'twiddling their thumbs' and that all are engaged in productive activity. As Roland Chaplain puts it, 'Timing in a lesson is everything, be it related to the speed at which you speak, when equipment is given out or when students are asked to start work on their own' (2003: 124). If, furthermore, weaknesses in this regard are 'a potential recipe for management difficulties' in general (ibid.), it will be a particularly risky window of 'opportunity' for the disaffected learner who wants to demonstrate their lack of interest with disruptive behaviour. This is something of a tightrope walk for the teacher, however, is it not? As Deborah Blair puts is 'While the teacher is still the coordinator and designer of classroom musical experiences, the teacher does not need to direct every activity every moment': the effective teacher who wants to really stimulate thought and learning in the classroom needs to leave time for 'what the students will figure out' (2009: 44).

What is the best general approach to navigating this difficult path? Anyone with practical experience of teaching whole classes in mainstream schools is likely to agree that a crucial timing decision is how long to work in a 'whole class' mode and then, when the time is right, whether to switch to individual, paired or group work (and, of course, how to make that transition). Ted Wragg – certainly one of the most widely respected commentators on education of the last fifty years – outlines a classic schema for this in his *Class Management in the Secondary School*. At the outset of the lesson, Wragg proposes whole class teaching 'to set the scene' and explain what is required of groups when, imminently, the class divides up. Next, group work (five learners per group is proposed in a particular example he offers) might involve planning and dividing up responsibilities within the group, with learners taking a driving role in their own self-organisation. Finally, individual work can be undertaken which, unsurprisingly (given that Wragg is picturing an English lesson), is proposed as a writing activity (2003: 52).

How well does this map on to a music classroom? Much of it can work well, with a whole class introduction being rather essential for any teacher, really, given that learners (particularly in the lower years of the secondary range) will typically need to be reminded what they are doing and how it is to be done. To what extent this whole class moment should be prolonged will certainly depend on what is being taught, and I offer some concrete examples from my own practice in the next chapter, describing different ways I tackled this question when using DJ decks in the classroom. What I will say, for now, is that I am in full agreement with Blair when she says that effective music teaching often 'requires that the teacher step back and no longer be the centre of the musical experience, responsible for all the thinking and doing and musical decision making. It requires', she goes on, 'the teacher to trust and enable the students' budding musicianship, rather than requiring students to mimic their teacher's musicianship' (2009: 44). If Blair is correct, and I am sure she is, then it will not always be essential that the teacher knows more about DJing than certain learners do: it is OK for the enthusiast DJ to 'be the teacher' and, indeed, if this enthusiast also happens to be a troubled and troublesome young man, the experience can be transformative.

What of the rest of the class, though? As I have said, they must not be left in a passive state, simply listening to the music in a non-reflective manner for the bulk of a lesson. We need to remember, that said, that listening does not *have* to be a passive activity. Blair, for example, suggests that challenging learners 'to find broad and specific musical ideas when listening' is not contradistinctive to the teacher 'carefully crafting lessons' (2009: 44). The point, however, is to frame it: as I hinted in Chapter Two, the child-centred classroom, if and when it is an effective learning environment, does not leave children to flap like a lost butterfly but, rather, helps them to find their way to the nectar (and helps them to decide what, for them, musical 'nectar' might actually be).

Does listening have to result in writing in order for evidence that the learning has taken place? For pragmatic reasons, given the contemporary climate in the UK at least, this will often be wise. This pragmatic move, however, does not necessarily need to be placed at the heart of a lesson: as we noted above, talk is important and, therefore, recording learning through written work might well be a summative rather than a formative aspect of a lesson. Again, though, much research suggests that a child-centred pedagogical method will be valuable here: 'to enhance the role of talk in shaping and developing learning requires interaction patterns which reduce the teacher's role as orchestrator or controller of classroom talk, and instead reposition the teacher as an enabler of talk for thinking' (Myhill 2006: 21). *Talk for thinking*: it is an appealing idea, but one which could make professional teachers in mainstream classrooms (teachers, that is, who feel the breath of Ofsted and the school leadership upon their necks) rather anxious. How can we be sure that the talkers are 'on task' and not just chatting? How, furthermore, can we check that the thinking is moving in productive and fruitful directions?

Any teacher worth their pay should want to ask these questions (even if, following the child-centred paradigm, they wish for the learners themselves to make the last analysis as to what 'productive and fruitful' thinking actually is). I would suggest that we *can* make such checks (and, furthermore, that we can do it without destroying the child-centred element which this author values). Aside from rushing around the classroom attempting to interact with every group and check that they are on task (and I will admit that lessons involving DJ decks were particularly likely to leave me dripping with sweat at the end of a sixty-minute session), other strategies are available. Galton, Hargreaves and Pell, for example, insist that 'as part of training pupils to work effectively in groups it is vital that teachers brief and debrief the class so that they can begin to gain metacognitive awareness of what it means to be part of a group' (2009: 134). The debrief is 'particularly important because [learners] not only evaluate how individuals responded in the groups but they also call for participants to make suggestions about suitable strategies for improving the situation on future occasions'. This, I agree, is vital: for one thing, it contributes fruitfully to the overall 'learning environment' such that group work in the music classroom – whether practical music-making or listening-based talk for thinking – is more likely to be productive in subsequent sessions. It could also feedback, furthermore, into the 'written recording' of the learning which has taken place. (Given the affordability and availability of audio-visual recording equipment in schools today, that said, it could be justified – particularly if one is working with a very low ability group in terms of literacy, as I often was – to simply video record the debrief conversation as a demonstration of learning.)

Should the debrief occur within a 'plenary' at the end of a lesson? In most cases, this will make perfect sense. We should acknowledge, that said, that there can be pitfalls with this element of lesson timing. Consider, for example, an account of 'a lesson inspection conducted by two assistant headteachers during a mocksted' discussed in *The Guardian* newspaper on Saturday, 20 February 2016 under the headline 'I see Ofsted for what it is – a purposeless farce'. 'The lesson was graded as "good" so I asked [the assistant head teachers] what I could do to make it "outstanding"', the writer reveals. 'They looked blank and eventually suggested I should have spent a bit longer during a discussion section of the lesson', he goes on. 'I pointed out that this would have reduced the time for plenary reflection – the latest targeted initiative – and they agreed'. Despite this discrepancy, 'I never did get a clear answer on whether it was even possible to make the lesson "outstanding"'.

Should we throw up our hands at the recounting of such a tale and perhaps even declare teaching work itself a 'purposeless farce' too, given such a peculiar and self-contradictory meta-structure sitting in judgement of our work? I will say that I never regarded my teaching work as purposeless, although certain requirements of the job did leave me wondering if the leadership (in the school, in Ofsted and in the government) had taken leave of its senses. As I have said, though, teachers walk a tightrope in a number of senses. When it comes to – wait for it – timing, one can err in any number of ways *but* – when it is done well, as in great comedy as well as great teaching – it can work like thunder. How does one improve, in this regard? Practice, doubtless; but, also, by observing the learning which is taking place before you and striving, always striving, to support it, nurture it and extend it.

I will give concrete examples of time management methods I used when teaching with DJ decks in the next chapter. For now, however, I want to make some remarks in relation to space – also vital for engaging children in music education.

Management of space in the classroom

On the occasions where I knew a supply teacher would be covering some teaching work for me, I made a point of covering the DJ decks with a sheet. Why? Because the very sight of them excites many young people: they are suggestive of something which many students believe perhaps shouldn't be allowed, for one thing, and represent music which many young people love, for another thing. At times like this, but at all times in fact, controlling the classroom space is vital for the music teacher. The same is true of any classroom, actually: 'it is worth thinking carefully about how to use the space at your disposal', Ted Wragg has asserted, adding that 'Time spent planning an effective classroom layout, given the amount of time spent there, will be a wise investment' (1993: 60). Wragg is honest enough, however, to admit that 'Many teachers work in classrooms that are less than ideal'.

The first classroom in which I delivered lessons involving DJ decks was a 'prefab' which my about-to-retire colleague would openly refer to (with good reason) as 'a shed in the carpark'. Heating, in the space, was noisy but just about adequate and the main classroom was actually quite large. I tried numerous different layouts in the room after my colleague retired (at which point I became, as music teachers will sometimes say, a 'one man band': the Head of a Department consisting of one teacher, that is). The classroom design I settled upon as my default layout allowed me to have students sitting at desks facing me with keyboards in front of them. I made sure there was enough 'circulation' around the room to allow headphones, splitters and exercise books to be handed out quickly and efficiently without significant downtime between my explanation of some practical task and the commencement of practical activity by the learners. Fortunately for me (and my classes), the room was sufficiently big that I could bring a class of thirty to the front for singing, positioning them sideways so that they had their backs to the fire door and the desks (with keyboards on them) were off to the side of them.

The DJ decks, meanwhile, were squirrelled off to the far side of the room, near the fire door (thus being behind the class when singing was taking place and to one side of the learners when they were sat at desks facing me). They were always visible, as a result, but not too distracting when other kinds of musical work were being undertaken. Sometimes the decks would be covered in a sheet, as I have said; this was essential if I had particularly lusty learners in the class who were desperate to 'gan on the decks' (as they say in the North East). The DJ decks made their presence known, I would say, but my classes knew that this equipment would only be used in certain lessons. When an Ofsted inspection took place, I made a point of positioning her chair next to the decks: the topic of the lesson was actually related to one of the oldest songs in the (early) English language, 'Sumer is Icumen In', but I wanted the inspector to see that all musics were welcome in this space. One of the deputy heads told me that the inspector burst into the heads' office immediately after this and, in front of the schools' senior management as well as the other three visiting Ofsted inspectors, proclaimed excitedly that she had 'just seen an outstanding music lesson'. Clearly, then, the inspector saw some value in the use which the class and I were putting the space to, without the DJ decks which were right in front of her having caused any problem from her point of view.

A year or two after this, I was moved from 'the shed in the car park' into an actual building made of bricks in the heart of the school. Again, I was lucky enough to find myself with a very large main classroom, sufficient to accommodate keyboards on desks, a singing area at the front and a designated space for DJs and MCs towards the back of the room. Even more helpful was a table on wheels which I managed to acquire. Sufficiently large to accommodate the two vinyl decks, the mixer and some powered speakers, this wheeled table meant that I could quickly bring the DJing equipment to the front of the room at any time and (sometimes with a semi-theatrical flourish, I will admit) transform the vibe of the classroom.

It is just this kind of careful utilisation of space which can pay dividends for the teacher of music, I would argue. In music teaching, indeed, space is probably even more important than most other disciplines. (Maths work, for example, probably rarely requires the level of quick-fire transformations of the classroom which a music teacher might need to make during the course of a working day.) What benefits can arise from this? I am in agreement with Chaplain that 'A learning environment that looks good is no substitute for good teaching' (2003: 124). Nevertheless, as he also remarks, 'there are a number of ways that the physical environment can be manipulated to enhance' social skills as well as the children's academic learning (125). His advice is sound, I would judge: 'Paying attention to where students are sitting, how they are grouped, their proximity to the teaching "hub", how often you interact with them, the nature of the interaction and so on' are crucial, he suggests.

Furthermore, 'Reflecting on who is sitting where, and the reason for doing so, can provide the basis for thinking of how to develop positive relationships with students who are at risk of social exclusion' (ibid.). This is quite so, I would say, but if those 'at risk' students are also enthusiasts of hardcore EDM (as often was the case in my years of teaching), the question of what *equipment* is sitting where also becomes vital.

We need to be creative with the space in our music classrooms, then, and particularly so if we want to introduce perceived-to-be-foreign equipment such as the DJ decks. My numerous experiences mentoring PGCE student-teachers have led me to recognise some truth in Chaplain's suggestion that 'Changing layouts seems to present a problem for some teachers… almost as if the desks are welded to the floor, or moving them might release the Golem' (2003: 125). For our purposes, it is interesting that Chaplain even suggests a possible classroom layout which he calls 'The Nightclub' (129–30): for work involving DJ decks, this might work well, I would say. Moreover, though, I would contend that we need to be willing to open up the space in our classrooms to radical change (even if only for a day or two, or a single lesson come to that) if we want to throw forth the possibility for a lesson around the DJ decks. Indeed, the thing that really works, I found, is that it certainly wasn't (isn't) 'just another boring music lesson': this alone is worth the hassle of a little classroom re-organisation, I would suggest.

Conclusion

Ted Wragg has argued that 'the ability to control behaviour, in whatever manner, is a "threshold" measure – if you have enough of it you are over the threshold and can display the rest of your repertoire of professional skills'; however, 'too little of it and these may never become apparent' (1993: 6). These, I think, are wise words; and without doubt classroom management is a key element within this effort to control behaviour. I am also in full agreement with Wragg's proposal that 'children tend to prefer teachers who… are interesting and provide a variety of stimulating work' (22). For the music teacher, the DJ decks can be a highly valuable source of such stimulation, I would add. After all, if we are 'aware of the difficulties of engaging all pupils in learning', and if a 'bracketing out of their voice' is a causative for the problem in question, as Wragg has asserted elsewhere (2004: 178), bringing this music-making equipment in to the classroom might well be a highly valuable solution to the problem at hand. If 'the continued failure to critically educate and to creatively stimulate working-class students is little short of criminal' (150), it ought to be at least worth giving urban music and hardcore EDM a try, ought it not?

In this chapter, however, I have tried to caution that the effective music teacher who would bring DJ decks into their classroom should handle their classroom management carefully. For one thing, one needs to keep an eye on the (pernicious, according to many) influence of Ofsted: a teacher who pays no heed to the expectations and preferences of the inspectorate might not remain in post for long, it seems. That said, I have tried to show here that the classroom *can* be managed in a manner which pleases Ofsted inspectors: the main thing, I would suggest, is making sure that time and space are well used in the classroom.

What is most vital, overall, is what I have called the 'whole class challenge'. If the teacher only has one set of DJ decks (as I did), this will be particularly big challenge, but in any case the decision as to how a whole class should be engaged, and how long for, is vital in mainstream teaching work. In music-specific terms, I have tried to emphasise that listening does *not* have to be a passive activity and that work involving talk can have legitimacy although, pragmatically, written work can be a useful manner of recording learning. It is, I found, possible to keep a whole class engaged with a lesson based around one set of DJing equipment, but there are potential errors and pitfalls which – having made them myself – I would certainly encourage another teacher to try to avoid. I turn to my own experiences more strongly in the next chapter wherein I discuss issues around assessment, lesson content and the specific demands of the UK's Key Stage 3 curriculum for music.

Note

1 We can note with interest that they also state that 'Only a few pupils chose to exploit the more disruptive aspects of electronic sound!' (Pitts and Kwami 2002: 217). Such pupils are very much of interest from my research vantage point, of course, and I think it is telling that Pitts and Kwami seem to assume that the pupils would 'exploit' electronic sound purely for 'disruptive' purposes. Might it not alternatively be the case that the apparently disruptive sound is of intrinsic interest to students for purely timbral/aesthetic reasons (that the pupils want to 'exploit' the sound in the sense that we would say a composer exploits his sonic resources, in other words)? The possibility is at least worth considering, I would think, and is very likely the case, I might add from experience.

References

Blair, Deborah V., 'Stepping Aside: Teaching in a Student-Centred Music Classroom', *Music Educators Journal*, 95/3 (2009), 42–5

Burnard, Pamela, Finney, John, *Music Education with Digital Technology* (London: Continuum, 2007)

Burns, Chris, Myhill, Debra, 'Interactive or Inactive? A Consideration of the Nature of Interaction in Whole Class Teaching', *Cambridge Journal of Education*, 34/1, (2004), 35–49

Cain, Tim, 'Theory, Technology and the Music Curriculum', *British Journal of Music Education*, 21/2 (2004), 215–21

Chaplain, Roland, *Teaching without Disruption in the Secondary School: A Model for Managing Pupil Behaviour* (London: Routledge, 2003)

Galton, Maurice, Hargreaves, Linda, Pell, Tony, 'Group Work and Whole-Class Teaching with 11- to 14-Year-Olds Compared', *Cambridge Journal of Education*, 39/1 (2009), 119–40

Hardman, Frank, Smith, Fay, Wall, Kate, '"Interactive Whole Class Teaching" in the National Literacy Strategy', *Cambridge Journal of Education*, 33/2 (2003), 197–215

Lever, Colin, *Understanding Challenging Behaviour in Inclusive Classrooms* (Essex: Pearson, 2011)

Mills, Janet, Murray, Andy, 'Music Technology Inspected: Good Teaching in Key Stage 3', *British Journal of Music Education*, 17/2 (2000), 129–56

Myhill, Debra, 'Talk, Talk, Talk: Teaching and Learning in Whole Class Discourse', *Research Papers in Education*, 21/1 (2006), 19–41

Pitts, Adrian, Kwami, Robert Mawuena, 'Raising Students' Performance in Music Composition through the Use of Information and Communications Technology (ICT): A Survey of Secondary Schools in England', *British Journal of Music Education*, 19/1 (2002), 61–71

Smith, Fay, Hardman, Frank, Wall, Kate, Mroz, Maria, 'Interactive Whole Class Teaching in the National Literacy and Numeracy Strategies', *British Educational Research Journal*, 30/3 (2004), 395–411

Wragg, E.C., *Class Management in the Secondary School* (London: Routledge, 2003)

Wragg, E.C., *The RoutledgeFalmer Reader in Teaching and Learning* (London: Routledge, 2004)

6
REMIXING THE KS3 CURRICULUM

'Key Stage 3', in the UK, is the period between the September after a child's eleventh birthday and the July before a child's fifteenth birthday. Some schools are now truncating this period of time to two rather than three years (thus concluding KS3 in the summer before a child's fourteenth birthday). In any case, though, this is the period of time, within typical mainstream schooling, *after* primary school finishes but *before* GCSE options are undertaken. The UK does retain some 'Middle Schools' which cover a 9 to 13 years of age range, but these are very much the exception rather than the rule: for the vast bulk of children in the UK, KS3 will be the first years at 'big school' (secondary school, that is) where children from several different primary schools are tumbled in together.

Music being a 'foundation' subject (as opposed to the perceived-to-be-more-important 'core' subjects English, Maths and the Sciences), this can be a very tricky period. For one thing, the learners are likely to have had very widely differing experiences of music in their primary schools: some children will have had very limited exposure to music teaching whilst others will have encountered non-specialist teachers who seriously struggle to deliver the prescribed National Curriculum at KS2. Another issue is that many children come to feel that the core requirements of the KS3 National Curriculum – singing, in particular, but also the clumsy expressiveness which tends to be a necessary first step when a person begins to make music – are an embarrassment. The literature on this 'transition' is too vast to recount here, but we can certainly note with interest a few specific findings from Dimitra Kokotsaki's *Improving the Primary-Secondary Transition in Music Education* report of 2015 (funded by the Nuffield Foundation).

Highly pertinent, for our purposes, is the revelation that 'pupils felt more positive about music during the first term of Year 7 [11–12 years of age], but these positive attitudes declined as the year progressed' (Kokotsaki 2015: 28). This, of course, is the 'honeymoon period' wherein even the most troubled and troublesome children have not much started to 'rise', normally speaking; most teachers will agree that the decline in question often reaches epidemic levels by the end of KS3. We can also note with interest that 'it was quite common for at least one pupil in each focus group to report disengagement and boredom with music in primary school' ('We never did proper good stuff, only maracas and things that you hold'; 'We only had one piccolo between 60 children ...') (32). Attitudes towards secondary school music seem more positive in Kokotsaki's findings, but we can note with interest that some pupils (Kokotsaki specifies that they were boys) stated that they 'disliked singing in class quoting reasons including singing not being a "manly" activity and feeling embarrassed to sing in front of their friends in class' (35). Few music teachers will be surprised to hear this, I believe: indeed, even TV personality Gareth Malone (famous for encouraging singing in schools) is reported by *The Independent* newspaper on 3 September 2008 as acknowledging that 'There are real gender issues around that difficult age when [biological] change is looming. You don't want to be perceived as unmanly.'

I lack the space here to look at Kokotsaki's report in much more detail, but I would say that many of the themes within my argument are reflected in her findings (one example, selected almost at random: a child is reported stating that they 'would like to do more up-to-date songs and listen to different types of music instead of just a little bit of classical and little warm ups') (2015: 38). How, though, is the effective music teacher to combat disaffection, disengagement and the slow drift which results in uptake of music at KS4 being a fraction of the available student population in so many schools? (The National Foundation for Educational Research have reported that music is 'the most problematic and vulnerable art form' at KS4 and that 'pupil enjoyment, relevance, skill development, creativity and expressive dimensions were often absent' [Hargreaves and Marshall 2010: 265].) Clearly my argument is that a child-centred approach which engages with contemporary urban music/EDM in general and which integrates DJ decks in particular can aid us in the struggle against disengagement from music at KS3 (and, I might add, at KS4, but I will explore that later 'Key Stage' in Chapter Seven). What *specifically* should the music teacher do with this stuff, though? This is my topic in the present chapter. I begin with a range of examples drawn from my own teaching practice. In the second section, I look at some more specific research around music education at Key Stage 3, going into some detail about the demands and specificities of the current National Curriculum for music. Thereafter, towards the end of the second section, I draw upon some examples of classroom work which were discussed by respondents in the case studies already mentioned in Chapter Four herein.

What are we doing today, sir?

It's a question which all good teachers ought to expect to hear: 'what are we doing today, sir/miss?' If the work is varied from lesson to lesson, from week to week, the learners will not assume that the content of each lesson is going to be a *fait accompli* (a 'done deal', that is). The ideal thing, I would argue, is for the class to arrive with a degree of excitement, or at least interest. One might give some indication, at the end of a lesson, as to what work will be undertaken next time, of course. Even then, however, it is fair to hope that some intrigue will linger in the minds of learners such that the lesson, when it arrives, will hold some surprise.

Because many of the learners I worked with were excited by the DJ decks and the felt-to-be-semi-illicit music which they associated with the decks, I would often be asked 'are we gannin' on the decks today, sir?' ('Gan' is a popular North East substitute for the word 'go'.) Sometimes I was able to say 'yes' but obviously (I think the necessity is obvious, at least) I could not turn every lesson over to a 'session' on the decks. Sometimes I had to say 'no' because, for example, we might be in the midst of an extended project on Indian music, the Beatles, folk music or whatever; other times, I had to decline in order to keep the classroom work varied.

Where, in a scheme of work, *can* equipment like this most suitably be employed? Obviously a topic around dance music gives ample room for the DJ decks to be explored, and I came to habitually make dance music the central topic for Year 9 in that long period between Christmas and Easter. Year 9, in the school where I worked at least, was the last year in KS3, meaning that many learners had already decided that they would not proceed with music at KS4. Unsurprisingly, many of them became less easy to work with during this period of time ('why do I have to do this lesson when I haven't picked music?', the pupils would remonstrate). By focussing on dance music, however, I found I could keep the enjoyment and attainment levels reasonably high with a diet of work which didn't feel like too much of a repetition of that which had already been learned; studying the DJ decks and EDM was certainly valuable to this.

It is perhaps worth offering a breakdown of the scheme of work I developed on dance music, so that the reader can get a sense of the context in which I embedded work relating to the DJ decks. With one hour per week with each class, I would begin the first lesson on dance music with a discussion around tribal drumming, basic types of instruments (for example, hollowed wood with animal skin across it) and the likely origins of music. Predictably enough, I would then divide the class into groups, working on Djembe drums and other percussion in different spaces (practice rooms, my cupboard if necessary, corridors if really pushed, in the main classroom obviously) on 'tribal rhythms' (with the meaning of this couplet being left largely open to practical interpretation). The following week, we would look at renaissance forms such as the Pavan and the Galliard: with keyboards set to 'harpsichord', a rudimentary Pavan would be attempted in pairs on keyboards, often with reasonably pleasing results. (Copying an idea from my retired ex-colleague, I would even sometimes get the students out of their seats to do a procession-dance whilst we listened to a recorded Pavan.) Thereafter we would visit the Waltz (with the low-high-high pattern providing ample opportunity for formative guidance), the Charleston, the Jive, and so forth. Always, I attempted to situate the practical music-making in a cultural context; I certainly wasn't shy of discussing the Pogo as a form of dance (even going as far as to demonstrate in class, if the mood struck me) and made efforts not to pejoratively prioritise any form of dance music over another.

Working in this somewhat chronological way, I would inevitably pass through Disco and arrive, eventually, at Rave/Techno/'Acid House': the EDM which emerged in the late 1980s and early 1990s, that is. Typically, I made space for two consecutive lessons on this theme. Firstly, I would play pioneering musical examples of DJing skills such as 'The Adventures of Grandmaster Flash on the Wheels of Steel' by Grandmaster Flash (1981) and of MCing skills such as 'Rapper's Delight' by the Sugarhilll Gang (1979). The opening minute of the former of these tracks was ample for a lengthy discussion of DJing techniques such as cutting, scratching, blending and beatmatching. Indeed, the way Flash selects Queen's 'Another One Bites the Dust' as a juxtaposition to the bass riff from 'Rapper's Delight' provides an excellent opportunity to discuss key musical principles such as tempo, key, syncopation and so forth. 'Rapper's Delight', meanwhile, seems to retain a remarkable level of respect and credibility amongst young EDM/urban music enthusiasts despite the fact that rapping, as an art form, has morphed and changed so much over the last thirty-five years.

Having set the scene with whole class talking time (see the previous chapter herein for pedagogical justifications of the employment of talk in class as a learning mode), I would show the class the decks and ask them what they knew about the way this equipment works. Some questions I found valuable were:

- How does the sound get transferred from the vinyl record into the speakers? (Key terms are of course needle/stylus, tone arm, groove, signal, vibration, amplification, speaker cone and so forth.)
- What is the thing sitting between the decks called and what is it used for? (Key terms here are mixer, cross fader, cutting, blending, headphones, monitoring and 'stereo phono jacks'.)
- What happens to the sound when the disc spins faster or slower? (Here, the concept of pitch can be very helpfully emphasised, because the increase or decrease in tempo is more easily recognised by the average young person whereas the change in pitch is less easily recognised by ear.)
- What happens to the sound when I manually turn the disc anti-clockwise rather than clockwise? (Here, a considerable amount of time can gainfully be spent exploring the different sounds which arise from different moments on a record; the raw sound will certainly excite and intrigue most young people, I found.)

When working in this way, I would typically ask for a volunteer to, say, put the needle in the opening groove and press the start/stop button, or to push the speed control up and down. I made a point, at this early stage in the session, of requesting volunteers who had never before touched DJ decks (the enthusiasts, if there were any in the class, would get a chance to show their skills later in the lesson). Often reticent at first, I found the class would usually warm to the task: in any case, it never ceased to amaze me that even the rowdiest of classes would quietly observe with interest as soon as the decks were placed before them. In the rare cases where the sight of the decks did not cause the class to 'settle', I would simply place the stylus in the groove of the record and make one or two loud 'scratch' noises. (The DJ scratch does not literally require a scratching of the disc in the sense of damaging it, of course: the DJ simply makes a physical movement of the disc, controlled by hand, back and/or forth such that a short segment of sound is presented in a manner which effectively distorts the sound in a sonically intriguing way.) Without fail, this sound would get them listening attentively. A disc I found particularly helpful for scratching was 'Wild Thing' by the Troggs – more specifically, the downward glissando on electric guitar at the outset of the track – which I always kept handy next to the decks.

Once some discussion of the decks as musical equipment had been undertaken, I would explain that the two turntables and mixer had normally been used, up until the late 1970s, to simply play one record and then, at the end of that disc, to segue to another. The remarkable innovation of the pioneering African-American DJs of the late 1970s was, in short, to 'cut' records into pieces in the sense that, say, a drum break might be looped, through the use of two copies of the same disc, *ad infinitum* such that an MC could be provided with a continuous and funky rhythm over which to rap. Such DJs might also leave a track unmolested but, whilst that piece of music was playing, cut in sounds from a second disc. In order to demonstrate the way this can be done even by a novice (which, I would remind them, I was), I frequently used some unambiguous piece of dance music on one turntable and, on the other, 'I Want to Break Free' by Queen. As with 'Wild Thing' by the Troggs, this was simply a disc which I had picked up for a minimal sum (50 pence, if memory serves correctly) at a 'car boot sale'.

The advantage of the Queen track in question was that it breaks down, eight seconds in to the song, to a voice, unaccompanied by instrumentation, singing 'I want to break free-ee'. As it happened, I had used this song for whole class singing the previous year, thus I knew that all members of the class would be *au fait* with the tune. Because the line is unaccompanied, it could be placed above another 'tune' (piece of music, that is, and usually I would rely on happy hardcore tunes as these were the taste of a very large minority of my learners) without sounding too cluttered. I could thus get a learner to cue up the disc and then to pick a moment at which to 'drop' (ie play) the vocal fragment before using the cross fader to cut the Queen track back out of the mix. Typically, pupils found this quite hard to do. However, given my training as a musician and, it is fair to say, my above-average musical skills in general, I found that I could then demonstrate a fairly effective dropping of the fragment across the dance tune such that a reasonably satisfying 'mash up' (mixture, essentially, that is) of Queen and happy hardcore was accomplished.

Typically, I would then show them the distinctive guitar break which appears at 1.34 in 'I Want to Break Free'. Again, the fact that the guitar is unaccompanied makes it ideal for the DJ to blend it into another track. The synthesiser-recalling sound (indeed, I think the sound may actually be played on a synth with a pitch-shifting function) is also ideal for scratching and, therefore, I often would then move to scratching the guitar break across the dance tune. I found that any learner with at least a bit of rhythmical sense could cut in some 'baby scratches' in a reasonably satisfying manner; it is easier than it looks to baby scratch passably, although harder than it looks to do it well.

Because there were so many DJ enthusiasts in the inner-city school where I worked, I would often then allow a member of the class to deliver a short DJ set for the listening pleasure of the rest. On some occasions, if the timetable of a really serious DJing pupil could allow it (in other words, if I could persuade a colleague to consent to it), I would bring in a DJ from another class to demonstrate his skills for the timetabled class. (Consent from colleagues for the DJing enthusiasts to be excused from their classes was often quite easily gained because, in truth, these were typically some of the most disruptive young people in the school.) On other occasions, there would be no DJs but one of the class might have skills in MCing. If that were the case, I might leave whole tunes playing whilst the MC (or, as sometimes happened, MCs) rapped over it. If possible, I would move to the back of the room at this juncture and hope that the children would forget that I was present.

Here, that said, we arrive at a risky point in the lesson: as discussed in the last chapter, the teacher who leaves the bulk of a class apparently idle whilst one or two individuals perform at the front is not likely to be approved of by Ofsted (nor the senior management of schools who answer to them). How can this problem be resolved? One possibility, which I often employed, was to set some form of paper-based work for learners to accomplish whilst the DJing set was being undertaken. My plenary, at the end of the lesson, would then be delivered without the DJ decks being in play: instead, we might recap on key points which had been discussed in the lesson. The paper-based work would be differentiated depending on the class. The least able classes, some members of which had a 'reading age' (let us leave this spurious concept unremarked upon for now) more than two years behind their chronological age, needed more support: for them, a set of key words and a writing frame might be offered. More able learners could be set research tasks, text to read through and comment upon or opportunities to 'link the learning' with acoustic principles which, I was aware, they had touched upon within the KS3 Science curriculum.

Quite often, I would challenge learners to annotate a worksheet featuring an aerial view of the DJing equipment. Again, this can easily be differentiated so that more able learners are given opportunities for more technical and more detailed annotations. In the plenary, meanwhile, I would also attempt to link the learning with our larger theme of dance music through the ages: why does happy hardcore (and techno, bouncy house, dupstep and so forth – the whole panopoly of dance-based contemporary urban music, indeed) make people want to dance? A question like this can in fact prompt some very valuable talk amongst a class.

As stated above, I might extend the DJ-related work across two lessons within my scheme of work on dance music. The second lesson would often begin with a discussion of 'acid house' and the free party scene which arose in the UK in the early 1990s. I would show the class newspaper clippings (culled from the Internet) from the era in question, perhaps discussing the tragic death of Leah Betts in 1995 or some such discussion-provoking historical detail (the British 'Reclaim the Streets' movement of the 1990s, for example, which took dance parties to the streets as a ludic political statement in opposition to 'car culture'). I would also draw the learners' attention to the 1994 Criminal Justice and Public Order Act's legislation against music involving 'repetitive beats'. In the middle of the lesson, some more practical work around the DJ decks often would be developed, perhaps focussing less on DJing techniques and more on the musical content. For example, I might encourage the learners to consider the perceived 'spirituality' (according to some ravers, at least) of the music and the somewhat trance-inducing 'repetitive beats' already mentioned. We can note, on the spirituality question, DJ Frank Owen's complaint that 'We live in a culture that's embarrassed by spiritual ecstasy ... [as being] something from the middle ages' and yet 'incredibly intense eruptions' can be found 'in raves'; world-renowned DJ Moby responds that 'As far as spirituality goes... House culture and rave culture are all about ecstatic expression and opening yourself up' (Ross et al. 1995: 98). Naturally, I would seize the opportunity to warn the learners of the dangers of drug misuse although, in an inner-city context, several of them will have known more about drugs by the end of KS3 than the rest of us will ever know, to be truthful about it.

Written work in a session like this would often focus on questions around Health and Safety: for example, what makes a nightclub safer and preferable for a 'rave' as compared with an *ad hoc* gathering in a warehouse (aside from the purely legal issue)? I was always keen for the music to be evaluated and discussed in a culturally specific context, with reference to socio-economic and cultural-political factors. That said, I was also always keen to develop music-specific skills amongst learners. Because of this, I would sometimes transcribe the melodic pattern from one of the hardcore tunes onto a stave and use it as the springboard for practical work on keyboards. One of my favourites for this purpose, which I had acquired on vinyl for teaching purposes, was a tune known as 'Love in Paradise', recorded in Spain in 1998 and issued under the name Virtual Reality on the DJs At Work label.

'Love in Paradise' is a typical 'Mákina' tune, very well known and much loved in the North East of England. As leading magazine *Mixmag* put it on 8 April 2015, 'Mákina is Spain's take on happy hardcore, and it had a huge following in Newcastle in the late 90s and into the 00s, with sets recorded at raves one week and sold on tape in the market a few weeks later'. In an article on Mákina published by *noisey .vice.com* on 1 June 2015, it is argued that 'a whole host of people hate [Mákina] but will still know it as the North East's sound', adding that 'the voice of the MC is a true representation of the life they lead'. It is distinct from grime and other forms of contemporary urban music coming from the UK because 'Most of the lyrics are about partying, but they also talk about stealing cars, doing drugs and getting chased by the police. Nobody talks about Rolexes, shifting drugs, or pulling women' (ibid.).

The young people who enjoy Mákina will typically be known in the North East as 'charvas' or 'charvs'. I know, from direct experience of a quarter of a century of living in the North East, that these descriptors were in regular usage in the North East long before the term 'chav' became known more widely in the UK. With good reason, therefore, 'Geordies will argue the term was born here and should always be pronounced "charv"' (as local newspaper the *Evening Chronicle* put it on 2 December 2010, citing the Oxford English Dictionary in support of its claim). Mákina, according to *factmag.com*, is 'proper, in-the-foundations-of-the-city, cross-generational folk music, a sound that serves its function perfectly and has no need to change'.

Starting out from a repetitive 'donk'-based beat, 'Love in Paradise' presents a highly melodic phrase from about one minute in to the track. Although I would use a stave to present the tune to learners, I would also typically offer them the note names too so that they might easily be able to translate it onto keyboards. Presented in this way (and transposed to A minor for the convenience of learners), the tune would be A-B-C, C, C, then C-B-A, A, A, then C-D-E, E, E, concluding with B-A-G, G, G, with each phrase being played twice. (Here, I have used hyphens to indicate quavers or, as they say in the USA, 'eighth notes' and commas to indicate crotchets or, in US terms again, 'quarter notes'.) Even the untrained eye should be able to see that this is melodically rather simple: A-B-C is followed by C-B-A, meaning that even a learner who is baffled by the geography of the keyboard should have a reasonable chance of playing the opening phrases of the tune, so long as they can find the note A.

That said, the tune would nevertheless prove too much for some learners. Determined to leave no child behind, I therefore offered a bass clef with the notes for the root notes of each implied triad: A for the first phrase, F for the second, C for the third and G for the fourth. Setting the keyboards to a square synth tone setting ('the rave sound', as many of my learners would put it) and holding each of these notes whilst silently counting to four in their heads, even the most struggling learner could usually re-create the bass line of the tune. If they then added a 'techno' beat (available on most keyboards today), this task allowed the learners to develop real musical skills: following a bar structure, locating beat one within the bar, navigating the geography of the keyboard's black and white keys and so forth. Often I would then be able to match a less able student, who could only manage the bass line, with a more able student, who might have learned the main tune, thus creating a reasonably satisfying duet. Sometimes, of course, I would encounter students with exceptional facility with music (and sometimes, I should add, such a student would be in the lowest set due to delayed literacy/numeracy skills). These students could be challenged to attempt the bass line with the left hand and the tune with the right, perhaps using the 'synchro start' button to make the tune 'kick off' with a rhythm at a particular moment. Some learners could manage this, but in any case it delighted most classes to see a middle-aged man in a suit playing a reasonably convincing reiteration of Mákina/happy hardcore on a cheap keyboard: the impact on motivation of using such (child-centred, given the particular location I was in) musical material as the basis for learning was unmistakeable.

The tune from 'Love in Paradise' became something I would hear on keyboards in the school all the time. Boys would sneak into practice rooms and play it on the pianos; new entrants to the school in Year 7 would be playing it before I had had time to show them it, having been 'learned it' by an older brother or sister who had accomplished the piece in lessons with me the year or two before. Eventually, I came to use the tune in question and the DJ decks for preliminary teaching in the first year of KS3, developing further knowledge and skills in subsequent years. It was important not to overdo it, but I found that 'Love in Paradise' had enough complexity to justify revisits (and often higher levels of attainment when learners returned to this musical material). In terms of the decks, meanwhile, judicious use of this equipment (alongside a range of other musical equipment, naturally) in class meant that the question 'what are we doing today, sir?' was worth asking: the answer, I believe my learners felt, was far from a certainty.

Delivering the National Curriculum at 160 BPM

What do the government want us to teach in music? Cynical teachers will say that the goalposts are moved with alarming regularity. We can note, for example, that the National Curriculum attainment levels have been abolished in 2016, following the arrival of a new National Curriculum in 2014. However, the content of the National Curriculum had already been re-drawn in 2008 and there can be good reasons for criticising the (newest) new deal. We can note, for example, a complaint by Sir Peter Williams, vice-president of the Royal Society, that 'it is clear from international comparisons that in this country we are prone to accelerate steps in our educational processes to ever earlier ages, contrary to practice elsewhere – notably in Finland and Japan.' More promisingly, that said, Dominic Wyse and Anusca Ferrari have argued in relation to the national curriculum that 'connections with creativity were more frequent in the visual arts and music than in languages and literature (Wyse and Ferrari 2015: 38).'

This should be good news for music teachers who want to maximise on creativity in their classrooms, of course. The trouble, however, is that – particularly given the removal of National Curriculum attainment levels – there is now something of a lacuna in terms of assessment strategies and, consequently, in terms of curriculum content. Granted, the new National Curriculum gives some indication of curriculum coverage: playing music, composing it and improvising, reading music, identifying and using the expressive and sophisticated dimensions of music, listening to music and developing depth of understanding of music which is performed and/or listened to (including its 'history'), in short. How, though, is the music teacher to judge the attainment of learners at KS3 now that National Curriculum levels can no longer be referred to? And how can a fit be made between assessment, on the one hand, and curriculum content, on the other hand, when there is at present no clarity as to what level of attainment should be granted which grading on the basis of what curricular work for the purpose of assessment?

At the time of writing, the situation is very confusing. I have undertaken some *ad hoc* (and, doubtless, therefore potentially faulty) research by asking practising music teachers how things stand at present. This *ad hoc* research suggested that many music teachers are currently being asked to use the UK's new numeric grading system for KS3 assessment levels. With regard to this numeric system (one to nine, with nine being the top grade), government agency Ofqual have announced on 12 September 2014 that 'it is not right to say simply that a new grade 4 will equal a current grade C'. This is because 'The read across is at the bottom of each grade, so that broadly the same proportion of students will get 4 and above as currently get C and above'. This is claimed as a 'subtle but important difference'; personally, I would add that it is so subtle that I cannot myself see the difference. Indeed, if 'where grade 5 sits within the grading scale will place it above a current grade C' (ibid.), is this not essentially a B grade by any other name?

Doubtless the position will become clearer over time. In any case, it is worth remembering that assessment in the arts, whether measured with a number, a letter or a percentage, is not an entirely scientific process. This author will not pretend to have found the traditional letter system for assessment to have been perfect. I always thought that the idea of an 'A★' made about as much sense as Chief Inspector at Ofsted Michael Wilshaw's pronouncement, quoted by *Gov.uk* on 6 January 2012, that for a school to be graded as satisfactory 'is not good enough'. (The A★, to my mind, equates to the advertising slogan that 'the best just got better'. Even if the claim were true, the best remains the best no matter how many stars you add to it: it is hard to imagine that the status of a '9' in the new GCSE assessment system is being misunderstood by school children and teachers when, predictably enough, they call it the equivalent of 'A★★'.) Moreover, for the purpose of the present chapter, our concern is how these changes impact upon assessment, curriculum and the possibility of bringing more urban music into the classroom.

With that in mind, we should go into some more detail about the six things which, according to the new National Curriculum for music, 'Pupils should be taught to' do (I merely sketched these a moment ago). To what extent can the kind of work discussed in the first half of the present chapter be understood as delivering these things? Let us analyse them, with that in mind, one by one. The first listed reads as follows: 'play and perform confidently in a range of solo and ensemble contexts using their voice, playing instruments musically, fluently and with accuracy and expression'. Presumably when MCs use their voices to rap over beats provided by a DJ, it is an ensemble of a certain stripe, is it not? (We must insist that the DJ decks, when they are used to effectively 'remix' music in real time, are a musical instrument.) We might recall that Mike Challis's research found that DJ-orientated work 'does wonders for their self-esteem' in a PRU where disaffection and low self-esteem were rife (see Chapter Five): this music-making allows them, in other words, to 'play and perform confidently'. Rhythmical accuracy is valued highly in this form of music-making and, in short, I would say that those who don't find the music expressive of the young people's feelings simply aren't listening appropriately: 'accuracy and expression', in other words, are often bountiful in the contexts in question.

Secondly, the new National Curriculum proposes that pupils should be taught to 'improvise and compose; and extend and develop musical ideas by drawing on a range of musical structures, styles, genres and traditions'. Clearly a diet of *only* EDM/contemporary urban music would not encourage this. That said, there is every reason to think that, for example, the musical structures found within the style/genre/tradition of happy hardcore can be profitably used in composition work. For example, the 'kick off' which, as mentioned above, I would demonstrate with judicious use of the 'synchro start' button, would quite often be subsequently used by learners as they developed their own compositions. The scratching on DJ decks which I encouraged learners to attempt, meanwhile, was certainly improvisational and developed on-the-spot musicianship skills amongst those students who were willing to attempt it, certainly. My scheme of work on dance music (see above) unquestionably developed learners' understanding of 'a range of musical structures, styles, genres and traditions' – including contemporary EDM.

The third stipulation of the new National Curriculum is that learners should 'use staff and other relevant notations appropriately and accurately in a range of musical styles, genres and traditions'. As noted above, I would use staff notation of hardcore Mákina tunes in class, finding that levels of motivation were extremely high amongst learners precisely because my child-centred methods had resulted in a very high level of fit between pupils' tastes and the musical notation from which they were working. I very much agree with the architects of the National Curriculum that notation should cover a wide range of styles, genres and traditions and, therefore, I would challenge students to use staff notation to learn melodies from Beethoven, Deep Purple and Scott Joplin as well as the EDM tunes which, in truth, were closer to the actual tastes of most students. The mention of 'other relevant notations' is most welcome, although we should note that DJing has largely been a non-notated art form. (DJ-specific forms of notation have been developed in relatively recent years, but many leading DJs, such as Qbert, regard DJ-specific 'notation as [being] outside of the hip hop tradition' [Miyakawa 2007: 98].)

Fourthly, the new National Curriculum calls for students to 'identify and use the inter-related dimensions of music expressively and with increasing sophistication, including use of tonalities, different types of scales and other musical devices'. On this point, we can note that 'Love in Paradise' uses the Aeolian mode and thus a different tonality from much classical and popular music. Beyond the fact that an interesting musical scale is being employed by this tune, I would say that the work on keyboards I have described above brought greatly increased sophistication to the music-making of many of the children I worked with. There is no question that Mákina and hardcore EDM allowed these young people to use various dimensions of music expressively: sometimes they expressed anger and aggression through their

MC rapping and DJing, sometimes a sense of joy (*jouissance*, one might even dare to say), but the crackle of expressivity was always abundantly apparent, to me at least.

We have already discussed in Chapter One the new National Curriculum's fifth demand, namely that children should 'listen with increasing discrimination to a wide range of music from great composers and musicians'. All I will do here, therefore, is to underscore the general position I have already outlined: a classroom wherein the great composers rub shoulders with underground EDM (the latter often being the music of taste for a certain class of young person, I have argued) is likely to be a classroom where teacher and disaffected student can respect each other. Without an effort towards such mutual respect, there is likely to be an indiscriminate rejection of 'great' music rather than any 'increasing discrimination'.

Sixth and lastly we have the new National Curriculum's insistence that young people should 'develop a deepening understanding of the music that they perform and to which they listen, and its history'. By talking to the young people with whom I was working, I found that the music they performed and to which they listened was normally contemporary urban music, whilst hardcore EDM was particularly popular with a very large minority. However, there was a limit to how much knowledge these young people had of the history of the music to which they listened. For example, I noticed that MCs would often recite the following lines, learned from old tapes of raves I believe: 'the Meadow Well, that's where I'm from, remember the riots in 1991?' It turned out, however, that not many of them knew where the Meadow Well is (just across the Tyne from the school where I was working, in fact) nor did they have much idea as to what happened in the 1991 riots, nor why those riots had occurred. (That said, one female pupil did pipe up, memorably enough, that 'me auntie was there throwing bricks at the coppaz [police]'.) There was also a lack of awareness of the history of rave music moreover, for which reason the work discussing acid house, Reclaim the Streets and the Criminal Justice Act (see above) was highly valuable for the delivery of element six within the new National Curriculum for music.

I would conclude, therefore, that all six of the core elements just discussed can legitimately be claimed as being addressed by the kind of work I discussed in the first half of this chapter. As I acknowledged in Chapter One, such work is best mixed with other, more 'traditional' kinds of musical activities. I would suggest, however, that a hostile Ofsted inspector would struggle to deny that the kind of focusses for lessons I described in this chapter would support the core requirements of the new National Curriculum. Suppose one wanted to teach raps in a similar manner to that of Rawz (see Chapter Four herein): could this too be legitimate for KS3 teaching? In Rawz's words, 'When I do it, the kind of first techniques I teach them is the basic principle of what makes words rhyme with each other, so kind of breaking things down into syllables'. Subsequently, 'if you're writing to a beat' then the crucial thing is 'keeping the amount of syllables to a line to be roughly the same', he explained. Are such tasks best suited to the English department rather than music? As we saw, Rawz found that this was where he was more often placed, but

I would suggest that – if learners are to 'compose' and 'extend and develop musical ideas by drawing on a range of musical structures, styles, genres and traditions' (the second detailed element in the new National Curriculum for music) – such work is very well justified.

What of the kind of work which Spencer Hickson does (again, see Chapter Four)? We will examine some elements of his work in more detail in Chapter Nine when we look at the newest technologies which can be introduced into the classroom when attempting to engage learners with urban music and EDM. For present purposes though, we can note with interest that Spencer had clear concerns in regards to keeping learners engaged when working with limited 'kit': 'from the first sessions, I realised that not everybody was engaged at the same time because we'd only got one console'. 'I knew', Spencer explained, that he 'needed a few more laptops and a few other mixers and then they could sit there with headphones'. This, he found, 'would accommodate some of the less-engaged people who didn't really want to be up there doing it through the speakers'. The advantage of this, as Spencer notes (with the sensitivity of a natural teacher, I would say), was that 'they can do it at their own speed with nobody, kind of, watching them – the pressure, y'know'.

That given, it is fair to say that a teacher is at a disadvantage, for engagement purposes in particular, if they lack the kind of extra equipment which (as noted in Chapter Four) Spencer was able to secure with some funding from Cheshire East council. Does this mean that a music teacher can be excused from bothering with urban music and EDM? I would suggest otherwise. Certainly the amount of teaching time which can be turned over profitably to this kind of work is probably best reduced if limited resources are available. However, the potential gain in terms of engaging learners with tastes at the peripheries of mainstream popular music surely means that some introduction of the kinds of music and music-making under discussion are to be encouraged. To employ the language of the new National Curriculum for music, meanwhile, it is certain that Spencer was able to encourage the disaffected young people he worked with to 'play and perform confidently', to 'improvise and compose' and 'extend and develop musical ideas', to develop 'increasing sophistication' and so forth.

Conclusion

It is easy to feel critical of government policy on education. As we noted in Chapter Two, there has been a steady drift towards governmental prescription and away from teachers' autonomy since the mid-1970s. As a result, many teachers are frustrated by a sense of powerlessness in their own classrooms. In fact, though, I would argue that there remains quite a lot of room to manoeuvre within the KS3 National Curriculum: one just has to be a little creative in one's interpretation of its descriptive terminology.

KS3 is certainly a crucial time in the lives of young learners: the transition from primary to secondary school can be a difficult one for students, as noted by

Kokotsaki (2015) amongst many others. When the honeymoon period wears off, KS3 music can become a lesson which many young people find unstimulating. The challenge for the teacher, therefore, is to keep things fresh and interesting such that young people look forwards to their 'entitlement' (in the UK, at least) of one hour per week of dedicated music learning. In my own classroom, I was able to maintain gratifyingly high levels of this interest and freshness by varying the work such that contemporary urban music in general and hardcore EDM in particular rubbed shoulders with the works of 'great composers' as well as more mainstream forms of popular music. I have outlined some of my work herein in the hope that researchers and teachers might find the descriptions of interest. I have also tried to show that other educators such as Rawz and Spencer Hickson (both of whom we encountered in Chapter Four) can be argued to have provided classroom work which both engages learners with urban music *and* responds to the demands of the current National Curriculum for music.

I also afforded some space to a discussion of the pressures for assessment at KS3. As I showed, the current situation is not entirely clear in the UK, due to some significant changes at KS4 which have led to the abolition of National Curriculum attainment levels at KS3. The risk in this, I would argue, is that KS3 learning achievements could begin to be seen as being valid only insofar as they suggest a potential for success at GCSE/Level 2 BTEC work. Many schools have replaced National Curriculum levels with a numeric KS3 level which is supposed to indicate the likely grade the student could attain at KS4 (one to nine, using the new system, that is). Consequently, there is a serious risk that teachers will make assessments based upon a skill set which would be required for post-KS3 work at the expense of the broader requirements of the KS3 National Curriculum. If this happens, there is a greater and greater risk of disengagement prior to the end-of-key-stage 'options' process. When teachers feel obliged to allocate a numerically low assessment grade (given that the learner in question would stand little chance of doing well at GCSE or BTEC), disengagement from music at KS3 amongst the *general* student population is only like to worsen.

What can the individual music teacher in a mainstream secondary school do about this? Very little, I am inclined to think. That said, we are surely obliged – ethically as well as professionally – to not forget that overall body of learners who want to develop musical skills, knowledge and understanding even though they might not have the abilities that would permit them to undertake a GCSE qualification. Bringing equipment such as DJ decks into the classroom, and bringing contemporary urban music into the classroom, can allow that larger body of learners to make progress in terms of musical skills but also just to *enjoy music lessons*. This alone, I would think, justifies the introduction of such music and music-making equipment into the mainstream classroom at KS3. What of KS4, though? Can DJ decks, MCing and EDM/urban music be valuable at that level? It is to this question that I turn in the next chapter.

References

Hargreaves, David J., Marshall, Nigel A., 'Developing Identities in Music Education', *Music Education Research* 5/3 (2003), 263–73

Kokotsaki, Dimitra, *Improving the Primary-Secondary Transition in Music Education* (Nuffield Foundation–funded report, 2015)

Miyakawa, Felicia M., 'Turntablature: Notation, Legitimization and the Art of the Hip-Hop DJ', *American Music* 25/1 (2007), 81–105

Ross, Andrew, Owen, Frank, Moby, Knuckles, Frankie, Cooper, Carol, 'The Cult of the DJ: A Symposium', *Social Text* 43 (1995), 67–88

7
REMIXING THE KS4 CURRICULUM

The UK's 'Key Stage 4' (KS4, henceforth) is the point where music education no longer remains compulsory: instead, students can opt into a 'Level 2' qualification (or Level 1 for those with weak literacy skills) in Music, or opt out of musical activities altogether. As noted in the previous chapter, the majority opt out whilst 'pupil enjoyment, relevance, skill development, creativity and expressive dimensions were often absent' according to a report from the National Foundation for Educational Research (Hargreaves and Marshall 2010: 265). However, Hargreaves and Marshall have also suggested, in 2010, that the 'levels of pupils' reported enjoyment of and engagement in school music activity may have increased over the last 5 years or so' (272). Furthermore, 'our analysis suggests that [capitalising on this success] is best accomplished by encouraging [learners] to think of music as something within the reach of all, rather than as a specialised activity: that everyone can be a "musician" at some level' (ibid.).

If Hargreaves and Marshall are correct, and I'm confident they are, then DJ decks should have some utility in school-level education: after all, it is surely the case that anyone can be a DJ 'at some level', is it not? Here, perhaps, we hit a stumbling block, however: is a DJ *really* a musician in the proper sense? The reader will not be surprised that my own view on this question is entirely affirmative: good DJing requires high levels of skill and/or musical sensitivity, without argument, in my view at least. Nevertheless, there are quite a large number of people (the majority, perhaps) within what is known as 'the music establishment' for whom a DJ is simply a person who plays records, not a musician *per se*. Querulous attitudes towards the level of musical skills in DJing even exist within the EDM field, furthermore. Deadmau5, for example, has been reported by *Rolling Stone* on 20 June 2012 complaining of 'button-pushers getting paid half a million'. (This is 'not to say I'm not a button-pusher', Deadmau5 clarifies; 'I'm just pushing a lot more buttons'.) The antipathy of the 'classical' establishment (if we can speak of such a thing, which I'm inclined to think we can) is probably the largest problem in regards to KS4, however. Even if a music teacher is sympathetic to DJing and MCing as valid modes of music-making, after all, surely the exam boards are not going to accept such music-making for GCSE performance work?

As a matter of fact, they are: at present, all three of the UK's exam boards for GCSE music (OCR, Edexcel and AQA) give specific detail as to how rappers/MCs can be assessed whilst two of those three exam boards give plentiful detail as to how to assess a performance on DJ decks. GCSE, furthermore, is no longer the only available Level 2 qualification available within the UK: BTEC qualifications are now on offer, and these too provide structures for DJs and MCs to be formally assessed.

There is no excuse, then, for these long-established modes of EDM-orientated music-making to be excluded from the contemporary KS4 classroom; and yet, in practice, very few DJs and MCs proceed with music education beyond KS3, I have reason to believe. One can understand some of the concern, from the teacher's perspective: how is one to assess this stuff? As someone who doesn't play any brass or reed instruments, I sometimes found it rather difficult to make proper assessment judgements for GCSE performance work. If so, however, I could then rely upon the judgement of my peripatetic teachers as to the difficulty of some particular piece and the accuracy or flair of a performance. Most schools don't have a peripatetic teacher specialising in DJing and MCing and, therefore, recourse to expert opinion is more problematic.

As an excuse, though, this is flimsy. Would we think it acceptable for a music teacher to show reluctance to assess the performance of, say, a 5-string banjo player if and when no banjo expert were readily available? As I will show in the present chapter, contemporary specifications for GCSE and BTEC music at Level 2 are precise enough that even a music teacher who knows absolutely nothing about DJing and MCing should have a reasonable chance of making a perfectly adequate assessment of strengths and weaknesses in a performance of rapping. When teaching to the OCR and AQA specifications (but not Edexcel, admittedly), a performance on the decks should also be easy to assess. All that is required, I would say, is a bit of effort: if one has never heard of a 'scribble scratch' or some such thing, it really isn't hard to find out what one is thanks to the Internet (YouTube, for example). The benefits, meanwhile, are potentially immense: 'pupil enjoyment, relevance, skill development, creativity and expressive dimensions', which the National Foundation for Educational Research (NFER) found to so often be lacking from music education at KS4, could suddenly become available in abundance, I would suggest. In any case, if the musical interests of our learners are not worthy of effort on our part as teachers, what are we in this job *for*?

Before offering some discussion of the detail of GCSE and BTEC specifications in regards to DJing and MCing, I begin the chapter with some general discussion of the situation for music education at KS4. How does the UK's KS4 compare with KS3? What are the views of GCSE music from those who have studied it? What prejudices and assumptions exist beyond the teaching profession, and how do these impact upon student perceptions? How far did GCSE move towards a 'level playing field' for KS4 music study, when it replaced O-level/CSE in the late 1980s, and how does the arrival of a Level 2 BTEC music qualification relate to that attempted levelling process? These are the key questions for our first section.

Heard the one about the GCSE music student...?

'What a joke', railed a *Daily Mail* headline on 8 August 2008: 'Pupils can get an A at GCSE music without knowing a crotchet from a quaver'. According to the article, the *BBC Music Magazine* had revealed that 'a knowledge of bars, crotchets, quavers and treble clefs is not necessary to do well'. The tone of the article seems to encourage us to be shocked that improvisation and 'non-standard notation' are acceptable 'across all boards' at GCSE level. Extra opprobrium is given to the OCR board for allowing compositions to be submitted 'only in recorded form'. Edexcel and AQA are given a little more implied credit because they 'require a score – a written record of the music'. Given, however, that 'Edexcel doesn't mark it' whilst AQA will accept a description of the piece in words (as if musical notation were something other than a form of writing in any case) or a diagram (as if the rising and falling representation of notes were other than diagrammatic), the *Daily Mail* journalist makes no secret of her disapproval.

No lesser an authority on the highest quality of music than Damon Albarn (vocalist of pop group Blur, apparently) is approvingly quoted as insisting that 'anyone interested in music should be *forced* to learn [to read and write notation] as without it you will never be able to articulate' [sic; emphasis added]. What would be articulated to what is not mentioned: the point, it seems, is simply that we must be forced 'to articulate' because articulating (whatever that means) is intrinsically important. Clearly, I am lampooning the inarticulacy of the quoted comment, but I think the remark is actually revealing of the central point. Notation *is* an articulation, in fact, because it provides (and, importantly, provided to musicians before the advent of recorded sound) a connection whereby a composer can illustrate a musical idea for a performer. The rhetoric of the *Daily Mail* article, however, treats notation as an end in itself: a musical skill the importance of which is articulated to itself, as it were, and without which musical skill is essentially unimaginable. The editor of the *BBC Music Magazine* just about sums it up for the *Daily Mail* journalist's purposes: 'Notation is the foundation of music and without it a student will never be able to play an instrument well or ever really understand music itself.'

Irving Berlin ('White Christmas', 'Putting on the Ritz', 'Face The Music', to name but three of his world-famous compositions), Lennon and McCartney, Jimi Hendrix – naturally one could go on and on and on – these people could not play an instrument well and never really understood 'music itself', if Oliver Condy of the *BBC Music Magazine* is right. Since the musicians and composers just mentioned have sold millions of records and have won the respect of countless musical 'experts', however, perhaps Condy is completely and irrevocably wrong-headed – perhaps it is he, in fact, who has no proper grasp of the vast scope of what 'music itself' could be. The problem for our purposes, that said, is that there are a large number of people who read and believe the rhetoric one can find in the periodicals in question. Beyond this, those of us who would contend that musical notation is not the be-all-and-all of music (despite being a handy device for recording musical details, and one which I am personally glad to have acquired skills in) are faced with a further problem. The issue in question is that the kind of people who share the world view of the *Daily Mail* and the *BBC Music Magazine* tend to be in very powerful positions in a perceived musical establishment.

So, we could point out that 'crotchet' and 'quaver' are simply *words*. We could add that they are words which are not much used in North America (where 'quarter notes' and 'eighth notes' are instead spoken of) and which need not be known in order to grasp the musical experience (of beats and bars) which most if not all in the West understand in practical terms. It would be impossible to DJ or MC without a practical understanding of crotchets and quavers, we could remark. However, these protestations would only miss the central myopia of not only the (still extremely powerful) music establishment but also, and crucially, the 'common sense' view of a simultaneously prejudiced and ignorant petit bourgeoisie. The myopia in question is that traditional methods and modes of instrumental and music education should remain the benchmark or 'gold standard' for what happens in schools. One might let them sing 'fun stuff', or even experiment with music a bit, at primary school and KS3. By KS4, though, we need to be preparing our young people with the kinds of musical skills which will allow them to go to a conservatoire or 'good' university to study music; post-GCSE study must involve notational skills, therefore GCSEs must prepare students for those skills.

Naturally the A-level class will be even fewer in number than the (typically miniscule, relatively speaking) GCSE music class. Of course there are nowhere near enough professional UK orchestras to employ anything more than a tiny fraction of the number of graduates which UK conservatoires churn out each year. Obviously the majority of us who did the pre-GCSE 'O-level' in Music found the composition of Bach-style four-part harmony an alien experience wherein we had little or no real grasp of what the harmony would actually sound like. Actually, one can complete a Level 3 BTEC in Music and even a BA in Popular Music without knowing how to read and write music. None of this is important, it seems. What is important, one feels encouraged to believe, is that a mass of young people continue to learn, now and in the future, the harmonic methods which were effectively codified by Bach in the sixteenth century. It is essential, apparently, that teenagers who have taken the time to learn to perform from notation are awarded the highest grades at GCSE and A-level. The traditions of music education, many seem to believe, should not only be carried forward but also maintained as the ideal, against which all other possibilities in music education should be measured.

I hope the reader will forgive my sarcastic tone. The subject at hand is something I happen to feel strongly about, precisely because I have seen so much damage wrought upon individual children by the kind of wrong-headed rhetoric discussed above. I am no ideological opponent of traditional methods in music education: I found the Bach chorale an alien process as a teenager, but I eventually became grateful to have learned to construct four-part harmony on a stave. As I have made clear in previous chapters, I commonly used notation as an element within my teaching, from KS3 onwards. However, it is simply a fact that excellent musicianship is possible without notation and, therefore, notation is only one musical skill amongst many.

Why is all this pertinent to our central concern in regards to the use of DJ decks and MCing in KS4 study? Because, in short, the DJ works by ear and from memory, as is typically the case in popular music; the MC is usually much the same, although some will use notebooks for lyrics. As noted in the last chapter, there have been efforts to develop forms of notation for DJs (Miyakawa 2007). According to Miyakawa, 'recently, some turntablists [DJs, that is, essentially] have shown an interest in "legitimizing" turntablism as "art"'; within this effort, 'notation has been one of the key tools turntablists have used to facilitate their entry into the "art" world' (81). This effort has met 'some resistance ... within the DJ community because it is seen as an unnecessary "academic" or "scholarly" tool' which has only been added retrospectively to a *de facto* area of musicianship which required no notation to successfully develop its skill set (92). DJ notation such as 'TTM' (Turntablist Transcription Methodology) has brought some credibility to individuals such as John Carluccio (described by *Time* magazine as one of the 'next innovators in music', 93) and has some pedagogical value for those of us who would like to better understand what a DJ is actually doing (91). The celebration of 'the first concerto piece in the history of classical music that features the turntable as an actual musical instrument' (98), however, is a world away from the taste in music-making of the inner city youths I worked with in the North East of England.

Does DJing require such supposed legitimisation? Perhaps, if Miyakawa is right that 'few musicians outside of hip-hop culture equate turntablism with musicianship' (2007: 101). I'm inclined to think he is perfectly correct in this assertion as regards the (general lack of) credibility regarding the DJ's musical skills, but I also agree with him that 'the act of writing down works for turntable ... smacks of retrospect' (102). Is this not a paradigmatic case of what Derrida, updating a term coined by Ludwig Klages, called 'logocentrism' (Klages 2015, Derrida 1975)? The education system and the musical world at large needs to recognise the skills of the DJ *as they are*, it seems to me, rather than expecting that the work of the DJ should be re-branded as 'turntablism' and supposedly validated through a visual representation of something which actually has its most important manifestation purely as sound.

What of the MC? Here, again, a logocentric ideology can interfere with the actual musicality of the MC's creativity. We noted in Chapter Four that work on rap is often assumed to belong in the English classroom rather than the music department. We should not be surprised, therefore, to find that Wayne Au lists copious literature on 'using rap to bridge the cultural divide that exists between schools and students' home and community cultures' and on 'using rap as a tool for developing critical consciousness among students' but very little on using rap for teaching music (2005: 211). However, as Au reminds us, 'rap music can be studied like any other subject area' (216). Something I would be emphatic about, in regards to that general point, is that MCing/rapping is a *musical* activity, not just a literary one. If 'rap is an effective teaching tool when used to enhance the self-esteem' and is 'capable of affecting the values and attitudes of many of our young people' to the extent that 'it can inspire and motivate our youth to stay in school and receive relevant educations', it should doubtless be part of the curriculum (Powell 1991: 257). If it is to be more than a carrot on the string, however, it needs to also be respected in itself, does it not? And this, I would insist, involves educators remembering that this is music, not just poetry.

David Kirkland has shown sensitivity to part of this problem, remarking that 'Englishes, as opposed to English, are relevant to the twenty-first-century conversations of English education' (2010: 293). However, 'This does not mean that the "old" English education is irrelevant' – moreover 'promoting linguistic pluralism means fully appreciating the hybrid and textured nature in which English is practiced and performed by inner-city youth'. Can we say, in tandem, that we should speak of *musics* rather than music whilst recognising the hybridic nature of the single most popular area of contemporary music (EDM, that is, in North America at least)? I am inclined to affirm that such is the case, and particularly so at KS4 where young people are making decisions about their educational pathways with potentially far-reaching consequences.

How popular is the GCSE with actual learners? According to government documents from the mid-1980s, the original shift from O-level to GCSE in the UK was supposed 'To encourage imaginative teaching in schools and foster a greater understanding of music through more direct experience of the creative processes involved' (Spencer 1993: 74). Surveying 164 responses from undergraduate (and thus necessarily high-achieving) music students who had been amongst the first cohort to sit GCSE in 1993, Piers Spencer found three concerns with the new qualification. Firstly, 'The GCSE as a whole was perceived by the majority of this high-achieving cohort as an undemanding examination'. Secondly, and relatedly, 'an inappropriate alignment between the GCSE and the demands of subsequent musical study, particularly at A-level' was perceived. Thirdly, 'The survey revealed a picture of many teachers ill-prepared for GCSE' with 'unclear objectives and sloppy assessment procedures in both the composing and performing components' having arisen (ibid.).

Well over a quarter of a century since the GCSE was introduced, it is fair to assume that the third of these problems should have eroded by now. The first two, however, remain a perceived problem, as we saw at the top of the present section of this chapter. The problem, in a nutshell, is that GCSE is too easy for some (a minority, it is fair to say) and yet, as much as being too 'hard' for the rest (the majority of 14- to 16-year-olds at large), it is largely irrelevant to their interests and needs. The backdrop to all this was not lost on that first cohort of GCSE students which Spencer based his research upon: 'The study of the Genesis set work was completely pointless. I assumed it was included for the pupils who were to attain "CSE" grades' (1993: 76). For younger readers, or those outside of the UK, it is worth clarifying that the CSE was a sister qualification, of sorts, to the O-level (which was actually named the 'GCE'). In theory, a Grade 1 at CSE was 'equivalent' to a C Grade at GCE O-level; in practice, a CSE marked you out as a weaker student, at least as far as most employers and educational institutions were concerned. (I have rarely bothered to include my Grade 1 CSE in French when filling out job application forms, assuming that it is barely worth mentioning.)

At the end of the 1980s, GCSE was supposed to do away with such inequities. However, BTEC qualifications, which were once delivered only in colleges of further education but have been ever-increasingly widespread in schools since the 1990s, have brought back something of a two-tier system. Roy Fisher's excellent PhD study of *The Vocational Curriculum in England 1974–1994* refers unambiguously to 'the widespread belief that a BTEC student is generally someone who is, academically, second class', for example (1999: 253). Anecdotally, I can add that my son's secondary school Head of Music is reported, by my wife, to have snorted derisively when she recently enquired whether a BTEC was on offer in addition to the GCSE course.

Why has BTEC developed this reputation? An indirect clue may be provided by some data offered by David Bray in 2000 (83). Noting a 6.8 per cent national average uptake of GCSE Music, Bray draws our attention to the fact that amongst a sample of forty schools with a larger uptake (of 20 per cent or more), a significantly large proportion were grammar schools (relative to national proportions of grammar schools to non-grammar schools). Bray also notes a low proportion of comprehensive schools and metropolitan schools were achieving 20 per cent uptake of GCSE Music (relative, again, to national averages). It would seem to be the case, then, that music was struggling – at that time at least – to maintain a reasonable level of engagement at KS4 in non-grammar schools. Indeed, Ofsted had revealed (three years prior to the publication of Bray's research) that 14 per cent of UK schools did not offer music as a GCSE option (ibid.).

Why would uptake of music in KS4 be less in comprehensive/metropolitan schools relative to the grammar sector? After all, the introduction of the GCSE was supposed to have encouraged 'a greater percentage of future adult populations being able to "derive deep satisfaction from their leisure pursuit of music"', according to government documents from the mid-1980s (Wright 2002: 228). Has the GCSE not been successful in this regard? Ruth Wright's research from 2002 would suggest that it has not, offering 'strong evidence … to suggest that pupils do feel that they are at a disadvantage on a GCSE Music course unless they receive instrumental tuition outside the classroom' (238). We can also note with interest that 'Pupils did not see GCSE as a logical progression from their earlier [ie KS3] studies in music' (240).

On the one hand, then, we have GCSE students who feel that their course of study leaves them ill-prepared for A-level but, on the other hand, we have a perception amongst learners that the course may be too difficult (even for those who have achieved well at KS3) for learners who are not receiving extra-curricular tuition on instruments. 'It is perceived by many pupils as being élitist and by others as being insufficiently academically challenging', Wright concludes from her evidence (2002: 240). Her hope, she reveals, is that the picture might look different 'in ten years' time' (241). Has the ever-increasing popularity of Level 2 BTEC music certificates plugged the gap and made that change? Only up to a point, I would suggest. It is to the relative character of GCSE and BTEC specifications for music that I turn in the next section, with a particular focus upon the extent to which they may or may not welcome DJs and MCs onto the programmes of study.

Is one permitted to spit in school?

Just under ten years ago, when I became Head of Music at the school where I worked (due to the retirement of a colleague), GCSE Music was unceremoniously dumped from the options for KS4. This was done without any consultation with me and much to the chagrin of a small cohort of girls who were, in fact, the highest achievers in their year group. When one of the girls' parents complained about their daughter's restricted choices, I negotiated with the school's senior management team to pay a peripatetic teacher to come in for a two-hour after-school class once per week. The plan was that this after-school class would culminate, after two years, in a GCSE qualification for the six girls who had opted in.

The peripatetic teacher was a senior member of the local music service at the time and, it is worth mentioning, was leading an adult choir at Newcastle Cathedral. In spite of these impressive credentials, the classes were fairly disastrous. One of the six girls immediately dropped out, despite being a passionate music lover who had done extremely well in my KS3 music classes. After numerous complaints from the girls about the quality and character of the teaching, I asked the head of the music service if an alternative peripatetic teacher might be available. No such thing being feasible, the music service head offered to observe the teaching and learning and concluded that, although there was something of a 'culture clash' going on, he could see no serious problem with the teaching. However, when the peripatetic teacher indicated to me that he perceived that his task was virtually impossible since only one of the girls read music with any fluency, I decided to step in and run the after-school class myself.

Two years later, three of the girls walked away with A grades whilst the other two achieved B grades. Clearly, then, there *had* been a teaching and learning problem with the peripatetic work – or, more accurately, a teaching problem (the grades the girls achieved show that there was no learning problem). It is worth noting that two of the girls went on to study non-musical disciplines at Russell Group universities – no mean feat when one has attended a school in the bottom 3 per cent for national measures of socio-economic deprivation.

Does this reflect the general situation up and down the country? Perhaps so, if some of the statistics and research findings quoted in the previous section of the present chapter are to be believed: lots of schools are not offering GCSE music and, of those which do offer it, uptake is significantly lower in the comprehensives and metropolitan (or 'inner-city', one might reasonably say) schools. The research showing that far more girls than boys take music is well known and well reflected in the anecdotal account just given. Has the Level 2 BTEC redressed the balance at all? I am inclined to tentatively propose that it has, but only up to a point. However, before discussing the BTEC specifications for Level 2 (GCSE equivalent, that is – or ostensibly equivalent, at least), I want to demonstrate that all three UK examination boards for GCSE Music provide explicit guidance for the assessment of DJs and MCs.

Turning firstly to the OCR specification for the new 'GCSE (9-1)' specification (see the last chapter for detail as to the shift from A*–G to 9–1 grades), we can be pleased to note that 'DJ-ing' is the third of four available study instruments. Voice (the second of the four) 'can include styles such as rapping or beatboxing' whilst 'sequencing – realisation using ICT' is also mentioned (being the fourth available study instrument). Within the 'Difficulty Mark Criteria for Groups of Instruments' section, meanwhile, we can note the DJing, 'Rapping/MCing' and 'beatboxing' remain in the list. Interestingly, and unsurprisingly enough I would say, they are at the bottom of the list (with the exception of 'sequencing') – but they are there, nonetheless.

The detail of the criteria for awarding a 'difficulty mark' for MCs/rappers – those who like to 'spit', that is, to use the currently popular term for rapping – is admirably precise. A piece with a low mark of 0–2 will involve 'simple rhythmic ideas using simple rhymes', 'a steady beat in a simple structure', 'simple demands in terms of vocal technique' and so forth. A higher mark can be earned if the rap is 'more complicated rhythmically with syncopation including breaks' and, understandably I think, 'faster pieces requiring technical dexterity in order to articulate faster movement of words' will deserve the higher mark. Extra credit, meanwhile, should be given to raps 'using long words'. The 'use of articulation, vocal inflections and phrasing' is also required for the highest marks.

There are elements we might query here. For example, the encouragement of higher marks for the 'addition of a hook line being sung' is questionable: I know of no evidence to suggest that, say, Chuck D of Public Enemy is capable of convincingly singing a hook line, and yet he is (or at least has been) one of the world's top MCs. We can also note logocentric thinking at play with the demand for 'long words', but the requirement is understandable given the academic context. Overall, it is fair to claim this as helpful guidance for the assessment of MCs/rappers and the encouragement of such students for inclusion within GCSE programmes: even a teacher who knows next to nothing about rapping should be able to glean the gist of the requirements for higher or lower marks, I would think.

What about the DJs? Again, I would judge the guidance as being very helpful indeed. The first statement, that said, is a little confusing: 'This should be a FREESTYLE performance using Vinyl, CD, or a suitable software package' (capitalisation retained). What do OCR mean by 'freestyle'? The word does not appear in the glossary of *You Can Make It as a DJ* (Parker and Parker 2003) nor the indexes of *How to Be a DJ* (Hoggarth 2002) and *Groove Music: The Art and Culture of the Hip-Hop DJ* (Katz 2012). Wikipedia, in March 2016, lists 'freestyle' as a sub-genre of hip hop. I do not believe, however, that OCR wish to refer only to this particular sub-genre: rather, it is fair to guess, OCR mean that the records should be tampered with in real time and not simply played one after another or using pre-programmed re-mixing. If so, the insistence is reasonable but could have been expressed more clearly.

OCR's insistence that the DJ set should be filmed, ideally 'looking over the learner's shoulder', is wise, I think. (An aerial view would also make sense, and would actually be more in keeping with the clips one can find online for aspiring DJs to learn from: one needs a good view of the exact position of the faders to best judge the precise agency of the DJ.) We can note 'the absence of a score' is no impediment to the DJ, in principle: 'a list of the sound sources (songs)' is insisted upon as a sub-stitute, but no direct conformity is made to the prejudices of Damon Albarn and the *Daily Mail* (see the beginning of the previous section in the present chapter). The assumption that sound sources will necessarily be 'songs' is perhaps unhelpful (some DJs are known to use BBC-released albums of sound effects in their sets and such like). Beyond this, however, I would say that the OCR specification makes it very clear what the DJ needs to do for a GCSE-level assessed performance.

For the lower marks, OCR specify that 'some control' must be shown with 'simple application of beatmatching' and 'basic application of "traditional" FX' such as EQ. If the DJ is scratching, baby scratching (helpfully defined by OCR as 'simple rhythmic scratching') will be done 'in time to beat'. The specification shows valuable sensitivity to the specificities of EDM cultures by acknowledging that scratching is 'primarily used in Hip Hop' whereas other DJs 'may use no or very little scratching techniques'. Clarifications such as this reflect the fact that every effort has been made to support even the music teacher with very little knowledge of EDM and DJ culture, it seems to me. It should be easy enough, for example, for even a musically-untrained person to recognise a DJing 'performance incorporating frequent changes between many sections and tracks', the 'regular use of the cross fader between all the available sources' and suchlike for the highest marks to be awarded. It is true that a little 'homework' would be required for the average music teacher to recognise specific skills such as 'drum scratching, forward and backward scratching, chops/stabs, crab': thanks to Youtube and the like, however, the music teacher should not face much difficulty in acquiring such knowledge. However, many of the high-rated (by OCR, at least) skills such as 'manual beatmatching' (as opposed to 'automatic sync'), 'inventive use of sound sources' and a 'wider range of material' should be easy to recognise, I would argue.

On balance, then, I would argue that OCR's specification in regard to DJing and MCing/rapping is extremely helpful. This is less the case with Edexcel's specification, wherein music technology is tolerated but presented as involving 'synthesisers, virtual instruments and amplified instruments, such as guitars using pedals (including loop pedals), audio samples, and other processors': no direct reference to DJing equipment, then. Indeed, only one direct mention of the possibility for 'a performance with DJ decks/turntables' is made in the entire specification. Rapping is covered in a little more detail: for Edexcel, the performance 'should demonstrate clarity of diction, secure breath control, tonal contrast and some extended vocal techniques' we are told, but considerably less precise detail is offered as compared with the OCR specification. The problematic prioritisation of a 'sung hook' appears again in the Edexcel specification, we can note.

The AQA specification lies closer to that of OCR than that of Edexcel. For example, the possibility of a DJ performance is detailed enough to emphasise the need 'to manipulate tracks and demonstrate an understanding and use of a range of techniques'. Some skills are mentioned which do not appear in the OCR specification, indeed, such as 'cue stuttering', 'rewind/spin-back' and 'looping (using digital buttons)'. In terms of the information regarding advanced scratching skills, the detail is particularly impressive: transforms, flares, chirps and orbits are all listed. That said, OCR's helpful disambiguation of hip hop and other, less scratching-orientated styles of DJing is not replicated by AQA. Nevertheless, their mapping of specific DJing skills to more traditional Instrumental/Vocal Grades 1-5 is extremely helpful: at a glance, the teacher can calculate an appropriate difficulty mark for the learner's performance piece on DJ decks.

To summarise, I would suggest that Edexcel's specification is by far the least welcoming towards DJs but, nonetheless, it would not be impossible to squeeze the work of a DJ into the confines of their GCSE assessment scheme. AQA is the least welcoming to rappers but, again, it would be feasible for a rapper/MC to be assessed by a teacher following the AQA specification. OCR is the most welcoming to both DJs and MCs but AQA arguably offers more valuable detail for the assessment of DJs, at least in regards to scratching skills. In my opinion, AQA's placement of value upon the DJ's 'sensitivity towards the expressive and interpretative demands of the music' is particularly welcome: the issue at hand, it seems to me, is whether the right music has been selected and appropriately handled (a somewhat undervalued DJing skill which will be discussed further in Chapter Eight).

How, then, does the DJ or MC fare in the BTEC specification? At KS4, the BTEC First qualification is suitable for Level 2 learners (or, for those aged over 14 but with weaker literacy skills, a Level 1 qualification is available). The BTEC First is designed 'to aid progression to further study and prepare learners to enter the workplace in due course': this is, in other words, a vocational qualification whereas the GCSE is more 'academic'. Unit 5, 'Introducing Music Performance', lists 'DJ techniques' amongst more traditional musical performance elements. The techniques in question are listed as 'beats per minute, pitch control, phrasing, spin backs, button stopping, crossfading, drop-ins, cutting' – a comparable repertoire of elements compared to the GCSE specifications discussed above although a little less detailed than one finds in the AQA and OCR documents.

On paper, it looks as though a KS4-aged DJ or MC might fare just as well in a GCSE course as in a BTEC, one might conclude. In practice, however, many teachers – especially those who work in schools within localities facing severe socio-economic deprivation, as I did – find the BTEC more workable. A respondent within some research by Jonathan Savage and Martin Fautley summarises the options bluntly but in a manner which I recognise for its broad veracity. Specified by Savage as a teacher in 'a multi-ethnic inner-city school', the respondent remarks that the suitability for her students of the GCSE has 'got much worse; the new syllabus is rubbish' (Savage and Fautley 2011: 147). By contrast, the BTEC syllabus means that 'They can do undeveloped pieces as well as a final piece, but the process, that is vital, and thinking about process helps them get a better final product' (ibid). Savage and Fautley argue that such broad attitudes are particularly common for 'teachers in urban environments' (148). I would add that such a learning mode is often particularly well suited to DJs and MCs who, in my experience, strive with amazing determination to hone their craft: given BTEC's greater emphasis on process rather than just assessable product, the syllabus will often be more suited to such music-making, I would assert.

Conclusion

In the 1980s, the replacement of CSEs and (GCE) O-levels with the GCSE was designed, as we have seen in this chapter, to encourage 'a greater percentage of future adult populations being able to "derive deep satisfaction from their leisure pursuit of music"'. It would be hard to sustain an argument that the GCSE has had much if any success, in this regard: music remains a marginal subject in secondary schools, studied by few and enjoyed by fewer. The programmes of study for GCSE seem to have become increasingly remote from the actual listening tastes of the population at large. As Savage and Fautley have shown, the GCSE is widely perceived by music teachers to have become increasingly prescriptive: 'You've got to do a waltz. My kids go "Why have I got to [do a] waltz? I don't want to do a waltz." And I don't know why they've got to [do a] waltz either' (2011: 144). This has led many teachers, particularly in urban/inner-city environments, to prefer the BTEC course, Savage and Fautley have argued (2011).

Whether a music teacher selects one of the GCSE syllabi or a BTEC, however, there are options for DJs and MCs within the specifications, as we have seen. This is less the case with the Edexcel specification than the AQA and OCR GCSE specifications, but all offer at least some potential room for DJs and MCs to perform in their chosen styles. There are no good reasons, therefore, for music teachers to reject such music-making from the classroom if a learner wishes to continue studying music at KS4.

Or are there? This question hinges, in large part, on what the purpose of education is *in general*. If music is to be studied for purely vocational reasons, it makes sense for DJing and MCing to be welcome in the classroom because EDM is now the single biggest-selling area of music in the world's leading marketplace (the USA, that is). Working as a DJ is, in fact, a paying 'gig' which is not unfeasible even for underprivileged young people today; many of the UKs most successful MCs grew up in environments of socio-economic deprivation. What, though, if a young person wants to study music 'proper' (as opposed to the nominally implied-to-be-peripheral 'popular music') at university? What if their ultimate ambition is, say, to provide instrumental tuition? In these cases, skills in reading notation (the importance of which I have, I admit, queried in this chapter) will become more valuable than they otherwise might.

We need to remember that sometimes the daughter (or even son, although it was nearly always daughters in my years of practice) of a bricklayer or plumber might find that Mozart was simply the musical creator whose work 'speaks' in a special way for that young person. What of these actually-existing individuals, if notation is sidelined in music education? The implications of the issue at hand are particularly important when one considers the weight of research discussed in the present chapter to suggest that non-grammar and inner-city schools are less likely to offer the (notation-friendly) GCSE qualification than the (less traditional) BTEC.

Anecdotally, I can mention that I moved from GCSE to BTEC myself in my last two years of school teaching (2010–12) in the hope of better engaging the interest of my learners. The senior management of the school had insisted that the restriction of my available teaching hours (as the sole music specialist in a small and under-subscribed school) meant that I could either run a KS4 class in the (higher achieving) X-band or the (lower achieving) Y-band but not both. I was aware that the overwhelming majority of the DJing and MCing enthusiasts were in the Y-band but was not confident that there were sufficient numbers to allow a class to actually run. Meanwhile, it was evident to me that there were enough learners in the X-band who were desperate to continue with music, including several boys. This being the case, I felt I had no option but to instruct the senior management team to make music a KS4 option for the X-band only. The choice to offer a BTEC rather than a GCSE also felt like no choice at all, in practice; and yet it saddened me to see an exceptional pupil struggling to pass her Grade 5 theory paper when so little traditional music theory (none, effectively) was being covered in class as part of her BTEC course.

What can an individual music teacher do about all this? Very little, in fact: we are the victims of political machinations which are beyond our control, just as much as the learners are, I would argue. That said, it is of course the learners (and especially learners from socio-economically deprived backgrounds) who suffer the worst consequences of government meddling in education. At this point, it would feel wrong not to mention the introduction by the Conservative government of the English Baccalaureate ('EBacc') KS4 schools' performance measure in 2010. To achieve an EBacc a learner should gain a 'good' (in other words, A★–C) GCSE pass in English, Maths, two sciences, history or geography and a language. What of music? This 'non-core' specialism, one assumes, will be taken forwards in the twenty-first century by the grammar schools and the independent schools which the grammar schools so often ape.

In my last years of school teaching, I was aware of senior management persuading young people (and their impressionable, typically semi-educated parents) that choosing history or geography over music would make a significant difference to the future prospects of 'little Johnny'. Never mind if little Johnny loves to play his guitar, or his oboe, or the DJ decks: he needs to think of his future. The truth, of course, is that it is the senior management who are far more likely to prosper, now and in the future, from little Johnny's decision to study geography instead of music. The 'performance measure' in question is currently far more valuable to whole schools, for league table purposes, than to the individual prospects of individual learners: a university is hardly likely to be more impressed by a GCSE profile which includes a 'good' pass in geography than a profile which perhaps includes a 'very good' pass in music. (Will little Johnny do as well in geography as he has done in music, if the latter is his passion? One can doubt it.) We can note, on the question at hand, that the UK's 'Russell Group' of (more prestigious) universities have explicitly stated that the EBacc combination 'is not currently required for entry to any Russell Group university' (2015: 22).

Such things are beyond the powers of individual teachers, as I have acknowledged. What we can do in our own classrooms, that said, is to attempt to provide a KS4 diet of music education which welcomes all contemporary musics, including EDM. With the latter area in mind, this chapter has shown that KS4 can offer options for DJs and MCs (and even 'beatboxers') in both GCSE and BTEC courses. What, though, of the advanced MC or the exceptional DJ? What are the skills we might expect them to acquire (or have acquired)? What were school music experiences like for now-successful DJs? What are the options for DJs and MCs at universities and colleges? These are the questions to which I turn in the next chapter.

References

Au, Wayne, 'Fresh Out of School: Rap Music's Discursive Battle with Education', *Journal of Negro Education* 74/3 (2005), 210–20

Bray, David, 'An Examination of GCSE Music Uptake Rates', *British Journal of Music Education*, 0/1 (2000), 79–89

Derrida, Jacques, *Of Grammatology*, translated by Spivak, Gayatri Chakravorty (Baltimore: John Hopkins, 1976)

Fisher, Roy, *The Vocational Curriculum in England 1974–1994: A Socio-Historical Study of the Business and Technology Education Council's National Diploma in Business and Finance*, PhD thesis, University of Huddersfield, 1999

Hargreaves, David J., Marshall, Nigel A., 'Developing Identities in Music Education', *Music Education Research* 5/3 (2003), 263–73

Hoggarth, J., *How to Be a DJ* (London: Penguin, 2002)

Katz, Mark, *Groove Music: The Art and Culture of the Hip-Hop DJ* (New York: Oxford University Press, 2012)

Kirkland, David E., 'English(es) in Urban Contexts: Politics, Pluralism, and Possibilities', *English Education* 42/3 (2010), 293-306

Klages, Ludwig, *Cosmogonic Reflections: Selected Aphorisms from Ludwig Klages* (London: Arktos, 2015)

Miyakawa, Felicia M., 'Turntablature: Notation, Legitimization and the Art of the Hip-Hop DJ', *American Music* 25/1 (2007), 81–105

Parker, Steve, Parker, Alan, *You Can Make It as a DJ* (Essex: Miles Kelly, 2003)

Russell Group, *Informed Choices: A Russell Group Guide to Making Decisions about Post-16 Education* (4th edition, 2015)

Savage, Jonathan, Fautley, Martin, 'The Organisation and Assessment of Composing at Key Stage 4 in English Secondary Schools', *British Journal of Music Education* 28/2 (2011), 135–57

Spencer, Piers, 'GCSE Music: A Survey of Undergraduate Opinion', *British Journal of Music Education* 10/2 (1993), 73–84

Wright, Ruth, 'Music for All? Pupils' Perceptions of the GCSE Music Examination in One South Wales Secondary School', *British Journal of Music Education* 19/3 (2002), 227–41

8
ADVANCED DJING SKILLS

So far in this book, I have often emphasised the broad appeal of EDM and urban music, encouraging the reader to see DJ decks in particular as something which can often aid the re-engagement of disaffected and/or underachieving learners in mainstream educational environments. Such an opportunity is certainly worth talking about and promoting. We need to remember, however, that MCing and DJing require very high levels of rehearsal and skill to be done well: even beat-matching is harder than it looks/sounds, and this is something of an 'entry level' DJ skill; the rhymes of an MC may sometimes be rudimentary, but delivering a convincing rap is far from being easily done.

In this chapter, therefore, I want to explore advanced DJing skills. I am prioritising DJing over MCing in this discussion, partly because I have found there is more available literature on advanced DJing skills upon which to draw, but also (and this may be why the amount of literature on DJing is larger) because the skills involved in MCing are (in my view, at least) harder to pin down. There are innumerable different styles of rapping: old school, grime, freestyle/spitting, semi-sung styles, battle rapping and many more besides. For information on the specific musical skills involved in MCing/rapping, the interested reader could probably do no better than to consult Adam Krims' *Rap Music and the Poetics of Identity* (2000). My purpose in the present chapter, moreover, is in the 'high end' abilities of the successful and/or ultra-committed DJ, the learning practices which allow them to attain such skills and the way those skills and learning practices relate to the field of education.

In the first section, I discuss some of the particular skills which are required of the advanced DJ: not only scratching and mixing techniques but also the question of 'moving the crowd' with appropriately-chosen recordings. The latter, I will contend, is a much under-discussed ability which has been too little considered within much literature (including scholarly literature) but which is becoming more apparent now that new technologies have rendered traditional DJ skills as more facile than ever before. In the second section, I turn back to the educational question. What space is there, not only in schools and colleges but also in universities, for DJs with advanced skills? To what extent do DJ skills even belong in the academy? Is this really just vernacular music which, being so commercially successful, requires little of no coverage in 'scholarly' contexts? These are the key questions for the second section of the chapter.

Move the crowd

It is not my intention, and in any case it would be beyond my abilities, to itemise in this section the full range of advanced skills which a DJ might want to accomplish as they become more proficient. There are numerous texts available which can assist the interested reader if they wish to gain serious detail on this general topic. These range from the rather frivolous (Parker and Parker 2003) to the more serious (Hoggarth 2002) and the scholarly (Katz 2012). There is also, of course, literature available on the Internet and, most valuable of all for the school-based educator I would say, innumerable clips from which the interested person can acquire knowledge in regards to basic, intermediate and advanced DJing skills.

However, I will offer some observations in regard to some of the particular skills and skill sets which I have observed in the most advanced DJs, not only in the school where I taught but also when liaising with professional DJ educators in different parts of the country. A crucial first distinction to make, and one which we already noted within the OCR GCSE curriculum (see previous chapter), is the distinction between DJs who scratch (more common in hip hop contexts) and those who don't. For those who *do* scratch, particular styluses will be required in order to avoid skipping and other problems. As far as I am aware, the Shure M44-7 is the most popular stylus with scratch DJs. Adjustment of the tone arm is also recommended and a stable surface is important, possibly gained by pushing a table up against a wall (Hoggarth 2002: 40, 83). Most mixers will be adequate for scratching but the faders will need to be in excellent working order because most advanced scratches combine one hand on the vinyl and the other on the fader or cross-fader: DJs need to be confident that the mixer will not let them down if they are to relax to a sufficient extent.

We have noted in Chapter Seven that the baby scratch is regarded as a basic skill. Slightly more difficult is the stab/chop, in which a very short segment of sound is repeatedly replayed. For this scratch, the fader enables the DJ to wind the disc back without the reversed sound being audible to the audience; thus two hands are required, one on the disc and the other on the cross-fader. Chirps are essentially a variation on the stab/chop except that they are slightly more difficult to achieve due to the disc being played both forwards *and* backwards (with the mixer cutting the sound intermittently such that the slowing down and speeding up of the disc's rotation is not audible). The crab is a more significant step up in skill, due to the manual dexterity required for its successful performance. Essentially, the thumb holds the cross-fader to one side (so that no sound will come from the speakers) whilst the other fingers on the same hand are drummed against the cross-fader, one finger after another, causing a stuttering sound as the thumb is repeatedly pushed back a fraction to allow sound from the vinyl to escape into the mixed output. Much harder than it looks, this scratch is definitely indicative that a scratch DJ has ascended into the higher realms of skill: only with rehearsal can this scratch be accomplished convincingly.

Numerous other scratches are available, some of which are simply variants of the aforementioned scratches (for example, the twiddle – a variant on the crab involving only two fingers with the thumb). I will not itemise these here. It would be wrong, however, if we did not pay at least some attention to the transformer – 'probably the most important scratch developed in the 1980s', according to expert Mark Katz (2012: 114). As with the crab, the fader is used to cut the sound in and out of the mix to produce a stuttering effect (although typically with just thumb and index finger being employed, unlike the crab). In addition to this, however, the DJ typically uses their other hand to push the vinyl back and forth. This being done manually, the sampled sound can have its pitch and timbre altered as the sound is played back and forth, allowing a wide range of expressive options to the scratching DJ. From the point of view of assessment of skill levels, this expressive range is extremely helpful: both rehearsal and imagination/creativity are required and should be readily recognisable when they have been deployed.

According to Katz, 'Transforming had a huge impact on DJs' (2012: 115). World-leading DJ Qbert concurs: 'When transforming came out, it just flipped the whole scratching world around' (ibid.). It is certainly vital to the DJ 'battle' in which DJs alternately perform routines for the judgement of the crowd as to who is the winner: almost any clip of DJ battles will demonstrate the indispensability of the transformer scratch. When Katz mentions the possibility of the 'line switch' on the mixer being used for the transformer, however, an interesting issue comes to the fore which we will have reason to pay close attention to in the present chapter. According to Katz (and I am very confident that he is correct), some DJs feel that transforming with the mixer's line switch is 'close to cheating because it's really no harder than flicking a light switch on and off' (114).

Why would something being easy present a problem for a musician? As a matter of fact, I am confident that we can find comparable issues arising in more traditional modes of music-making. I recall, for example, my jazz guitar teacher insisting that I use a particular chord voicing rather than a bar chord shape precisely because the latter, being so commonly used in rock, would lead 'any decent [that is, jazz-playing] guitarist in the audience' to disapprove. This has stuck in my memory for thirty years because the voicing in question actually replicated four of the six strings found in the bar chord, meaning that the preferred chord essentially *was* the bar chord but with two notes removed. Less is more? What was important to my teacher, I believed then and still believe now, was that the approved voicing was a more awkward shape for the fretting hand and didn't (visually) send out the generic signals which the bar chord shape, by contrast, would. In the end, though, shouldn't the sound a musician attains be more important than the means to acquiring that sound? The difference, in the case of using the line switch for the transformer scratch and the bar chord shape alike, is more one of the *eye* (and the mind) than the ear, I would contend.

We will have more to say about the question of technical difficulty shortly. Firstly, however, we should at least say something about the DJ's advanced mixing skills which are separate from the scratching skills discussed so far. Most important to the non-scratching DJ is the skill of beatmatching. In short, this entails matching the BPM of two tracks so that both can be played simultaneously and live cutting between the two can be enacted such that either a blend of the two is created or a smooth segue from one to the other is presented.

The latter is the most common usage of beatmatching for the 'club DJ' who, unlike the scratching/battling DJ, mostly just wants to *move the crowd* (to excite the audience with a flow of agreeably-matching tracks, that is). Quite often, within a club set, the DJ will offer only a few bars where the two tracks are both playing simultaneously: the new track will be 'dropped' (introduced to the audience) during the closing bars of the previous track, enabling a brief overlap between the two. Sometimes, however, the DJ will give little hints of the forthcoming 'tune' much earlier in the previous track, whetting the appetite of the audience. Beatmatching is valuable here because the hints of the forthcoming tune can then be integrated without dancers being confused or thrown off balance, as it were.

As well as being a valuable skill for this practical purpose, beatmatching is fairly tricky as a skill in itself – with vinyl decks, at least. This trickiness arises because, even if the two tunes are using electronically created (and thus metronomic) beats, which typically is the case, there is every chance that the mechanically driven turntable will fractionally misalign the beat so that a 'double beating' effect is created (similar to the sound created by a galloping horse). To avoid this, the vinyl DJ must keep one ear to the headphones and one hand to the disk, regularly touching the latter to fractionally speed up or slow down the rate of spin such that the double beating effect is dispelled. The more skilled DJ will be able to do this whilst using his free hand to cross fade between the two tunes, giving occasional 'tastes' of the newly-introduced disc.

With a little rehearsal, entry level DJs should be able to do a little beatmatching, but becoming capable of more prolonged integration of tunes through beatmatching requires fairly significant amounts of rehearsal. As a school teacher, I encountered one or two students whose more advanced skills at beatmatching genuinely amazed me: to acquire the skills they had in dropping sections of one tune onto another, these students must have spent many hours honing their craft. Beyond this, however, I would judge that the students must have also had high levels of natural musical skill. Interestingly, this natural skill (if one can speak of the 'natural' so confidently, which is arguable I admit) often did not manifest itself in more typical classroom work such as performing on keyboards or hand percussion, we should note. However, the musical skills which had not been manifest in the classroom heretofore became recognisable in many DJ-enthusiast students when they would perform on the decks.

Because the students I worked with were not enculturated in hip hop, they usually did not do any scratching, but we should note that the most advanced beat-related skill is probably beat juggling. The potential range of beat juggling skills is too vast to be captured in the present context, but the core requirement is essentially scratch related: the disc is repeatedly paused, re-wound or interfered with such that a new and different beat is created from the raw material of a pre-recorded beat. Because the DJs I worked with were not scratchers, they would not offer any beat juggling, but the interested reader can consult a large range of online clips where the remarkable possibilities of beat juggling are demonstrated by innumerable different DJs.

So far in the present chapter, I have written as if vinyl decks remain the dominant mode in DJing. Certainly DJs were largely responsible for the continued pressing of vinyl in the lean years after the 1980s when the popularity of CDs led many to proclaim (incorrectly, as it has turned out) the death of vinyl (Osborne 2014). However, in recent years CD decks have become more prominent, with Digital Vinyl Systems (DVS) perhaps offering the best of both worlds. DVS allows a special vinyl disc to trigger samples from a laptop: Traktor and Serato are arguably the most well-known systems, but naturally a range of manufacturers have products on the market. Whether DVS or CD decks, many 'old school' DJs object to the new technology on principle: 'Some veterans criticize the technology for making DJing too easy, for allowing younger DJs to get away without paying their dues' reports Katz (2012: 219). As Kai Fikentscher puts in his '"It's Not the Mix, It's the Selection": Music Programming in Contemporary DJ Culture' (in Attias, Gavanas and Rietveld 2013), today 'beatmatching and mixing can be (and often are) achieved through the push of a software sync-button'. As a result of this, 'programming can be said to have returned as an important way to distinguish a DJ' (125).

This question of the DJ's skills in programming (selecting particular records and playing them in a particular order, that is) has certainly gained in perceived importance. However, we should note, before discussing this recently-returned higher esteem for programming, that not all commentators are persuaded that new technology removes DJing skill. For example Chris Christodoulou argues, in his 'DJs and the Aesthetic of Acceleration in Drum'n'Bass' (in Attias, Gavanas and Rietveld 2013), that 'the widespread use of virtual DJ software that can automatically detect and "sync" track BPMs' has actually 'added another means by which a drum'n'bass DJ can demonstrate skill' (212). This, he argues, is achieved through the 'double-drop' (simultaneous climax of two tunes, by Christodoulou's definition) which requires 'the ability to make creative decisions quickly and spontaneously'. That said, Christodoulou acknowledges that 'DJs who can perform double-drops using only CDs and vinyl records are given particular acclaim' (ibid).

More strident, as regards the possibility that new (post-vinyl, as it were) DJing technology might actually allow *greater* musicianship, is a DJing respondent within Jonathan Yu's 'Electronic Dance Music and Technological Change: Lessons from Actor-Network Theory' (in Attias, Gavanas and Rietveld 2013). 'From my perspective', the DJ argues, 'the digital formats … enable the new DJs to do way more complicated transitions and include way more complicated parts to the transitions and to their pieces' (155). In his view, 'the transitions that a vinyl DJ would do are not even a fucking split on what a digital DJ would do with Ableton or Traktor in terms of the technical aspect and the musicality of it'. For this reason, the 'deep resentment' of DJs who use digital equipment is 'completely unfounded' (156).

Such arguments are possibly best left to the various online debates which DJ enthusiasts will indulge in. For our purposes, the main point is that there is at least some debate to be had in regards to the question as to how great a level of skill is required for relatively new DJing equipment (CD decks, DVS, 'launchpads' and so forth) as compared with 'old school' vinyl decks. Beyond all this lies the question of *programming*: are technical skills even the heart of the *real* skill of a successful DJ? Here, the debate is particularly important from an educational point of view: are the kinds of skills which normal methods of academic assessment in music tend to prioritise (see the last chapter, for example) even *pertinent*? If it is the case that the real skill of the DJ is simply 'reading the crowd' through the selection of records that will get them moving, perhaps not. (DJ veteran Mike Tull states emphatically that 'I don't care what skills you've got, if you can't read the crowd you can't DJ worth shit' [quoted in Elafros 2012: 468].) Here, then, we need to tread carefully.

The general question at hand arises in numerous chapters (some of which we have already been drawn upon above) within Bernardo Alexander Attias, Anna Gavanas and Hillegonda C. Rietveld's *DJ Culture in the Mix* collection (2013). According to Fikentscher, it is clear that 'programming ... is an aspect of DJ musicianship that may be considered both artistic and salubrious' (145). For Yu, we need to resist any 'technological determinism where[by] an artistic practice ceases to be artistic' and to eye suspiciously the idea of a 'moment where supposedly there is no longer any skill or creativity involved in the craft, such as when button pushing replaces earlier notions of DJing' (170). Instead, he suggests, we must 'examine the new creative practices and discourses that emerge and how these contribute to an on-going redefinition of musicianship' (ibid). Within Yu's chapter, that said, we can note that some DJs consider it 'so hard to be different from everyone else because everything's just the same. Everyone's got the same set, the same plugins, the same software, the same samples' (162). There is, then, at least a perceived rut into which the DJing world has fallen, according to some. How can the DJ rise above this and show their worth?

According to Mirko M. Hall and Naida Zukic's 'The DJ as Electronic Deterritorializer' chapter in *DJ Culture in the Mix* (Attias, Gavanas and Rietveld 2013) 'DJs must understand their beloved equipment is only a means; their playing and programming still requires a fair amount of musical intelligence (a knack for a groove) and analytical precision (technical aesthetic know-how)' (115). To support their argument, Hall and Zukic quote A DJ names Sasha who argues that 'Even though DJs are playing other people's records, it's the way you play it, the records you choose, the way you drop records, the way you program it, and your style' which can mark a DJ's quality (ibid.). Because of this, Sasha argues, the technology is valuable despite the fact that it makes DJing easy: the real skill is not too closely related to the kind of technical skills which so often get emphasised in discussions of DJing but, rather, in programming a DJ set and delivering it nicely. Hall and Zukic are in broad agreement, speaking of the effective DJs 'magical ability to "work the crowd" with the right record at the right time' (110-1). For Yu, 'Part of the preparation work of the DJ is to collect' records: simply to undertake 'crate digging' (searching through old boxes of vinyl) and other forms of music hunting (some of which today can be 'virtual', doubtless) and demonstrate DJing skills by playing the music which has been selected through this process (169).

Could such skills ever be satisfactorily caught in an educational setting, however? As I have hinted above, the current emphasis in GCSE curricula (see Chapter Seven) on the technical skills of the DJ over and above their programming skills makes a poor fit with the kinds of skills which are emphasised in the last two paragraphs. Can a teacher seriously (and objectively, moreover) appraise the *taste* of a DJ? It is hard to see how this could be done without high levels of subjective judgement coming into play. Given the prioritisation by a range of different commentators quoted above upon the importance of the DJ's ability to move/read/work the crowd, perhaps a partial solution could be to assess a DJ set delivered in front of an actual audience. Video recording could feasibly assist this process for the purpose of external assessment. However, how could an exam board ever be sure that the audience was not just the DJ's friends who, one might reasonably guess, would therefore lack an objective response to the DJ set? We can also note, on this topic, a respondent in *DJ Culture in the Mix* remarking that 'It's sad and kind of comical watching DJs trying to do 20–30 minute sets' (Attias, Gavanas and Rietveld 2013: 131). If 'real-life' vocational skills are as important as much of the contemporary rhetoric around education would imply, the DJ will really need several hours in front of a club audience in order to replicate something along the lines of the skills in programming and responsiveness to a crowd which are essential for the actual 'jobbing' DJ.

It is hard if not impossible, however, to see how such a thing could be captured and measured for assessment at KS4, KS5 or even, to some extent, in a university context. How, after all, do we distinguish between a first class or A*-standard dropping of some particular club tune after some other particular piece of music relative to the way another DJ programmes their set? It may be the case that 'It comes down to song choice. Everybody knows when the DJ is terrible. People don't want to dance' (Attias, Gavanas and Rietveld 2013: 155). *Which* 'people' don't want to dance, though? It is hard to escape the arbitrariness of audiences: one crowd might be 'mad for it' (as they say in the UK) with one tune, another might have differing preferences. In the end, making a fair judgement of the differing programming skills of DJs might turn out to be an impossible.

Speaking, however, as someone who taught in schools and then, latterly, has lectured in universities, perhaps the key to this problem is for curricula at school level to encourage more of the kind of 'critical reflection' capacity which seems to me to be afforded more importance in universities. If, for example, a DJ can create a setlist, justifying the choice of tunes and reflecting on the impact that the programming has had upon an actual audience, will this not be rather a valuable skill for them to demonstrate? And, furthermore, is it not feasible that assessment needs could be reasonably well supported by the reflections and justifications this would generate?

I would suggest, based on the survey of GCSE and BTEC curricula which I offered in Chapter Seven, that the BTEC curriculum (as it stands at present) already offers a reasonable chance for such skills to be figured within assessment processes. I am inclined to add that, in the longer term, GCSE and A-level exam boards should consider the issues at stake in regards to programming. If the exam boards are really serious about opening up the curriculum to new technologies and new modes of music-making such as DJing, it will be necessary to consider further broadening the curriculum in order to better engage with the actual skills which are often most highly merited amongst DJs and fans of EDM.

In the short term, though, we are where we are. What, then, are the prospects for DJs in the educational scene *as it currently stands*? We can note with interest that the DJ quoted a moment ago with the remark that 'Everybody knows when the DJ is terrible' because 'People don't want to dance' is actually a (regrettably) rare example of a female DJ. Perhaps more interestingly still for our purposes, she is revealed as a 'classical bassoonist turned pop musician and beginner DJ' (Attias, Gavanas and Rietveld 2013: 155). The fact that someone would turn from a 'classical' orientation to not only a pop one but, moreover, an EDM orientation is particularly interesting because it raises a question about educational provision and learner expectation. To some extent, we are back to the question of learner-centred pedagogies, of course. Moreover, though, in the next section I want to explore the question as to whether DJing really even fits at all with schools, colleges and universities. If it does fit but only partially, which do we change: the music culture or the educational system?

We don't need no education … or do we???

A revealing moment in Jonathan Yu's chapter in *DJ Culture in the Mix* arises when one of his DJ respondents remarks that 'At the end of the day I say, if you need to be taught, don't bother' (Attias, Gavanas and Rietveld 2013: 161). The context for this remark is a discussion of younger 'kids' who have taken up DJing: older and more experienced DJs, who had to learn their skills without the help of YouTube training videos, sync button facilities and suchlike, tend to be critical of the more youthful fraternity, it is fair to say. Beyond this somewhat generational chauvinism, though, I also observed some discomfort amongst older DJs during my research when I asked, for example, whether they thought there should be grades available for DJing in the style of the ABRSM grades for more traditional musical instruments. Most were merely hesitant on this particular question but one DJ educator, who had also worked for countless years as a jobbing DJ, was emphatic that grade exams for DJ decks would be a terrible idea. When pushed, he was unable to give a coherent rationale for his antipathy, but the strength of his negative feeling about the idea was unmistakeable.

Why *shouldn't* there be a possibility for a DJ to apply to university with a grade 8 certificate in DJing or, come to that, MCing? Perhaps no such thing should happen precisely because DJing is, as they say, 'a whole other thing': the brass player will find it gradually more difficult as they pass through grades which demand higher and higher pitches (and thus more and more challenging *embouchure*), whereas the skills of the more or less advanced DJ are not so transparent. Is the DJ not rather 'shooting himself in the foot', however, when he takes this stance? After all, nearly all school music teachers have been trained in university music departments. If we don't do more to legitimise DJing as a practice, therefore, how can we ever get more teachers into schools who are *au fait* with the decks and thus start to break the cycle whereby teachers and (a significant minority of) learners face each other with mutual musical incomprehension?

My suspicion, in any case, was that the reluctance to consider the possibility of DJing grade exams had a rather more deep-seated basis. In short, I suspect that DJs often feel that they (and their music) *just do(es) not belong in mainstream music education*. It's all very well, the unspoken argument seems to me to go, for some after-school or out-of-school DJing training to take place. The idea, however, of formalising the DJing skills such that the decks take a position next to the violin, the oboe and even the electric guitar – is such an idea not anathema for this marginal music? It is worth remembering the resistance to Carluccio's *Concerto for Turntables and Orchestra* which we noted in Chapter Seven above. It would seem evident, then, that not everyone within the broad EDM field finds 'classical' legitimisation to be something which the field should seek.

The trouble is, though, that EDM *isn't* marginal music: it is now the biggest-selling music in the USA, as noted in the introduction above, and has been wildly popular in Europe for a long time. That given, we need to recognise the actual musical interests of learners today and, if child-centred learning has any legitimacy at all, we need to make some adjustments to the whole educational scene such that learner interest and curriculum content are not too problematically out of step. As we have seen, many in power think that child-centred pedagogy is *not* legitimate; and, moreover, there is good reason to suspect 'the music establishment' (if we can be permitted to speak of such a thing) are very likely to resist progressive ideas such as, say, graded exams on DJ decks. (The 'establishment' in question, incidentally, arguably includes elements of the 'popular' field; or, at least, we can guess that some popular musicians will be resistant to the idea of DJ decks as musical instruments. Bernardo Alexander Attias, for example, has written of a 'resistance among some more traditionally skilled musicians – particularly in the rock'n'roll world – to consider the DJ an artist in any capacity at all' [Attias, Gavanas and Rietveld 2013: 30].) Nevertheless, I would contend that we ought to at least consider the possibility that the DJ decks might deserve a more prominent position within music education, now and in the future.

Assuming that this should be accepted as a fair proposal, what then are the potential barriers to it being immediately implemented as an educational tendency? As I have already hinted in the present section, one such barrier may well be an internalised (and probably unconscious) assumption *on the part of DJs themselves* that the downgrading of DJ decks as a not-quite-proper musical instrument has some legitimacy. If so, from where does this sense of illegitimacy derive? It derives in large part, I would suggest, from the very music classrooms to which DJs (despite having long since completed their schooling) continue to feel excluded/misplaced. Consider, for example, the following remark from DJ Jazzie B: 'I didn't have any real professional sort of teaching or anything.... Learning an instrument held no real relevance to what I really wanted to do' (quoted in Burnard 2012: 103). It is telling, is it not, that the DJ decks, which he declares were his starting point for music-making, are not counted by Jazzie B as 'an instrument'? Jazzie B was the founding member of Soul II Soul, 'one of the most successful musical exports from the UK during the late 1980s and early 1990s' according to Pamela Burnard (103). His band achieved a top twenty album and top ten single in the US charts whilst he has been awarded an OBE in the UK. Nevertheless, Burnard raises the possibility that, in his school days, Jazzie B may have been 'asleep at the back of the class' (105).

Why is it that, to this author at least, Burnard's suggestion is entirely credible as a possibility and, indeed, a likelihood? It is credible, I think, because we all know that the decks aren't *really* a real instrument, at least from the overwhelmingly dominant perspective. Paul Thompson's 'empirical study into the learning practices and enculturation of DJs, turntablists, hip hop and dance music producers' makes the general position very clear (2012). According to Thompson, 'In formal educational institutions in the United Kingdom, … the practical study of dance music and hip hop genres has been unequivocally avoided in favour of more traditional Western Art music.' Meanwhile 'Rock-based popular musicians are more easily integrated into formal education institutions using Western Art pedagogical frameworks with a focus on instrumental tuition in combination with the study of music theory and composition.' However, 'The popular electronic musician … is less easily integrated into formal educational institutions, primarily because an instrument is not "played" in the traditional sense and technology provides the basis for compositional and performance methods' (2012: 43).

Thompson argues that, in the HE sector, 'many courses fail to integrate popular electronic music practices, such as turntablism or deejaying, into [their] taxonomy of musical study' and consequently 'the musical skills and knowledge required to compose, arrange and perform dance and hip hop styles of music have often been overlooked' (2012: 43). The solution, he suggests, is clear: 'Academic enquiry into the techniques employed in popular electronic music-making is necessary, not only to acknowledge these areas of popular music as worthy of study' but also in order to develop 'a greater understanding of the learning strategies involved' (ibid). Interestingly for the question as to whether DJs and EDM producers have some kind of internalised sense of their music-making as being less than entirely legitimate, Thompson draws our attention to 'some of the responses from the popular electronic musicians who until the study, had not considered their musical development as a learning process' (53).

Why does this happen? Thompson suggests that 'The intrinsic motivation of the musician and their focus on music-making creates a virtual imperceptibility that learning is actually taking place' (2012: 53). In other words, the DJs and producers are 'just really into it', as they might say: in their minds, perhaps, learning is never something one could do for pleasure and, therefore, the fact that they enjoy developing the musical skills at hand means that it can't really be 'learning'. That said, though, is it not revealing that one of Thompson's respondents remarks that 'My old music teacher used to call it noise ... he couldn't figure out why we liked it' (48)? If the educational establishment at large is responsible for the creation of a sense amongst countless generations that learning and enjoyment are mutually exclusive, it is nevertheless the responsibility of *individual* music teachers for mistaking music for noise, I would contend. Individual teachers need, then, to at least *try* to 'figure out' the appeal of this music: if we don't, it is surely likely that yet another generation of young people (or, at least, a significant slice of the generation) will assume that what gets called 'music' in the school is quite discrete relative to what *they* perceive as music.

Interestingly, all that said, Thompson's concluding remarks imply that he remains hesitant as to whether the 'learning practices and enculturation of DJs, turntablists, hip hop and dance music producers', upon which his research is focussed, can ever be successfully integrated into the overall music educational field. 'The popular electronic musician works directly with sound in a tactile fashion, either through the manipulation of a record or a digital audio file', Thompson points out; as a result, this electronic musician is 'making music in a way the musician playing a musical instrument does not' (2012: 56). There is plenty to argue over, here: after all, which instrument (other than the voice) excludes tactility? Surely a cellist, flautist or harpist also 'works directly with sound', do they not? Again, I feel, there is an extent to which the advocate of EDM and EDM-orientated music-making has created a self-defeating argument, here.

That said, I applaud Thompson's next statement: 'Formal pedagogical and assessment frameworks would require significant reconsideration' if we wish to expand 'the inclusion of the practical study of popular electronic categories of music into formal educational institutions (2012: 56). I am convinced that this is so: in a sense, we would need to 'bring the mountain to Mohammed', to use an old expression. By this I mean that, instead of prioritising technical skill, as is obviously done in grade exams, a proper integration of EDM and DJing into music education would require, for example, musical taste (which, after all, is what the DJ excels at when his programming allows him to move the crowd) to be more highly emphasised. To make a change like this really would be to move a mountain, I think; it is worth at least considering, however, if we are serious about better matching twenty-first-century music education to the twenty-first-century musical landscape.

After all, these are serious musicians: Thompson's research makes this fact unmistakeable. 'As you practise, your ears and hands work together without you noticing it', reveals one young respondent (2012: 48). 'I used to rehearse for something like 7 hours at a time when I started off', remarks one DJ whilst another talks of 'working on my own for hours and hours' (49). 'I was taught the basics [of beatmatching] by my brother, then practiced, practiced, practiced to refine the skill and train my ears' (49); 'I used to practice at 4 o'clock every day when I got home from school' (50). Can we seriously deny the status of musician to individuals who rehearse like this? Can DJ decks be anything other than a musical instrument if so many hours of rehearsal and practice are required to develop the appropriate musical skills? And yet we have observed already that Thompson counterpoises the DJ against 'the musician playing a musical instrument' (see above).

It is not just a matter of moving the 'mountain' of the musical establishment, then: DJs (and those who would advocate for them) need to remember that they *are* musicians and that the decks *are* a legitimate instrument, that they have every right to be recognised by the music establishment. If Mark Katz is to believed, the issue at hand has a long history (2012: 41). Katz challenges the common idea that 'hip-hop arose in part because there was little or no music instruction in the schools' of the Bronx (the latter being the birthplace of hip hop). On his view, 'the opposition/resistance theory of hip-hop's development' is problematic because, to look more closely at the issue at hand, 'Music never completely disappeared from the schools, and there's little to say that the kids who developed hip-hop would have participated in school music no matter how abundant the offerings'. Indeed, one of Katz respondents (DJ Disco Wiz) 'says he could have been a member of the school band. It just wasn't cool.' ('I had enough trouble just walking down the street without a fucking trombone in my hand', Wiz clarifies.)

The problem isn't only that school music wasn't/isn't cool, though: Katz questions whether 'the pioneering DJs even thought of what they were doing as musical performance, and thus as an alternative to playing in school ensembles' (2012: 41). Katz's argument, then, is that there was (and, I feel confident to say, still is) a *mutual antipathy/misapprehension*: 'Without minimising the poor state of public schools in the Bronx at the time, or the importance of school music programmes, it hardly seems that lack of opportunity was a prime motivator among DJs.' Rather, the pioneering DJs had means at their disposal: physical equipment (turntables, mixers, etc.) at more affordable prices than had been the case earlier in the 1970s but also, of course, 'imagination and ingenuity, drive and desire … and, above all, music' (ibid.). We know that this led them to create a new music-making mode which would soon become a worldwide phenomenon – but we need to remember that this was done quite separately from the school system and its offering for music education.

Does that historical fact mean that schools and EDM must *remain* wholly other to each other? I would dispute it (except, perhaps, in a Levinasian sense – see Chapter One). For one thing, DJ specialists are already making inroads into the educational scene (see Chapter Four). National curricular specifications, in the UK at least, are beginning to recognise key traditions from EDM such as DJing (see Chapter Seven). There is, in fact, a two-way flow of traffic, furthermore. We can notice, for example, that two of the four DJ case studies in Pamela Burnard's chapter on 'DJ Cultures' turn out to have been classically trained. DJ XUAN 'was identified as having "gifted" classical piano skills, and was accepted onto the Juilliard School's very selective pre-college division' (2012: 107). DJ Rob Paterson 'achieved high levels in grade music examinations for at least one of the several instruments he played, which included piano, trumpet and guitar' (112). Add to this the bassoonist already mentioned above and it is clear that it is perfectly possible for an individual with a 'classical' background to find EDM and DJing attractive as a genre/mode for music-making.

We should not be hasty about the situation at present, however: DJing and MCing opportunities in schools remain limited and most graduates of music degrees know little or nothing about DJ decks, I would assert. Is it satisfactory for this situation to continue, given that DJing has thrived without requiring mainstream validation for nearly forty years now whilst the classical tradition is, needless to say, older still? Doubtless the two worlds can survive without each other. However, are there not rather a few advantages for DJs (some of whom are now of a pensionable age) to be gained from greater legitimisation? Consider, for example, Mark Katz's revelation that Grand Wizzard Theodore (unquestionably one of the most important pioneers of hip hop DJing) 'told me very frankly that one of the reasons he started teaching at Scratch [the 'academy' which provides training for aspiring DJs] was because it finally allowed him to have dental insurance' (2012: 235). According to Katz, 'The association with the discourse and values of higher education sends the message that DJing is both serious and respectable and, by extension, a *real* art' (ibid, emphasis retained). If such is the case – and I believe Katz is absolutely correct here, for what it's worth – then who could deny that DJing has a place not only in the university sector but, moreover, in the world of music education at large?

Conclusion

According to Mark Katz, the twenty-first century has brought 'a world in which barriers to becoming a DJ have surely fallen away' (2012: 248). This might be encouraging for 'the managers and teachers of DJ academies', but the idea that anyone can be a DJ is only 'spoken with contempt by experienced DJs who have lost gigs to newcomers' (ibid.). As I argued at length in my monograph *Anyone Can Do It*, the apparent democratisation of catchy universalising slogans needs to be considered carefully and critically, therefore. If new technology has allowed novice musicians to do something musical where previously they could do nothing, I would insist that this is a good thing. We need to remember, though, that DJing has been developed through painstaking rehearsal and experimentation by pioneering practitioners: there are a whole set of technical skills which the committed DJ can acquire, some of which have been outlined in this chapter.

Beyond technical skill, however, there are also programming skills which are vital for the effective DJ. Recent scholarship on DJing (especially the chapters collected in Attias, Gavanas and Rietveld's *DJ Culture in the Mix*) has begun to note that such skills are arguably the heart of DJing in terms of the actual appeal of a DJ to an actual audience. In the words of DJ Groove Terminator, 'For me it was always about sharing great music with people'; the 'technical ability of the whole thing, which you can pick up fairly quickly' is less important than 'knowing what to play next [which] is, I think, probably 85% of DJing' (quoted in Burnard 2012: 116).

This being the case, a pedagogical question arises: if the real skill of the DJ is programming (rather than scratching, blending and so forth), how is the DJ to be judged for the purpose of assessment? This question is seriously problematic for the music education field, I would suggest: in the end, it undermines a value system which goes back at least to the formation of the Associated Board of the Royal Schools of Music (the ABRSM, that is) in 1889. The value system in question contends that 'a high standard of achievement' is what we should measure: the appraisal of DJs on grounds of their programming contradicts this by prioritising high standards of *aesthetic taste*, essentially.

Is this contradiction likely to be resolved in the near future? I very much doubt it. Indeed, although I will admit that I declined the encouragement of my instrumental tutors to take grade exams when I was a teenager (on the grounds that, then as now, I thought music was not about competition), I am not convinced that ABRSM grades have no validity for musical learning now and in the future. The example of *embouchure* which I raised above is probably as good an example as any: brass players need to develop the range of pitches they attempt a little at a time and many players will benefit enormously from the feedback which ABRSM examiners can give in regards to particularly skills such as articulation, intonation and so forth. I would not call, therefore, for a complete abolition of the grading system which has been so central to music education for the last century and more: it remains useful and worthy of significant respect.

Grades, however, are not the 'be all and end all' of musical capability. Duane Eddy, to pick an example almost at random, had hit records with guitar riffs which are far from challenging in a technical sense. Many of his riffs, indeed, could feasibly be played by someone who had never before touched a guitar, given that they require (or appear to require, at least) only one finger. The simplicity of his riffs did not prevent Eddy from acquiring a huge fanbase in the late 1950s and early 1960s, however. Could his true skill be claimed as musical 'curation', in a sense, therefore? Perhaps, I would argue; for the guitar work in question is more about collecting together predictable 'twangy' riffs, and presenting them for the delight of what turned out to be a considerably-sized audience, than it is about demonstration of advanced technical skill.

Was Jimi Hendrix just showing off a bag of tricks, or might it have been the case that his technical excellence actually came easily to him and, therefore, the guitar 'wizardry' was incidental to something far more *musical* which actually drove him to play the way that he did? The question is perhaps too big (and too musicologically contentious) to be handled in detail in the context at hand. What I would assert firmly, though, is that measurement of skill only captures part of what it is to be a musician.

The DJ, who curates music and musical sounds for the predilection of eager and often very large audiences, is unmistakeably a musician in my view. Clearly, at least, the DJ does a great service to music if and when their curation includes the esoteric and the less obvious or (as certainly often happens) helps us to recognise the truly great. DJs are of a much underestimated importance to post-war popular music, therefore: 'Everybody knows when the DJ is terrible. People don't want to dance' (see above). But can we *measure* that importance in individual DJs for the purpose of educational assessment? I have suggested above that such is perfectly thinkable in a university environment if and when assessment prioritises critical reflection, contextual awareness and suchlike. For these kind of skills to be recognised at school level is harder to imagine, given the lay of the contemporary educational field. I would insist, however, that the future is ours: and we must keep talking, therefore, not only about what music education is at the moment but also, moreover, what it could be in the future.

References

Attias, Bernardo Alexander, Gavanas, Anna, Rietveld, Hillegonda C., *DJ Culture in the Mix: Power, Technology and Social Change in Electronic Dance Music* (London: Bloomsbury, 2013)

Burnard, Pamela, *Musical Creativities in Practice* (Oxford: Oxford University Press, 2012)

Dale, Pete, *Anyone Can Do It: Empowerment, Tradition and the Punk Underground* (Aldershot: Ashgate, 2012)

Elafros, Athena, 'Locating the DJ: Black Popular Music, Location and Fields of Cultural Production', *Cultural Sociology* 7/4 (2012), 463–78

Hoggarth, J., *How to Be a DJ* (London: Penguin, 2002)

Katz, Mark, *Groove Music: The Art and Culture of the Hip-Hop DJ* (New York: Oxford University Press, 2012)

Krims, Adam, *Rap Music and the Poetics of Identity* (Cambridge: Cambridge University Press, 2000)

Osborne, Richard, *Vinyl: A History of the Analogue Record* (Farnham: Ashgate 2014)

Parker, Steve, Parker, Alan, *You Can Make It as a DJ* (Essex: Miles Kelly, 2003)

Thompson, Paul, 'An empirical study into the learning practices and enculturation of DJs, turntablists, hip hop and dance music producers', *Journal of Music, Technology & Education* 5/1 (2012), 43–58

9
USING NEW TECHNOLOGIES

To some educators and theorists of education, new digital technologies which can be used in the music classroom are a 'quick fix' for disaffection and, therefore, a godsend. For others, however, this new technology offers, at best, a 'double-edged sword' and, at worst, risks 'throwing the baby out with the bathwater'. This range of metaphors reflects the fact that, at present, the music education jury (as it were) is not in full agreement as to the value of technology. 'Today, anyone with loop-based software on her computer can make music', asserts Lauri Väkevä; but one can't help but feel tempted to counter that, yesterday too, anyone could make music if they have a voice or limbs and some imagination or commitment (2010: 61). 'What if students aren't taught the violin anymore, and instead, they only know how to use GarageBand?', queries a preservice teacher in research by Vratulis and Morton (2011: 405). However, one finds it hard to imagine that the introduction of such software into music education seriously threatens the continuation of the traditional instrument in question as a favourite for (some) school children.

There is confusion here, then, and a great need for dispassionate evaluation of the situation as it stands (and as it looks set to develop). Should music technology be embraced, rejected as a threat to tradition or placed alongside the existing range of established options in music education as, in short, another option which can aid general engagement? Those who have read the rest of my book will not be surprised to learn that I am strongly inclined toward the third of these three options. In my own practice, and in my observations of others' teaching practice, it seems clear that new technologies can really help to engage and stimulate young people, especially those who are enthusiastic about EDM (which is many if not most young people today, I would contend). This does not mean that all existing traditions in music education should now be abandoned; but it does mean that new technologies should be embraced as a musical tool which can make more learners feel that music is 'do-able' than traditional methods and modes of music education have been able to.

Having said this, I do feel sympathies not only with those who have embraced new technologies for music education with a proselytising zeal but also those who fear a consequent loss of support for that important minority of learners who respond with immense enthusiasm and passion to traditional music education. It is particularly important in inner-city schools within areas of severe socio-economic disadvantage, such as the school in which I taught music for nine years, that we remember that the latter kind of young person, although always a minority, can be found in any school. It would be a tragedy if only private and grammar schools provided violin lessons for young people, for example. Meanwhile, the zeal with which I personally brought new technologies into my classroom began to fade as I realised the existence of certain limitations which seemed to be inherent to the technology which is currently most readily available. Nevertheless, the excitement which accompanied the arrival of fifteen 'MacBooks' (replete with headphones and splitters, such that a whole class could work as individuals or with a partner on musical editing software) was remarkable. I had loaned the MacBooks for half a term from a nearby school around 2010, and the impact on engagement and enthusiasm was immense – initially, at least. Music technology is valuable, then; but we need to handle it carefully.

My aim, in the present chapter, is to give the most balanced appraisal I can muster in regards to the advantages and disadvantages of new music technology. By 'new music technology', I am primarily gesturing at computer-based music-making rather than, for example, the vinyl-playing DJ decks which I have tended to focus upon in much of this book. It is not uncommon at all, and is likely to become more common in the future indeed, for a UK school to have a computer suite (or, indeed, several suites) which can be used by music teachers to support an entire class for computer-based music-making work for a lesson or a series of lessons. This is a great opportunity, but it also needs to be handled carefully. All learners need to gain not only an experience of the range of up-to-date music-making options which are currently common but also to get a glimpse of the kinds of music-making experiences which have traditionally been available in schools. One reads a great deal of criticism of xylophones in contemporary literature on music education; speaking personally, however, I found group work around pentatonic scales on xylophones during my first term at secondary school in 1982 to be one of the absolute highlights of that year. Perhaps I was one of those gifted ones (whatever 'gifted' means) who are always perhaps going to be a minority in any given class. Even if such is the case, however, surely the hands-on lesson with beaters, melody and rudimentary harmony was a vital one for me individually, in that it unlocked certain interests (or at least, I believe it did) which were only beginning to emerge strongly in me at that time?

We need to remember that making music can be completely free of technology (as normally understood, at least), as in singing, then; and that 'old school' technology (such as shaping lengths of wood to create differing vibration frequencies, as is done with a xylophone) can still excite young ears and hands. We need balance; but we need to be aware that 2017 is not the same as 2007 or 1997 let alone being identical to the school education scene which I happen to have experienced in the 1980s. Music education can't stand still; but it shouldn't change everything too hastily, for traditional music education in schools has been exciting, to a life-changing extent, for countless individuals in the past. The trick, I should think, would be to find ways to expand the scope of school music such that more than just a tiny minority can engage with it and enjoy it in the future. I am quite convinced that new technologies can assist us in this ambition.

The chapter is structured into two halves. Firstly, I explore some of the many benefits which can arise from the introduction of new technologies into school-level music education. Some of this discussion is based upon my own practice, some is based upon published research and some is based upon conversations with DJ-orientated educators during my own recent researches. In the second half of the chapter, I engage with some critical viewpoints in regards to music education and new technologies: is this really legitimate music-making at all? I am quite convinced that new technologies are entirely legitimate, but I will suggest that some of the critical attitudes have legitimacy too. That given, the music education 'baby' really must not be 'thrown out with the bathwater': we can avoid doing that easily, I think, but we may want to look carefully and critically at the options as music education move forwards now and in the near future.

Engagement and purpose

Jonathan Savage's article 'Working towards a Theory for Music Technologies in the Classroom: How Pupils Engage with and Organise Sounds with New Technologies' is unambiguous about the benefits of new technology: 'At a sophisticated level, pupils began to explore the similarities and differences between sounds with a greater degree of engagement and purpose' (2005: 174). Any good teacher ought to prick their ears at the mention of such a thing. Savage assures us that 'the sounds that pupils made with the various pieces of ICT quickly captivated their imaginations' (171). How, though, was this possible? Few will be surprised by the answer: 'many powerful musical tools that were previously housed within the realm of the professional recording studio are now available freely over the Internet' (167): as a result, anyone can do it, it seems – provided they have a computer and an Internet connection.

The development in question does not necessarily render the role of 'teacher' obsolete, we should note: 'Inspiring starting points are vital in any creative activity' and, therefore, 'The choice of starting points can be made by teachers in the first instance' although 'there is also scope for pupils to define their own starting points' (Savage 2005: 172). We may not be out of a job quite yet, then; but child-centred methods (learners defining their own starting points, for example) are, at least in Savage's view, worth considering. Can we music educators afford to bury our heads in the sand and simply carry on with 'business as usual'? Not if Savage is to be believed: 'Compositional practice in the wider world has undergone a revolution that we, as educators, ignore at our peril' (178). The shift cannot be a drop in the ocean either: 'To embrace the true potential of ICT would require a *major* shift in the music education culture' (169, emphasis added).

Savage is not alone in this view. Teresa Dillon, for example, states that ICT 'has changed the nature of learning' in music education as it has elsewhere (2003: 893). According to Gall and Breeze, meanwhile, when given the chance to use ICT 'students felt that they had more control over the creative process than in larger group "traditional" settings' (2008: 36). Gall and Breeze suggest that the learners 'recognised that their increased confidence and ability to carry out tasks was related to the ease of using the software': because the ICT was easy to use, '*every* student could explore musical possibilities freely, whether or not they had formal musical skills' (36, emphasis added). This is not an isolated occurrence, Gall and Breeze suggest: 'The music coordinator's description of all pupils starting on "a level playing field" reflects other educators' suggestions of the "democratisation" of music afforded by the use of new music technologies' (ibid.).

The engagement and purposeful learning which Gall and Breeze speak of is explicitly associated with the extra-scholastic experiences of the learners: ICT 'enabled pupils to compose in contemporary styles with which they identified and which permeate their worlds outside of school' (2008: 36). This comes across very clearly in the quotes which Gall and Breeze offer from learners: previously the focus had supposedly been 'classical tunes but, like, we're into hip-hop and rock and stuff like that … so it's quite … strange for us, to hear the music we're into … it's new … it's good. It has a better beat!' (ibid.). In keeping with much of my argument in the present book, this EDM-/rock-recalling music-making brought 'excitement – particularly of a number of boys who expressed dislike for the largely singing and percussion-focussed "traditional" composing activities' (ibid.).

Gall and Breeze do not adopt an uncritically positive standpoint in regards to the benefits of such ICT for music education. They do ask 'what of creativity?', for example, but go on to argue that 'Our data suggests that possibilities for creative outcomes can be fashioned by the teacher through the way s/he plans the composition task' such that 'even though all the pupils were working to the same brief, they all produced distinctly different outcomes' (2008: 36). Creativity, then, does not seem to have been eradicated by the introduction of user-friendly ICT: 'To be completely original is not impossible' (ibid.). (The last quoted comment should 'always already' be challenged by a Derridean or post-structuralist thinker, but let us pass over the problematic in question for the time being.) 'For pupils in this study, producing music that sounded like music they would listen to at home was evidently important, and yet, all those who were interviewed felt that their pieces of music reflected their own creativity', Gall and Breeze suggest (38).

Fears about the introduction of new technologies into music education are unfounded, Gall and Breeze argue: 'Teachers' initial concerns that their pedagogies would need to be adapted when introducing computers into the music classroom proved unfounded'. Despite the fact that 'there was an inevitable requirement to consider practical implications, such as pupil grouping, the teachers were able to use and build upon their existing pedagogies' (2008: 38). New technologies can be used (up to a point) to enhance traditional music educational practices, indeed, as Lauren Char has shown in her 'Using GarageBand to Motivate Students to Practice' study (2009).

How solid are the foundations upon which such claims are made? To what extent, that is, are the research claims based on hard evidence? The doubtful reader can consult the original publications if they wish, of course, but I am happy to say that the evidence base seems very solid to me. I want to look for problems, nevertheless, in regards to the use of new technologies in music education, and I will do this during the second half of the present chapter. Before doing so, I shall outline not only some of my own experience within classroom practice but also, in the first instance, some ideas from Spencer Hickson (see Chapter Four above) relating to new music technology.

As we learned in Chapter Four, Spencer 'fell into' the provision of EDM-based practical workshops in educational 'alternatives' (PRUs and the like) some years ago and has had significant success as a teaching practitioner as well as a music producer in his own right. Spencer uses Novation launchpads (partly because they are 'colourful pads, so they light up', usefully enough for an educational context) in conjunction with Ableton. 'It comes with house, hip hop, drum'n'bass, dubstep and, y'know, genres like that – but then you can buy packs which are only £1.99, I've probably got twenty-odd different genres', Spencer informed me. These offer 'programmed loops so you start with drums, then you can add some bass, then your percussions, effects, you can do stabs...'.

Being unfamiliar with such launchpads, I asked if it was similar to software such as GarageBand: 'not in the layout; it's just like a block of squares', he responded. It also sounded to me as though the work was potentially less insular than the way many teachers would run a session on GarageBand or eJay: rather, Spencer spoke of the possibility for a 'huge jam' using a 'main controller with speakers and then I've got three laptops with mixers, two per console. And then I've got mini-amps, I've got four but you can get two on each, y'know, two sets of headphones'. Seeing that this seemed to allow only a handful of learners to be active at any given moment, I enquired how Spencer would cope with a class of thirty and he stated that 'it's never that big' but suggested that he could manage ten to fifteen. He could buy another five pads, he remarked, which would allow another ten people to actively make music – 'but then you've got to manage that', he acknowledged.

Spencer's long-term vision was 'to link them up [via Wi-Fi] so you could have it in a massive space, it's all BPM timed so there'd be nothing out of time. You could start and it just, y'know, evolves as more people start adding things. The sound, if everybody put drums on, would be ... [laughs] well, quite heavy, but I guess if you've got it into a sequencer then you can EQ some of that out and play with that later.' I found it hard, I will admit, to picture how this might go in a classroom situation (or, rather, I found it easy to picture this going horribly wrong with many of the classes I used to teach). That said, Spencer revealed that he had been in conversation with a representative of Ableton in regards to this ambition. Furthermore, he suggested that 'people are doing that now, y'know, but it's not … you're not able to [sync] it in the way you'd want to'.

The astute reader might guess that, as a teaching practitioner, this author is struggling to picture the flow of a session which operated along the above-described lines. Perhaps the approach he outlines will be the future for new technologies in music education. In a clarifying email (in response to my synopsis of our conversation as shown in the preceding paragraphs), Spencer stated that 'this vision I have is each user could control their own sounds and you'd get that kind of jam feel of people experiencing with sounds and effects live'. This certainly sounds exciting. If my research budget had allowed it, I would have liked to observe Spencer in educational action. Given that such was not possible, I will proceed by sketching out the way I would approach a computer-based session involving loop-based 'composing' (composing of a sort, that is) as well as giving some detail as to how I worked with the 'freeware' sound-editing software Audacity in whole-class situations.

Because my first opportunity to have a whole class working on computers involved MacBooks (see above), the GarageBand software which comes with Macs was an obvious place to start. Having said that, it should be noted that a wide range of other software with similar functions and presentation exists – eJay, Acid, Fruity Loops and so forth. Initially I was nervous about teaching on computers, not being much of a technophile myself: home recording in my teenage years and my twenties involved four-track machines and my entire background as a musician was in real-time performance with other players on traditional instruments. Fortunately, however, a secondary school very near to my own institution had a suite of Macs and a remit to support other local schools in developing music technology-based work. (Indeed, it was this school which lent me the fifteen MacBooks for a six-week half-term – in 2010, this seemed like a massively exciting opportunity although, by 2012, my school had its own suite of Macs.) I was thus able to take whole classes on foot to the nearby school, prior to gaining the MacBooks for my own classroom, and see how an expert teacher of music technology would use GarageBand as the basis of a morning's classroom work.

The first thing the teacher who I observed did was to play the class the opening moments of Fat Boy Slim's 1999 hit 'Praise You', drawing their attention to the way the track builds from solo piano to piano plus voice, then piano plus voice plus percussion and, finally, piano, voice, percussion and bassline all playing together. She then used a white board to present the thickening texture of the music as blocks, presenting the blocks in a similar way to how the loops would look on the screen when the children opened GarageBand. Significantly (to my mind, at least), the teacher used EDM-appropriate language by referring to the 'drop' around one minute into the track followed by a 'build up' and 'kick off'. All children were fully engaged with this starter activity, including those who were on the Special Educational Needs register for a range of emotional and behavioural educational disorders.

The teacher went on to demonstrate how to search through the 'loops' (fragments of drum beats, bass lines and so forth) which could be dragged and dropped into a mix. Pupils were left for a reasonably short period of time to explore some of the sounds, again with maximal levels of engagement from a class which I typically struggled to manage. (It is worth noting that senior management offered to exclude two of the pupils from the trip due to chronically disruptive and challenging behaviour. I made a judgement call that the opportunity to do something exciting in a music lesson would bring out the best in the two learners in question, however, and was delighted to see that the teacher at the neighbouring school – in conjunction with the technology itself – was able to engage these two 'difficult' children so well.) The teacher went around the room supporting learners and listening to the work they developed before stopping the whole class and demonstrating advanced techniques such as using the volume function to fade instruments in or out or to remix in other ways.

When I subsequently gained the MacBooks in my own classroom, I used the bulk of what I had seen done in the neighbouring school to structure a sequence of lessons using GarageBand. By the end of the scheme of work, the classes had developed extended pieces which I was then able to measure against specific National Curriculum attainment descriptors in order to make a judgement as to the NC Level which learners were working at. It is worth noting that nearly all learners were able to attain higher (and sometimes significantly higher) NC Levels than they had achieved from more typical summative assessments. However, we should also note that some of the learners with good or outstanding skills on traditional instruments were unable to demonstrate the skills and musical sensitivities which, during more typical classroom work, would see them attaining far higher NC Levels than their classmates. In at least one case, indeed, the GarageBand-based work which a 'gifted and talented' ('G and T') violinist produced was at a lower NC Level than she normally achieved.

Is this a major problem? Obviously not in regards to the overwhelming bulk of learners who, for once at least, were able to produce something in a music lesson of which they could be proud. (The way that learners would invite each other to listen to each other's pieces and express enthusiasm for what they heard was a delight to be hold, I might add.) As to the G and T pupils who were unable to show themselves as being so musically superior as they might normally have been able to appear, I am inclined to think this might be beneficial to those individuals. Is there not some advantage to us all, after all, if and when 'musicking' is seen as something which is within the reach of all rather than being a rare and special skill which is available only to a minority (Small 1998)? It is possible, I would suggest, for the labelling of the musically gifted as 'special' to be as much of a curse as a blessing. An above-average empathy for number, after all, rarely brings as much fuss as a special facility for music brings, and it is worth remembering that public performance is not always a pleasant experience for every musically-capable child.

That said, the 'levelling out' of abilities which music technology can sometimes bring should never be seen as an end in itself. If computer-based musical work can allow those who struggle to take pride in the products of their music classes to reverse that trend, naturally the teacher should be pleased. If, however, differentiation is at the heart of all teaching – as many will insist it is, of course – then we need to find ways to allow those who have differing and (felt-to-be) advanced skills to demonstrate/extend those capabilities.

One piece of software which I personally found excellent for this purpose was the 'open source' program Audacity. Although other programs for recording and layering sound may be preferable in that they are designed for musical use whereas Audacity is not music-specific software, the fact that Audacity was a free program made it highly appealing for my teaching practice. Technical staff were able to install it on all the students' laptops without expense, at a point where my department budget was already stretched to breaking point. In 2010, the UK government's Home Access Programme sought to challenge the 'digital divide' by providing free laptops to children from families in receipt of free school meals, housing benefits and other markers of economic disadvantage. In the school where I worked, so many of the children were eligible for the free computers (nearly the entire population of the school, in fact) that the Head took the decision to simply add a little extra funding from the whole school budget and provide a laptop to every child in the school without means testing.

This meant that I was able to ask whole classes to open their laptops, open the Audacity programme and click the circular red button to begin recording. We would then create a rhythm by stamping and clapping out a repeating rhythm such as that found in Queen's 'We Will Rock You' or some variant thereof (depending on the rhythmic capabilities of the class which faced me). I could then invite the children to explore the editing functions which Audacity clearly presents on screen: one can 'see' the beat, as it were, very easily, and thus one can cut a rhythm up and re-imagine it in innumerable different ways.

Classes based around the Audacity software would typically then develop into small group work whereby groups would head off to a practice room and attempt to layer up a piece and then remix it in differing ways. One advantage to this work, as compared with the GarageBand-based lessons, is that individuals with skills in singing, or with special facility for rhythmic work, or with the ability to play a traditional instrument, could demonstrate advanced skills. Perhaps more importantly, those learners who had the confidence and ability to do so could really get inside the music, as it were, altering its direction or radically re-imagining its character. Some learners would layer up pieces at home and bring them to me for evaluation; others would just mess around with the sound effects on a voice. In every case, I felt that the arrival of the laptops and the availability on them of Audacity meant that every child had a chance to develop musical skills in relation to new technologies.

However, there is more to musical life than technology, perhaps. Of course, one can say that music has always already had a technological dimension. For example, the tuning of a string was only ever a process of experimentation, evaluation and critical decision; the equally-tempered scale did not simply drop out of the sky,

God-given. Even the human voice, indeed, is technically controlled by the human subject in order to achieve the miracle of singing, in a sense. Such facts notwithstanding, it remains the case (if a range of scholars already quoted at the top of the present section are to be believed) that new technologies are (or at least should be) radically shaking up music education. That being the case, we need to tread carefully as we move forwards and, therefore, I seek a critical stance in regards to the many advantages of new technologies for music education in the next section.

Flattening out the hierarchies?

In Mirko M. Hall and Naida Zukic's chapter 'The DJ as Electronic Deterritorializer' within the *DJ Culture in the Mix* text, it is proposed that 'By flattening out the hierarchical stratifications of EDM culture, [new musical technologies] engender endlessly non-hierarchical movements of territorialisation, deterritorialization and reterretorialization' (Attias, Gavanas and Hillegonda 2013: 112). Bedroom DJs, they argue, can 'buy a MacBook, use GarageBand, produce new grooves and broadcast them online through social media technologies such as Facebook, MySpace and YouTube – potentially making a name for themselves in the world of entertainment' (117). 'There is something remarkably egalitarian about this', it is argued; 'It is true that DJ practitioners are always embedded within the matrix of late capitalist production, consumption and reception…. But there are also continually evolving opportunities within this very matrix that provide important conditions for the democratization of DJing' (117).

Readers who are unfamiliar with *A Thousand Plateaus* (Deleuze and Guattari 1987) could be mystified by Hall and Zukic's reference to 'territorialisation, deterritorialization and reterretorialization' in the above-quoted remarks. In short, the authors are making fairly legitimate and effective use of a 'continental' theory of Deleuze and Guattari's which proposes that a (broadly speaking) subaltern grouping, when faced with power from above, can flee in a 'line of flight' from the imposed power ('deterritorialization', that is). Subsequently, if and only if the deterritorialization is 'relative' rather than 'absolute', there will be a 'reterritorialization' through which subaltern power is reinvigorated in a manner which essentially evades the problems of hierarchy.

Although Hall and Zukic are thus making reasonable use of Deleuze and Guatarri's ideas, I am inclined to query the idea that 'endlessly non-hierarchical movements' can be possible. We could invoke the ideas of Derrida, perhaps Foucault and probably Marx too in order to problematise this proposal of a possible and facile escape from hierarchy, but to do so would be to divert from the main purpose of the present book, I feel. More directly, we should agree with Hall and Zukic that to 'buy a MacBook [and] use GarageBand' and getting involved in 'the world of entertainment' necessarily places one within 'the matrix of late capitalist production, consumption and reception'. That being the case, I am inclined to think that the label 'egalitarian' is too comfortably granted here: isn't there an extent to which hierarchy in general and capitalism in particular benefits from, say, most state schools in the UK acquiring a suite of Macs?

For Hall and Zukic, within the DJ culture 'everyday people make music for their very own pleasure by deliberately rejecting networks of late capitalist production and consumption' (Attias, Gavanas and Hillegonda 2013: 118); but I'm not so sure that the rejection in question is actually either deliberate or successful – or at least not entirely so. When we bring EDM into the classroom, we are certainly not waving away hierarchy and capitalism with an easy flourish, I would insist. Nevertheless, there are good reasons to bring this music into the classroom, I have argued. What, however, are the (inevitable, I would say) drawbacks which counterbalance the gains that arise from using new technologies for music education?

One good source for information on this topic, doubtless, is the voice of the learners themselves. We can note with interest, therefore, some comments from a learner as quoted by Louise Cooper in her chapter 'The Gender Factor: Teaching Composition in Music Technology Lessons to Boys and Girls in Year 9' within the *Music Education with Digital Technology* text (Burnard and Finney 2007). Regarding some classroom work based around the eJay program, the learner remarks that 'You don't really learn as much as you would if you were learning in class' (33). This, the boy goes on clarify, is 'Cos it doesn't tell you all the different notes that you use and things and notey and technical things' (34). Cooper adds that 'being limited by a series of set sounds in a set style of music ... made the pupils frustrated' specifically because, in the words of one learner, 'It's programmed so that only dance music is available' whereas 'If all styles were available it would be much better'. Another pupil remarks that 'I prefer to just use an instrument to using a computer because you can work on getting a melody out of it – getting a tune out' (ibid.).

There are reasons to hesitate, then, when bringing such technology into the classroom. That said, Cooper is emphatic that 'On the whole, students were incredibly focused in their music technology lessons and even the most difficult students seemed compelled to work hard' (Burnard and Finney 2007: 35). In the end, she is clear that eJay can be valuable as a 'starting block to give students confidence to compose' but, that said, the software 'represents music in a very superficial way' (39). Of course, we could critique this critique by pointing out that conceptualising the possibility for music to be represented in a 'superficial' way presupposes some universal agreement on the status of music as a non-superficial object. Given that no musicologist has been able to define 'the music itself' to the complete satisfaction of all other musicologists, this superficial characteristic is at best questionable in its status. (If music has no solidly objective status, that is, isn't it always a bit superficial?) Such a meta-critique might better be postponed for present purposes, however; Cooper's overall position (namely that eJay and, by implication, comparable software is not a perfect solution to the difficulties which often face the contemporary music teacher) is a valuable one for present purposes.

Cooper is far from alone in her doubts about the overall value of eJay, furthermore. In the same collection of chapters, indeed, we can note Teresa Dillon's ambivalence within her 'Current and Future Practices: Embedding Collaborative Music Technologies in English Secondary Schools' chapter (Burnard and Finney 2007). On the one hand, Dillon observes that 'While keyboards currently dominate secondary school music classrooms, further research is needed as to whether such instruments are the most appropriate to support general level musical skills and knowledge' (122). On the other hand, eJay's 'Samples tended to be predictive: the time signatures were standardized and could not be modified, which could lead to compositions sounding very similar'. The best ways to counterbalance these issues are carefully considered by Dillon, I would say: for example, the proposal that 'Tasks on keyboards and on computers need to be well structured. Setting clear task goals helps students to begin composing' (ibid.). Moreover, it is clear that Dillon, like Cooper, feels that new technologies are best seen as a complement to rather than a replacement for more traditional equipment in music education.

There are nuances at stake here which we do not have the space to unpick in detail in the present context. Against Dillon's concerns around standardization, for example, we can note Liz Mellor's argument, in relation to a study of computer-based composition in primary schools, that 'within the one identified vertical composing strategy which all the participants used, *creativity occurred within all the composing responses* regardless of the participants' musical backgrounds' (Mellor 2007: 61, emphasis added). For Mellor, creativity can be 'defined in terms of divergent thinking skills and problem solving skills and the extent to which each participant generated their own problems and "creative" solutions' (ibid.). The nuance to be potentially fought over, here, relates to this vital question as to what 'creativity' is, doubtless. However, as noted, space restricts me from ruminating at any serious length on that question. Summarising the overall position in the briefest possible manner, therefore, I suggest that we can at least conclude that, although some will find creative musicality to be recognisable when new technologies are employed, others will fear standardisation. We also need to remember, furthermore, that some students will desire more traditional opportunities from music lessons, such as the opportunity for an individual to sculpt out her or his own melody (see above).

New technologies such as GarageBand are not an individually perfect solution to the difficulty of engagement at KS3 (the period within UK education where every child is expected to develop skills in and knowledge of music, that is). New technologies, indeed, will not support every valuable dimension of musical teaching and learning but can doubtless have great value for most if not all teachers in the contemporary scene nonetheless. We should add that some have eyed GarageBand and comparable software critically beyond the educational field. For example, an article published by the influential website *Pitchfork* (written by Art Tavana and published on 30 September 2015) is titled 'Democracy of Sound: Is GarageBand Good for Music?' Admirably even-handed, the article points out that this software 'has engendered praise for its egalitarian simplicity as well as some ire for its creative limitations'. According to Tavana, 'GarageBand is the most clickable and widespread DAW in history, a fact that's subsequently added a whole new layer to the modern sound palette'. Consequently, 'even if GarageBand is not for everyone, its democratic ideals are universal'.

Such a claim seems dubious to me: after all, this is a commercially-driven piece of software which can only be accessed via computers and devices that are manufactured by a gigantic multinational corporation; if its 'democratic ideals are universal', why is it only on offer to Apple customers? To my mind, therefore, the *Pitchfork* article in question is not as critical as it should be, although we should be pleased that the article at least acknowledges some 'creative limitations' to the software in question. I feel much the same when I read Lauri Väkevä's claim that 'digital technology has brought the mixing practices to everybody's reach and offered a global distribution and exchange network for new mixes' (2010: 61). Has utopia really arrived so soon? Personally, I doubt it; for one thing, as even the *Pitchfork* writer is able to notice, new technologies have brought 'a host of musical products designed "in the key of easy", [these being] part of the GarageBand gene pool'. If the *Pitchfork* critique holds water (and one has to concede that *Pitchfork* has a fairly high quotient of credibility beyond the ivory tower) then Väkevä's utopianism starts to look dubious.

We can note, on this topic, Väkevä's argument that, if and when 'cultural commons' are in play, 'the primary tasks of the music educator would be to help the students to find interesting ways to employ these commons and to find new approaches to them that could amount to individual expressions' (2010: 62). Perhaps so, but if so then how is that educator to provide the 'help' in question? In my own teaching practice, I found that sessions using GarageBand often included students accusing each other of 'stealing' their ideas. The reason this problem would so often arise is that, as some researchers whose work I have drawn above have noticed, GarageBand offers creativity within quite a tight frame. This software's recording function is all well and good, but most KS3 learners are not sufficiently confident and developed to create original musical ideas on an instrument or using their voice and, therefore, they tend to rely on the bank of samples for loops to mix together. These loops are, of course, the restricted 'gene pool' to which *Pitchfork* refers (see above). As a teacher, I found that it was generally easier for the young people I worked with to create 'individual expressions' (as Väkevä puts it) on keyboards, xylophones or percussion than via GarageBand. The latter might be user friendly whilst the former might have tended towards an awkward clumsiness, but the musical products from GarageBand did not sound very individual to my ears: on the contrary, none of the pieces of work really stood out in the way that other student creations often would, I would suggest.

Conclusion

On the one hand, new technologies are valuable for music education: they allow us to engage students with music which is closer to the taste of a large number of young people (probably the majority) than most other kinds of classroom musical work will tend to be. Additionally, the product is likely to have a more 'finished' or 'produced' sound than anything which the same learners could probably achieve on traditional instruments: arguably, therefore, such learners can take a greater pride in what they have produced. On the other hand, however, there is a limit to how much individuality certain new technologies (such as those discussed in the present chapter) can offer to young learners: 'composing' by combining and remixing pre-programmed loops doesn't really allow the developing musician to 'get their hands dirty' with, say, melody and rhythm relative to, for example, a xylophone.

This being the case, are new technologies something of a 'red herring' for the contemporary music education scene? Is such software, in other words, an (apparently) easy solution to the problem of engagement but, when you get under the surface of actual music-making in concrete classroom situations, little or nothing about music is really being learnt? I would not agree with such an assessment. For one thing, there is a moment for all those who have struggled to master a traditional instrument, I suspect (or, at least, such a moment certainly arose in my own youth), wherein what seemed impossibly difficult suddenly falls into place and becomes easy. My own first experience of this was mastery of the 'bar chord' shape when I was about twelve years old and learning the guitar. Using a full-size 'Spanish' guitar with a fairly wide neck, and having less than full-size hands at that moment in my life, the chord shape eluded my capabilities for some time. Suddenly, one day, I found myself sitting at the bottom of the stairs successfully holding down the chord shape in question. Of course, I had a great deal more to learn before I could claim proficiency of any kind on the instrument, but that moment of achievement remains a palpable memory for me, well over thirty years later.

Don't all children deserve to have such 'I *can* do it!' moments of surprise during their years of compulsory music education? Is it not the small defeat of a technical challenge which allows us to face up to the next (bigger) challenge? To my mind, there can be no doubt on this question. If we have classes of children who think they have no chance of producing something satisfactory, disillusion and disaffection are bound to be rife. If, however, every child feels that they managed to produce at least one piece of music which was not devoid of value during their school years, I would contend that we are much better positioned to move forwards with ever increasing levels of self-confidence amongst the majority of young learners in mainstream classrooms.

New technologies are not a catch-all solution for problems around engagement and music education, but they have significant value as a tool for battling disaffection, therefore. On the other hand, those who critique the value of music technology often go too far in the statement of their scepticism. Take the following remarks from a teacher interviewed within the researches of Vratulis and Morton (2011): 'You can't just create music. Calling [computer-aided musical creation] music is like picking up a fork and banging it on the table and creating a beat and then saying, "Yeah, that is music" — but it's not, you know?' (407). The statement is shockingly bald, is it not? To be fair, the teacher goes on to say 'That doesn't mean you can't use it to teach students things about music, like how to create a beat'. In the end, however, he is emphatic that 'it is not music'.

As a matter of fact, one *can* 'just create music': the history of music (and especially of popular music, from Scott Joplin to Jimi Hendrix and beyond) is littered with individuals who seem to have produced something from nothing, just creating something where that something previously was unknown. A teacher who starts out from the assumption that 'you can't just create music' is not likely to get very far in the kind of inner-city school that I taught in, I might add. It would be rather better, would it not, to tell the young people that 'you *can* just create music'? I would add, furthermore, that banging an object (a fork, a bone, a stick, whatever) on another object (a table, a rock, a log) not only is music but is so fundamental to the human history of music-making that a teacher who dismisses it risks the most dangerous of dismissals one can imagine. Who, after all, is to say what music 'is'? The musicological jury, as noted above, is very much out on this particular question; and the ontological vulnerability of the object of music teaching (music, that is) should best be seen as a boon to our task than a hindrance, I would maintain. Do we not want young learners, after all, who have been emboldened to assume that they can re-imagine music as anything they wish to imagine it as? Let us embrace the vulnerability of the musical object, therefore, and invite our learners (in the first instance, at least) to tell *us* what music 'is'.

That said, I was always eager to expose my classes to the rich traditions of music from Europe, America and beyond (India, for example, which was always my first topic for the last year of the compulsory KS3 years). In my practice, therefore, new technologies were embraced with great enthusiasm but the traditional stuff – singing, playing percussion, finding C on a keyboard and so forth – were also a vital component of a diet of classroom learning and teaching which I always kept as varied as I possibly could. This, I would suggest, is the wisest general rule for the future in music education: embrace the new, maintain the best of the tradition(s) and always listen to the interests and tastes of the learners before making decisions about curriculum content.

References

Attias, Bernardo Alexander, Gavanas, Anna, Rietveld, Hillegonda C., *DJ Culture in the Mix: Power, Technology and Social Change in Electronic Dance Music* (London: Bloomsbury, 2013)
Burnard, Pamela, Finney, John, *Music Education with Digital Technology* (London: Continuum, 2007)
Deleuze, Gilles, Guattari, Felix, *A Thousand Plateaus* (London: Continuum, 1987)
Dillon, Teresa, 'Collaborating and Creating on Music Technologies', *International Journal of Educational Research* 39/8 (2003)
Gall, Marina, Breeze, Nick, 'Music and eJay: An Opportunity for Creative Collaborations in the Classroom', *International Journal of Educational Research* 47 (2008), 27–40
Mellor, Liz, 'Computer Based Composition in the Primary School: An Investigation of Children's Composition Responses using Dance eJay', *Journal for the European Society for the Cognitive Sciences of Music* 11/1 (2007), 61–88

Savage, Jonathan, 'Working towards a Theory for Music Technologies in the Classroom: How Pupils Engage with and Organise Sounds with New Technologies', *British Journal of Music Education*, 22/2 (2005), 167–80

Small, Christopher, *Musicking: The Meanings of Performing and Listening* (Hanover: Wesleyan University Press, 1998).

Väkevä, Lauri, 'Garage Band or GarageBand? Remixing Musical Futures', *British Journal of Music Education* 27/1 (2010), 59–70

Vratulis, V., Morton, C., 'A Case Study Exploring the Use of Garageband and an Electronic Bulletin Board in Preservice Music Education', *Contemporary Issues in Technology and Teacher Education*, 11/4 (2011), 398–419

CONCLUSION

On 21 September 2003, *The Guardian* newspaper quoted the then-newly successful rapper Dizzee Rascal as saying that 'I was in danger of being thrown out of [school] and, in the end, the music class was about the only one I went to because I had been excluded from most of the others'. I will not pretend that my years of teaching produced such illustrious alumni as this, but I know that there were some learners for whom music was the only (or one of the only) classes which they much enjoyed. This was not due to some magical skill or charisma which I happened to possess; it was simply the case that, in my classroom, the marginal tastes of a large minority of learners ('happy' hardcore EDM, that is) were welcomed as valid music for practical work and classroom discussion.

Music doesn't stand still, as years pass. It changes character such that older and younger people sometimes query what it is that makes the other group enjoy what they enjoy. Having said that, dispassionate appraisal of music shows that, even though it might be the case that 'one man's meat is another man's poison', and even though universal agreement as to what music *is* remains elusive in the last analysis, mutual respect and recognition are not necessarily unattainable goals in a practical situation such as a classroom.

Electronic Dance Music is different from much of the popular music which existed up to the 1970s; EDM's basic character tends to be 'a whole other thing', relative to more traditional music(s). Is it really 'wholly other' to non-EDM stuff, though? This question demands a decision which, with fidelity to a Derridean conception of 'justice', I will not foreclose (see Chapter One above). What I will say, however, is that I found plenty to do (or, more importantly, for learners to do) in my classroom in order allow/encourage young enthusiasts of EDM to develop musical skills not only within the musical sphere which they counted as their own but also in more general terms.

The theoretical background for this educational approach was the child-centred pedagogies which I had read around during my PGCE year. Child-centred methods have received serious criticism over the last thirty or forty years (see Chapter Two), but I maintain that they can have great validity for contemporary practice. That said, the practitioner who combines child-centred methods with a pragmatic 'realism' may well fare better in the contemporary educational field, as I have attempted to show herein, than an ideologue of child-centric teaching who responds uncritically to, say, the work of Ivan Illich.

Whichever way one looks at such pedagogical questions, I have tried to make an emphatic case in this book for the practical utility of EDM in general, and DJing equipment in particular, for the contemporary classroom. In Chapter Three, I presented this as an option which could literally have 'life and death' implications: given that 'at risk' children will sometimes wind up dead before they complete their teenage years, and given that hardcore EDM is sometimes the music of taste for such 'marginal' young people, bringing this equipment can make a world of difference to individuals. At a less dramatic level, encouraging young people to DJ and/or MC in school can help those who typically feel as though their urban culture is either invisible or virtually illegal to suddenly feel legitimate, welcomed, even celebrated.

In Chapter Four, I argued that the successes I was able to achieve in a mainstream music classroom are too rarely replicated in the teaching practice at large within the UK. That said, I offered some evidence to suggest that DJing and MCing *are* sometimes available as an educational option – but almost invariably this is either an extra-curricular option or, more commonly as far as I can tell, such music-making is offered in PRUs, remand centres and other environments beyond the mainstream of education. This, I argued, is not satisfactory – EDM/urban music is music and DJing/MCing have a long history which needs to be more well reflected in the content of teaching and learning in the UK.

In Part Two of the book I proposed more detailed methods for actually delivering teaching and learning based on contemporary urban music in mainstream schools. An important element within such delivery will certainly be classroom management, which I discussed at some length in Chapter Five. Making space for and setting up, say, vinyl decks in a classroom can be yet another demand on teachers who already feel greatly pressured by the demands of daily whole class teaching. The effort is worth the reward (namely great boosts to engagement levels amongst learners), I have argued, but I recognise that there are difficulties and challenges around classroom management for the teaching practitioner who would bring DJ decks into their classroom. It is hoped that Chapter Five could have some value to willing teachers, as well as to the researchers who monitor and comment on their work.

Practical utility for teachers and researchers is also the ambition behind Chapter Six, wherein I explored some particular issues around EDM-related whole class teaching at KS3. This was extended in Chapter Seven, where I looked at the post-compulsory KS4 period. Within the latter context, I showed that the mainstream exam boards for KS4 music *do* recognise MCing, DJing and other contemporary urban music-making practices (beatboxing, for example) as being valid for assessed performance at the present time. I strongly suspect, however, that very few teachers are consulting the GCSE and BTEC specifications in enough detail to see that MCs and DJs can legitimately be assessed without the teacher needing to inaugurate their own assessment procedures. I also suggested that an imbalance between BTEC and GCSE, comparable to the pre-1988 GCE/CSE divide, has been creeping back in to music education at least and probably into education more broadly. This would be a highly problematic drift which I would suggest requires urgent attention amongst researchers. I have not attempted any firm conclusions herein. However, I am acutely aware (especially so given my present lectureship for a BA in Popular Music) that the BTEC qualification equips students with a very different set of skills as compared with the GCE A-level. Sometimes this works very much to the disadvantage of individual learners who both need and want to extend their more traditional skills, although the situation is certainly complicated by the fact that many successful 'pop' musicians (most, I suspect) do not read and write music and so forth. (For the latter reason, the BTEC qualification probably has more 'real life' value for a pop musician, arguably – the situation is complicated, then.)

In Chapter Eight, I discussed advanced DJing skills but also asked whether a fixation upon technical skills is to ignore what many practitioners and theorists are beginning to recognise as the most vital component of effective DJing, namely 'programming'. If such *is* the 'true' heart of DJing, the implications for music education are immense: how, after all, do we assess a learner's capabilities in programming a DJ set, or in diverting from a planned programme in order to better 'move the crowd'? Here, perhaps, we reach a liminal point where music education cannot cope with the demands on conceptualisation which the new urban cultures of EDM have brought. I am confident, however, that my chapter merely scratches the surface of a debate on this topic which will continue to grow in importance in the coming years – especially at A-level/BTEC Level 3 and in universities.

In Chapter Nine I turned my attention to new technologies, arguing that they have many valuable aspects but should be regarded as a supplement for, rather than as an alternative to, traditional methods and modes in music education. Certainly there are limits to the efficacy of new technology for the stimulation of musical skills and understandings amongst young people. However, there is also a great benefit to offering young learners, who otherwise might struggle to demonstrate musical competency, a classroom option which can allow them to produce something of which they can easily feel proud.

According to Glenda McGregor and Martin Mills, 'the music teacher needs the skills of an expert DJ who can spin several records at once in order to create a RMXed curriculum' if that music teacher is to successfully confront issues around gender and education in the field of contemporary music education (2006: 222). I am confident that the statement is well justified and, indeed, I would add that a similar metaphor could be applied for the teacher who would confront issues around engagement and disaffection in contemporary music teaching and learning. I am not suggesting, therefore, that every music teacher in the UK would find it easy to provide options for DJs and MCs in their classrooms: on the contrary, I am sure that many would struggle with such music-making and, indeed, might lack enthusiasm for the EDM and urban music upon which DJs and MCs are typically fixated.

Being aware of this situation, indeed, was the major spur for the creation of the current book. I hope that my efforts herein might be of some utility for such teachers, and for the consideration of researchers. If we want to engage the broad population of twenty-first-century learners with music education, we need to open up the curriculum to cover modes of music-making which are relevant to the broad tastes of that contemporary majority. This means that EDM, DJing, MCing and whatever else falls within the spectrum of contemporary urban music needs to be granted at least some reflection within the contemporary curriculum. If and when this is done, I am quite sure that immense gains can be achieved not only for engagement but also for attainment. Without it, doubtless a minority of learners can be engaged in the manner which music education has heretofore achieved. Whether we should be content with this situation is something on which, in the last analysis, individuals must make their own decision. All I will say for now, in conclusion of all I have tried to say herein, is that a little openness to the unfamiliar and willingness to experiment can yield remarkable results in a music classroom, just as it can in so many other areas of life and education.

Reference

McGregor, Glenda, Mills, Martin, 'Boys and Music Education: RMXing the Curriculum', *Pedagogy, Culture and Society* 14/2 (2006), 221–33

INDEX

A
absenteeism 57
abused or neglected children 54–5
acid house 2, 67, 100, 103
A-level 115
AQA 113, 114, 122
Ark T 9, 70–1
assessment of DJing or MCing 140; EBacc 47; GCSE 113, 120–3, 133–4; grade exams 134–5; KS3 105–6, 110; *see also* Ofsted evaluations
Associated Board of the Royal Schools of Music (ABRSM) 140
Aston, Peter 47
Audacity 147, 149
autistic learners 68–9

B
baby scratching 121, 128
Badiou, Alain 24–5
beat juggling 131
beatmatching 85, 127, 130; assessment issues 121; moving the crowd 130; one learner's experience 67
Beethoven 28
behaviour management *see* classroom management
Biafra, Jello 60
Blair, Tony 43, 44
Brady, Di 6–7
Breeze, Nick 145
BTEC 115, 118–20, 122–3, 134, 159
Burnard, Pamela 84
Burns, Chris 87–8

C
Callaghan, James 42
Campbell, Rory 'Rawz' 70–1, 108
Cavicchi, Daniel 11
censoring rap lyrics 61, 71
Challis, Mike 84–5, 106
'charisma' effects on teaching outcomes 7, 26, 61
child-centred learning 34, 49–50, 158; balancing formal-informal strategies 49; contemporary ambiguities 46; critiques of 34–5; KS3 music disengagement and 98; progressive idealism 35–41; reactionary shift 41–6; role of talking 91; suggestions for practitioners 46–9; teaching DJing skills 68
Children in Need days 55–6
chirps 128
class sizes 45, 76
'classical' music skills 22–4
classroom management 83–5, 158; ICT resources 87, 88; mutual respect 83; Ofsted's influence 94–5; space management 92–4; time management 89–92; whole class teaching 85–90
Claxton, Guy 44–5
Clennon, Ornette 59–60
computer-based music-making *see* new technology
CoMusica project 8
crabs 128–9
creativity 105, 145, 152
criminal behaviour 59–60

162 Index

Criminal Records Bureau (CRB) checks 58–9
crotchets and quavers 104, 114, 115
CSE qualification 118
cultural knowledge and experience, pragmatic benefits of gaining 29–30
curriculum tensions: fear of Ofsted and 6–7; inclusion and respect for otherness 22–7, 32; popular music 19–22; right to one's own music 27–30; *see also* music education curriculum; National Curriculum; Ofsted evaluations

D
Dale, Paul 11–15
debriefing 91
Deleuze, Gilles 150
Derrida, Jacques 25, 116
deschooling 37–9, 49
deterritorialisation 150
dialects 29, 31
digital technology *see* new technology
digital vinyl systems (DVS) 131–2
Dillon, Teresa 145, 151–2
disaffected learners 2; Ark T project 70–1; basic argument for engaging 1; DJing/MCing-related positive behaviours 56–7; extracurricular DJing activities participation 57–8; Learning to Learn program 45; positive musical identity and engagement 26; preventing disaffection 78; socioeconomic deprivation 2, 54–5; students with preexisting DJ skills 52–3, 56
DJ equipment ('DJ decks'): availability in non-mainstream settings 66–7; basic argument for student engagement 1, 10, 35; classroom management 92–4; digital technologies 131–2; KS3 curriculum 99–101; as musical instruments 106; researching availability/use in schools 8–9; resource considerations 48–9, 87, 109; scratching tools 128; teachers' familiarity with 12; working with larger groups 85, 87; *see also* new technology
DJ Experience 78
DJ School UK 78
DJ Workshops Ltd 78
DJ-as-artist paradigm 1–2
DJing and/or MCing history 2, 101, 103, 108, 138
DJing grade exams 134–5
DJing notation 107, 116

DJing skills 2, 101, 127, 159; assessment issues 113, 120–3, 133–5, 140; author's background 12; author's teaching practice, KS3 100–5; balancing different musics 30–1; basic pedagogical questions 3; beatmatching 67, 85, 121, 127, 130; child-centred approach to teaching 68; digital technologies 131–2; experienced students 52–3, 102; female DJs 63, 134; gender differences 63, 84; guest DJ visits 58–9, 102; mainstream validation problem 134–9; mixing 130; moving the crowd 127, 130, 133; natural musical skills 130; programming 132–4, 139–40; resources for educators 128; scratching 101, 107, 121, 128–30; 'traditional' musical skills and 114–17; validity as 'music-making' 112–13; workshops for youth 67–9
DJing tutor 67
double-drop 131
drug use 59, 61, 64–5, 103
dubstep 62

E
EBacc 47, 124–5
Eddy, Duane 140
Edexcel 113, 114, 121–2
education, aims of 10, 34, 123–4
educational research methodologies 5–9
educational theory and practice 5–6
eJay 4, 88, 151–2
elaborated codes 21
electronic dance music (EDM) 1, 2; integration into formal educational institutions 136–8; popular music versus 157; *see also* hardcore EDM
Ellis, David "TC" 75–6
English dialects 29
Every Child Matters policy 46
extracurricular DJing or MCing activities 9; engagement in non-mainstream settings 66–72; participation of challenging students 57–8; positive musical identity and engagement 26; *see also* Pupil Referral Units

F
faders 128, 129
female DJs 63, 134
Finney, John 47–8, 84
folk music 30
'freestyle' 120–1
Freire, Paulo 38

Index

G
Gall, Marina 145
GarageBand 4, 88, 146, 147–8, 152–3
GCSE 20, 159; assessment issues 113, 120–3, 133–4; DJing/MCing and traditional musical skills 114–17; DJing/MCing validity as music-making 113; music uptake issues 117–23
gender differences 55, 63–4, 84, 120
Goodman, Paul 37
Goodson, Ivor 5
Gordon, Brett 70
grade exams for DJing 134–5
grading system 106
Grand Wizzard Theodore 139
'great composers and musicians' 19, 24, 108
Green, Lucy 12, 24, 25
'Groove Noise' 69
Guattari, Felix 150
guest DJs 58–9, 102

H
Hall, Mirko M. 132–3, 150, 151
happy hardcore EDM 2, 21, 48, 60, 62, 107
hardcore EDM 2, 84; aggressiveness 48; composition work using 107; curriculum inclusion issues 21; gender differences 63; racial considerations 60–2; social bias against 89; transcription exercises 27, 103; unpleasantness perceptions for teachers 26
Hardman, Frank 85–6
Hickson, Spencer 67–9, 109, 146
High School for Recording Arts (HSRA) 72–6
hip hop music 2; High School for Recording Arts 72–6; pedagogical uses of 60; racial and regional differences 62; social bias against 89
history of DJing and MCing 2, 101, 103, 108, 138
Holt, John 13, 35–7, 49–50
Home Access Programme 149
How Children Fail (Holt) 13, 35–6
Hunter, Matthew 43–4

I
ICT *see* new technology
Illich, Ivan 38–41, 158
'improvise and compose' requirement 107
inclusion 66; curriculum issues 22–7, 32; gender differences 63; learning from students 74; non-mainstream lessons for mainstream schools 75–8; non-mainstream settings 66–74; preventing disaffection 78; school policy on mobile devices 74–5
interactive teaching styles 85–9
Internet and education 39–40

J
Jamaican sound system culture 2
Jazzie B, DJ 136
Jourdain, Kathryn 25

K
Katz, Mark 129, 139
Key Stage 3 (KS3) curriculum 97–8; assessment issues 105–6, 110; author's teaching practice 98–105; 'improvise and compose' requirement 107; National Curriculum delivery 97, 105–9; new technologies and 109; 'play and perform' requirement 106–7; primary-secondary transition 97–8, 109–10
Key Stage 4 (KS4) curriculum 97, 112, 158–9; assessment issues 113, 120–3, 133–4; BTEC 115, 118–20, 122–3, 134, 159; DJing/MCing and traditional musical skills 114–17, 124; DJing/MCing validity as music-making 112–13; EBacc 47, 124–5; gender differences in student participation 120; music uptake issues 98, 112, 113, 117–23; OCR 113, 120–2; *see also* GCSE
Kirkland, David 60
Kokotsaki, Dimitra 97–8
Kwami, Robert 86–7

L
Lamont, Alexandra 26
language and music, right to one's own 27–30
larger groups of students 85, 87
learner identity transformation 26
Learning to Learn program 45–6
Lever, Colin 83
Levinas, Emmanuel 25, 27
listening and music education 20, 31, 90, 107
Lister, Ian 41
logocentrism 116
'Love in Paradise' 103–5
Lowe, Roy 41–2

M

MacBooks 147, 148
McGregor, Glenda 63, 159
Mákina 103–4, 107
Marx, Karl 40
mash up 101
MCing and rapping 1; associated skills 127; author's teaching practice, KS3 100; balancing different musics in classroom instruction 30–1; censoring offensive words 61, 71; creative writing 84; dialect 'correction' considerations 31; GCSE assessment issues 113, 120; gender differences 63; historical roots 2; racial and regional differences 61–2; 'traditional' musical skills and 116–17
Mills, Janet 88
Mills, Martin 63, 159
Minnesota's High School for Recording Arts (HSRA) 72–6
mixers 128
mixing skills 130
Miyakawa, Felicia M. 116
mobile devices *see* new technology; smartphones or mobile devices
Moby, DJ 103
'monkey' 14
Moore, Alex 10
moving the crowd 127, 130
Murray, Andy 88
music as 'universal language' 22–3
music education: DJing and EDM mainstream validation problem 134–9; examining purpose of 10, 34, 123–4; gender differences in student participation 55; researching DJ equipment availability/use in schools 8–9
music education curriculum: balancing different types 30–1; 'classical' harmonic rules 22; DJing/MCing validity as music-making 112–13; GCSE 20; gender considerations 63; inclusion and respect for otherness 22–7, 32; KS3 97–110; KS4 112–25; listening 20, 90, 107; National Curriculum statement 19, 23; passive listening 20, 90; popular music 19–22; right to one's own language or music 27–30; singing requirement 97–8; starting points 23; *see also* child-centred learning; Key Stage 3 (KS3) curriculum; Key Stage 4 (KS4) curriculum; National Curriculum
'Music for the Minority' 47

music notation conventions 104, 107, 114–16, 124
music production education, High School for Recording Arts (HSRA) 72–6
music skills, 'classical' 23–4
music teachers: author's background 11–15; 'charisma' effects on teaching outcomes 7, 26, 61; child-centred learning suggestions 46–9; DJ equipment expertise 12; effective teacher backgrounds 75–6; job challenges 55; learning from students 74; peripatetic 119
musical identity and student engagement 26, 28
music-making and criminal behaviour 59–60
Myhill, Debra 87–8

N

National Curriculum: contradictions and ambiguities 46; effect on teacher critical thinking capacity 5–6; 'improvise and compose' requirement 107; KS3 97, 105–9; music attainment assessment issues 105–6, 110; music education statement 19, 23; 'play and perform' requirement 106–7; singing requirement 97–8; *see also* Key Stage 3 (KS3) curriculum; Key Stage 4 (KS4) curriculum; music education curriculum
NC Levels 148
new technology 4, 142–4, 153–5; author's teaching practice 147–9; creativity and 152; critical perspectives 150–3; DJing equipment 131–2; Home Access Programme 149; 'just creating music' 154–5; KS3 curriculum delivery issues 109; a practitioner's vision 146–7; resource considerations 87; school policy on mobile devices 74–5; student engagement and purpose 144–6; using in workshops 68; whole class teaching and 87, 88; working with larger groups 85
North East England 54, 103–4
North West England 67
notation conventions 104, 107, 114–16, 124

O

OCR 113, 120–2
offensive words 61
Ofsted evaluations: of the author 14, 15*n*; effect on curriculum innovation 6–7; influence on classroom

management 94–5; punitive measures for already troubled schools 54
O-level 20, 117, 123
'other' music, inclusion of and respect for 22–7, 32
Owen, DJ Frank 103
Oxford area 8–9, 61–2, 70–1

P
parental permission slips 57–8
Paynter, John 47
pedagogy, child-centred approach *see* child-centred learning
peripatetic teachers 119
Pitts, Adrian 86–7
'play and perform' requirement 106–7
Plowden Report (1967) 13, 14, 34, 37, 46
popular music 19–22, 157
postmodern blackness 60
primary-secondary transition 97–8, 109–10
programming skills 132–4, 139–40
progressive pedagogy 35–41
Proudhon, Pierre-Joseph 40
public education, purpose of 10, 123–4
Pupil Referral Units (PRUs) 3, 9, 66–7, 84, 158

Q
Qbert, DJ 129
quavers and crotchets 104, 114, 115

R
racial considerations 60–2
racist words 61
rapping *see* MCing and rapping
Rascal, Dizzee 157
reading 60
regional differences in music preferences 61–2
Reimer, Everett 49
research methodologies 5–9
respect 58, 83, 108, 157

S
Sage Gateshead 8
Savage, Jonathan 144
scales 107
Scott, David 5–6, 7
scratching 101, 107, 121, 128–30
Seidel, Sam 72–5
self-esteem improvement 84
sexist words 61
Shakur, Tupac 60
singing 30, 97–8

smartphones or mobile devices 68, 74–5
see also new technology
Smith, Fay 85–6
Smith, Gary ('DJ G') 9
social constructivist theory 85
socioeconomically deprived youth 2, 54–5
see also disaffected learners
sociolinguist issues, right to one's own language or music 27–30
Söderman, Johan 60
software tools *see* new technology
sound system culture 2
spatial management 92–4
spirituality 103
stab/chop scratch 128
Stahl, Garth 8, 56
starting points 23, 144
student behaviour management *see* classroom management
students' right to their own language or music 27–30
styluses 88, 128
Sugrue, Ciaran 49
surprise 99
Swanwick, Keith 47

T
talking 29, 91, 100
teacher 'charisma' effects 7, 26, 61
teacher-as-researcher approach 5–9
teacher-centred pedagogy 43, 44–5, 49
technology *see* new technology
Thatcher, Margaret 35
Thompson, Paul 136–8
time management 89–92
tonality 107
Total People 67–9
'traditional' musical skills 114–17, 124
see also music notation conventions
transcription of electronic dance music 27, 103
transformer scratch 129
Traveller children 50
Trudgill, Peter 29, 31
TTM (Turntable Transcription Methodology) 116

U
UK National Curriculum *see* National Curriculum
urban music 1 *see also* electronic dance music; hardcore EDM; hip hop music
Urban Music Foundation 70–1
Usher, Robin 6–7

V
Väkevä, Lauri 153

W
Walker, Robert 24
Wall, Kate 85–6
Wharmby, Jaz 8, 61
whole class teaching 85–90, 100
Wilshaw, Michael 106
Woodhead, Chris 43
workshops 67–9
Wragg, Ted 90, 92, 94

written work 29, 84, 91, 103
Wyse, Dominic 105

X
xylophones 143

Y
YMCA 69

Z
Zorn, Jeff 27–8
Zukic, Naida 132–3, 150, 151